Contents

OVERVIEW   x

UNIT 1   WHAT IS A PARAGRAPH?   1

Example Paragraphs   2
   Writer's Note: Repetition and Simple Present Tense Verbs   3
   Writer's Note: Imperative Form   6
   Writer's Note: Use of *I* and Simple Past Tense   8

Building Better Sentences   9

Four Features of a Paragraph   9
   Writer's Note: The Title of a Paragraph   21

Building Better Sentences   21

Working with Paragraphs   22
   Language Focus: Identifying Verbs in Sentences   23
   Writer's Note: Checking for the Verb   24

Building Better Vocabulary   26

Original Student Writing   27

Introduction to Peer Editing   28
   Writer's Note: Once Is Never Enough!   28
   Writer's Note: Suggestions for Peer Editing   28

Timed Writing   29

UNIT 2   DEVELOPING IDEAS FOR WRITING A PARAGRAPH   30

Brainstorming   31
   Writer's Note: The Importance of Brainstorming   32

How Brainstorming Works   32
   Language Focus: Subject-Verb Agreement   37

Building Better Sentences   39

Building Better Vocabulary   40

Original Student Writing   41

Timed Writing   42

UNIT 3   THE TOPIC SENTENCE   43

Features of a Good Topic Sentence   47
   Controlling Ideas   47

Building Better Sentences 49

Working with Topic Sentences 51

    Writer's Note: Keeping a Journal for New Ideas 54

Building Better Sentences 55

    Language Focus: Sentence Fragments and Comma Splices 56

Building Better Sentences 59

Building Better Vocabulary 60

Original Student Writing 61

Timed Writing 62

UNIT 4   SUPPORTING AND CONCLUDING SENTENCES 63

Good Supporting Sentences 63

Kinds of Supporting Sentences 67

Building Better Sentences 68

Analyzing and Writing Supporting Sentences 68

    Language Focus: Using Pronouns for Key Nouns 74

    Writer's Note: Staying on Track 75

Good Concluding Sentences 75

Kinds of Concluding Sentences 76

    Restate the Main Idea 76

    Offer a Suggestion, Give an Opinion, or Make a Prediction 76

Analyzing and Writing Concluding Sentences 77

Building Better Sentences 80

Building Better Vocabulary 80

Original Student Writing 81

    Writer's Note: Selecting Important Information 81

Timed Writing 82

UNIT 5   PARAGRAPH REVIEW 83

Paragraph Review 83

    Features of a Paragraph 83

    Language Focus Review 83

Working with the Structure of a Paragraph 84

    Writer's Note: Proofreading Your Work 85

Building Better Sentences 88

Analyzing Paragraphs 89

    Writer's Note: Checking Your Supporting Sentences 90

Building Better Sentences 94

    Language Focus: Articles 94

Great Writing 2

Great Paragraphs

Great Writing 2

Great Paragraphs

THIRD EDITION

KEITH S. FOLSE
UNIVERSITY OF CENTRAL FLORIDA

APRIL MUCHMORE-VOKOUN
HILLSBOROUGH COMMUNITY COLLEGE

ELENA VESTRI SOLOMON
EMIRATES COLLEGE FOR ADVANCED EDUCATION
UAE

HEINLE
CENGAGE Learning™

Australia • Canada • Mexico • Singapore • Spain • United Kingdom • United States

Great Writing 2: Great Paragraphs
Keith S. Folse, April Muchmore-Vokoun,
Elena Vestri Solomon

Publisher: Sherrise Roehr

Acquisition Editor: Tom Jefferies

Senior Development Editor:
Yeny Kim

Assistant Editor: Marissa Petrarca

Director of Content and Media Production:
Michael Burggren

Marketing Director, U.S.: Jim McDonough

Director of Adult Education Sales:
Eric Bredenberg

Marketing Communications Manager:
Beth Leonard

Senior Product Marketing Manger:
Katie Kelley

Academic Marketing Manager:
Caitlin Driscoll

Senior Content Project Manager:
Maryellen Eschmann-Killeen

Senior Print Buyer: Susan Spencer

Composition: Pre-Press PMG

Library of Congress Control Number: 2009926618

ISBN-13: 978-1-4240-5100-7

ISBN-10: 1-4240-5100-2

Heinle Cengage Learning
20 Channel Center Street
Boston, MA 02210
USA

Cengage learning is a leading provider of customized learning solutions with office locations around the globe, including Singapore, the United Kingdom, Australia, Mexico, Brazil, and Japan. Locate our local office at:
International.cengage.com/region

Cengage Learning products are represented in Canada by Nelson Education, Ltd.

Visit Heinle online at **elt.heinle.com**
Visit out corporate website at **cengage.com**

Printed in the United States of America
4 5 6 7 13 12

Building Better Vocabulary 96

Original Student Writing 97

Additional Topics for Writing 98

Timed Writing 98

UNIT 6   DEFINITION PARAGRAPHS 99

What Is a Definition Paragraph? 99

Building Better Sentences 105

    Writer's Note: Quotation Marks 105

    Writer's Note: Citing Ideas to Avoid Plagiarism 107

Putting the Paragraph Together: Sequencing 108

    Writer's Note: Including Original Examples to Avoid Plagiarism 110

    Language Focus: Simple Adjective Clauses 111

    Writer's Note: Combining Sentences for Variety 114

Building Better Sentences 118

Building Better Vocabulary 118

Original Student Writing: Definition Paragraph 119

Additional Topics for Writing 120

Timed Writing 120

UNIT 7   PROCESS ANALYSIS PARAGRAPHS 121

What Is a Process Analysis Paragraph? 121

Building Better Sentences 126

Organizing a Process Analysis Paragraph 127

    Writer's Note: Using Index Cards to Help You Organize 127

    Language Focus: Transition Words and Chronological Order 127

    Writer's Note: Using Technical Terms 129

    Writer's Note: Checking Possessive Adjectives 131

Building Better Sentences 132

Building Better Vocabulary 132

Original Student Writing: Process Analysis Paragraph 133

Additional Topics for Writing 134

Timed Writing 134

UNIT 8   DESCRIPTIVE PARAGRAPHS 135

What Is a Descriptive Paragraph? 135

Describing with the Five Senses 136

    Writer's Note: Using Adjectives to Connect with Your Readers 143

    Language Focus: Adjectives 143

    Writer's Note: Using Adjectives in the Correct Place 144

Building Better Sentences 146

    Writer's Note: Using a Bilingual Dictionary 146

Using Denotation and Connotation to Describe 147

    Language Focus: Denotation and Connotation 147

Using Prepositions of Location to Describe 151

    Language Focus: Prepositions of Location 152

    Writer's Note: Word Order with Prepositions of Location 157

Building Better Sentences 158

Building Better Vocabulary 159

Original Student Writing: Descriptive Paragraph 160

Additional Topics for Writing 161

Timed Writing 161

UNIT 9   OPINION PARAGRAPHS 162

What Is an Opinion Paragraph? 162

Working with Opinions 163

    Writer's Note: Including an Opposing Opinion 167

Facts and Opinions 168

Building Better Sentences 169

    Language Focus: Word Forms 171

Choosing a Topic for an Opinion Paragraph 173

Building Better Sentences 173

Building Better Vocabulary 174

Original Student Writing: Opinion Paragraph 175

Additional Topics for Writing 176

Timed Writing 176

UNIT 10 NARRATIVE PARAGRAPHS 177

What Is a Narrative Paragraph? 177

    Writer's Note: Including Background Information 178

    Beginning, Middle, and End 178

Working with Ideas for Narrative Paragraphs 185

    Writer's Note: Using Vivid Language to Help Readers
    "See" Your Story 185

Building Better Sentences 188

    Language Focus: Verb Tense Consistency 189

Building Better Sentences 194

Building Better Vocabulary 195

Original Student Writing: Narrative Paragraph   196

Additional Topics for Writing   197

Timed Writing   197

UNIT 11   PARAGRAPHS IN AN ESSAY: PUTTING IT ALL TOGETHER   198

Getting to Know Essays   199

What Is an Essay?   199

Why Do People Write Essays?   199

How Are Essays and Paragraphs Similar?   200

How Are Essays and Paragraphs Different?   200

What Does an Essay Look Like?   202

An Essay Outline   204

Writer's Note: Varying Your Vocabulary   204

The Thesis Statement   204

Supporting Ideas   205

Different Kinds of Essay Organization   206

Putting an Essay Together   210

Building Better Vocabulary   213

Next Steps   214

Original Student Writing: Essay   215

Timed Writing   215

BRIEF WRITER'S HANDBOOK WITH ACTIVITIES   217

Understanding the Writing Process: The Seven Steps   218

Editing Your Writing   225

Capitalization Activities   228

Punctuation Activities   231

Additional Grammar Activities   238

Citations and Plagiarism   247

APPENDICES   249

Appendix 1   Building Better Sentences   250

Appendix 2   Peer Editing Sheets   265

INDEX   289

Overview

Great Writing 2: Great Paragraphs is the second book in the five-level *Great Writing* series of composition books. *Great Writing 2* offers introductory material on paragraph writing. This material includes a wide variety of exercises that provide serious practice in both learning the writing process and developing a final written product.

The book is designed for intermediate students; however, we have controlled the language as much as possible so that dedicated upper beginners and weak advanced students may also benefit from the instruction. Depending on the class level and the amount of writing that is done outside of class, there is enough material for 60 to 80 classroom hours. If a more substantial amount of writing is done outside of class, the number of hours for a faster group can be as little as 40.

Some of the highlights of *Great Writing 2* include the following:

- **Abundance of activities and writing practice** The new third edition contains 209 activities, including 30 suggestions for additional paragraph writing assignments and 31 supplementary activities that focus on sentence combining, capitalization, punctuation, and grammar in the Brief Writer's Handbook with Activities. New to this edition, the Timed Writing feature provides students with an opportunity to practice writing using a writing prompt with a time limit.

- **Step-by-step instruction** Some English learners are already good writers in their native language, and their writing skills may transfer to English when these students are given appropriate practice activities to bring their abilities out. However, other learners need work in the basic steps involved in the process of composing a paragraph. These students in particular will benefit from the step-by-step activities in *Great Writing 2*. Of special interest are Appendix 1, Building Better Sentences, which contains guided activities to improve students' sentence combination skills, and the new Editing Your Writing section of the Brief Writer's Handbook with Activities, which provides a step-by-step introduction to the process of identifying and correcting errors and rewriting drafts based on teacher feedback.

- **Contextualized activities** An important feature of *Great Writing 2* is the inclusion of 100 example paragraphs distributed throughout the units. Teachers and students recognize the importance of grammar in writing; however, we want to stress that while grammar is important, having good grammar is not all that is necessary for being a good writer. In this book, we have tried to avoid lengthy grammar explanations. When we provide grammar practice, it is done in the context of whole paragraphs of related sentences. In addition to providing relevant practice in the particular grammar (or punctuation or capitalization) area, these contextualized activities also provide learners with more input in English composition and paragraph organization and cohesion. We believe that this is a win-win situation for both teachers and learners.

- **Enhanced focus on vocabulary** A piece of writing is often only as good as the writer's ability to use a wide range of appropriate vocabulary. To help our learners achieve this important goal, this third edition includes more emphasis on vocabulary in six key ways:

  1. *More vocabulary items.* We have revised some of the paragraphs to include more focus on words that will help students improve their own writing.

  2. *More glossing.* We have glossed more vocabulary items after the paragraphs.

  3. *More recycling.* We have intentionally recycled vocabulary items from unit to unit. With increased exposure, students will learn not only the basic meanings of words and phrases, but also acquire actual natural usage.

4. *Practice of meaning.* New to this edition, each unit contains a Word Associations activity that allows students to check their understanding of the basic meaning of new vocabulary.

5. *Practice of collocations.* Also new to this third edition, each unit includes an activity on collocations, which are words or groups of words that naturally and frequently co-occur with a target word. Learning collocations will help students build on their bank of commonly used phrases, which is the first step to incorporating those phrases into their writing.

6. *Active use of vocabulary.* While knowing word meanings may allow for passive recognition in reading or listening, knowledge of word meanings alone is often insufficient for using the vocabulary accurately and fluently in writing (or speaking). Students need to practice the vocabulary items and collocations presented in these activities in their writing. To this end, students are instructed to use some of the vocabulary presented in the vocabulary activities as they write their Original Writing Practice assignment for that unit.

The teacher is always the best judge of which units and which activities should be covered with any group of students. We fully recognize that no one knows your students and their writing needs better than you do, so it is up to you to gauge the needs of your students and then match those needs with the material in this book.

Text Organization

Great Writing 2 consists of these sections: Units 1–5 deal with the elements of a good paragraph, Units 6–11 feature five different kinds of paragraphs and an introduction to writing essays, and the Brief Writer's Handbook with Activities and the Appendices contain ancillary and additional practice material.

Units 1–5

Units 1–5 teach, in general terms, how to construct a good paragraph. Some of the material in these units may be redundant for some students. Thus, teachers may want to use only selected material from Units 1–5 while moving more quickly into the specific paragraph practices in Units 6–10. The five units cover (1) what a paragraph looks like, (2) how to brainstorm, (3) how to write a topic sentence, (4) what supporting and concluding sentences do, and (5) how to write a simple paragraph. Students who are already familiar with what a paragraph is may begin with Unit 5, which reviews material presented in Units 1 through 4.

Units 6–10

Units 6–10 explain five different kinds of paragraphs: *definition, process analysis, descriptive, opinion,* and *narrative.* While it is not necessary to cover these five paragraph modes in this order, the current sequencing will allow for some recycling of grammatical and lexical items. We do not believe that learning to write by studying rhetorical modes is the only good way to learn ESL composition; however, we believe that rhetorical modes are the easiest, most efficient, and most sensible way to organize an ESL composition course.

Unit 11

Unit 11 helps students see how paragraphs and essays are related. Students are given both guided practice opportunities in writing missing paragraphs for an essay and original practice opportunities in the whole process of producing an original essay. (Students who need to master essays should use the third, fourth, and fifth books in the *Great Writing* series: *Great Writing 3: From Great Paragraphs to Great Essays, Great Writing 4: Great Essays,* and *Great Writing 5: Greater Essays.*

Brief Writer's Handbook with Activities

The Brief Writer's Handbook with Activities offers additional support in both the process and the mechanics of writing.

"Understanding the Writing Process: The Seven Steps" explains the seven steps in the process of writing a paragraph. However, rather than merely listing the seven steps as many books do, this section walks students through the step-by-step process of the assignment in Unit 6, Definition Paragraphs. (We chose definition paragraphs to illustrate this process because definition paragraphs are one of the easiest and most transparent rhetorical modes for learners at this level.) For the final assignment in this unit, a student has written a paragraph in which she defines a type of regional food. Each of the seven steps is explained, followed by the student's writing in that step, whether it be brainstorming, handwritten notes about the process, or a first draft.

New to this edition, the "Editing Your Writing" section guides students through the editing process. Teachers often spend considerable time marking and commenting on student work, but many students have difficulty incorporating teacher feedback as they write their next draft. While many textbooks offer general advice on editing, students often need more specific and explicit advice. This innovative section is meant to provide students with the step-by-step training they need to effectively integrate teacher feedback as they rewrite their drafts. In Editing Your Writing, students analyze three versions of the same student paragraph.

- Version 1 is an uncorrected draft of a student-generated, timed-writing assignment. Students read the assigned writing task and then the original paragraph to compare the task and the product globally. Students then read the paragraph for a closer inspection of the organization, grammar, vocabulary, and writing style.

- Version 2 is the same paragraph with instructor comments. In this version, students can see what the instructor has written. Students will see both positive and negative comments. An important point here is for students to compare their comments after reading Version 1 with the teacher's comments. Which comments are similar? Which areas are different?

- Version 3 is the second draft of the work after the teacher's comments. The writer has accepted some of the teacher's comments but appears to have rejected others, which is a very common occurrence in all composition classes. Through guided questions, students are asked to identify sections that were changed. Were the changes made in response to teacher comments, or were the changes original changes initiated by the student after rereading the writing?

The "Capitalization Activities" and "Punctuation Activities" sections provide a review of capitalization and punctuation rules. The "Additional Grammar Activities" section provides additional practice in some of the most persistent grammatical problems for English learners so that students' ability to express themselves in English is not hindered by their level of English proficiency.

"Citations and Plagiarism" is new to this third edition, but the topic it addresses is not a new concern: citing borrowed information and avoiding plagiarism. In addition to teaching notes within the units, we have included a separate section on citations and plagiarism. For many students, the notion of plagiarism is new. Many English learners find it difficult to paraphrase material because they either do not understand the original material well enough in the first place or they do not have enough vocabulary knowledge to express the same idea in their own words. Whether writers use a paraphrase or an exact quote, they need to learn how to cite this information to avoid plagiarism.

Appendices

Appendix 1, Building Better Sentences, consists of twenty exercises that help students build better sentences in English through sentence combining. Some students' writing contains many simple sentences that rarely go beyond subject-verb-object or subject-*be*-adjective constructions. While such sentences may be correct, this type of writing lacks variety and appears very simplistic. Instructing students to write longer sentences may help them write more. A real advantage of these twenty activities is that they can be checked as a whole class, thereby reducing teacher grading time.

Appendix 2 consists of peer editing sheets for the final writing activity in each unit. We believe that for the peer editing process to work beneficially for both the reader and the writer, proper guidance is needed. These peer editing sheets provide structure and focused guidance to help readers make useful comments that the writer can benefit from. For those students who are able to go beyond the basics, several of the questions are open-ended and invite additional comments.

Contents of a Unit

Although each unit has a specific writing goal and language focus (listed at the beginning of the unit), the following features appear in every unit.

Example Paragraphs

Because we believe that writing and reading are inextricably related, the example paragraphs are often preceded by short schema-building questions for small groups or the whole class. Potentially unfamiliar vocabulary is glossed. Example paragraphs are usually followed by questions about organization, syntactic structures, or other composition features.

Writer's Notes

Rather than large boxed areas of teaching overflowing with information, *Great Writing 2* features small chunks of writing advice under this heading. The content of these notes varies from brainstorming techniques, to peer editing guidelines, to citing original sources, to using adjectives for better descriptions, to plagiarism.

Language Focus

This section directs students' attention to a grammar issue that is related to the kind of writing being practiced in that unit. Those students who need additional practice should work through any additional exercises in the "Additional Grammar Activities" section of the Brief Writer's Handbook with Activities.

Building Better Sentences

Periodically in each unit, students are asked to turn to Appendix 1 and work on building better sentences. Each practice is intentionally short and includes only three problems. In each problem, there are three to five short sentences that the students must combine into a single sentence that expresses all the ideas in a logical and grammatically correct manner.

Proofreading and Editing

Many of the units contain different kinds of proofreading exercises. A writer's ability to locate and repair problems in his or her own writing is key to successful independent writing.

Sequencing

Even in the early units, students are asked to read sentences and put them in the best sequence. Where appropriate, students are asked to analyze the connecting or transition words and phrases. One of the main goals of *Great Writing 2* is to teach writing devices, such as transition words, so that students will be better equipped to use them in their own writing. In addition, other activities focus on sequencing by asking the student to complete partial outlines of the material in a given paragraph.

Copying

In the early units, students are asked to put sentences in sequence or to supply the correct verb form of a given verb within a sentence. Students are then asked to copy these sentences in a paragraph format and add an original title. This exercise provides practice in what a paragraph looks like and the kinds of related information it contains. Some teachers may wish to skip these activities altogether depending on students' needs and proficiency level.

Analyzing a Paragraph

Students are frequently asked to read a paragraph and answer a series of questions about various aspects of writing at the intermediate level, for example, recognizing the topic sentence, identifying the use of examples as support, or discovering the writer's purpose for including a given piece of information.

Building Better Vocabulary

Before the Original Writing Practice in every unit, students will complete two vocabulary-building activities. In these activities, which are new to this edition, vocabulary words have been taken from each unit's writing, and special attention is paid to building schema and collocations. In the first activity, Word Associations, the student identifies words that best relate to the target vocabulary word. This allows them to build connections to more words and thus grow their vocabulary more quickly. The second activity, Using Collocations, helps students learn specific word combinations, or collocations, which will help their original writing sound more advanced.

Original Writing

The end of each unit includes at least one activity that requires students to do some form of original writing. In Units 1–5, students are often asked to write a paragraph of no specified rhetorical style. The purpose here is to practice developing a good paragraph from a solid topic sentence with good controlling ideas. In Units 6–10, students are expected to maintain the same standards while producing a different kind of paragraph in each unit. Unit 11 asks students to write certain paragraphs to complete an essay.

In Units 5–10, students are provided with a list of five additional writing ideas or assignments for a total of 30 additional original writing assignments. It is up to the teacher to decide whether all students will write about the same topic or whether each student is free to choose any of the five topics listed. It is our experience that having students discuss their ideas in groups of no more than five or six students results in maximum discussion in English, maximum exchange of ideas, and maximum participation from each individual.

Peer Editing

At the end of each unit, a peer editing activity offers students the opportunity to provide written comments to one another with the goal of improving their paragraphs. Appendix 2 offers a unique peer editing sheet for each unit that provides the guidance and structure that is necessary for students at this level to successfully perform this task. We recommend that students spend 15 to 20 minutes reading a classmate's paragraph and writing comments using the questions on the peer editing sheet. Since a certain amount of trust and cooperation is involved in peer editing, it is important to make sure that students work with peers that they feel compatible with.

Timed Writing

One way to improve students' comfort level with the task of writing under a deadline, such as during a testing situation, is to provide them with numerous writing opportunities that are timed. As a result, in this third edition, the final activity in each unit features a timed-writing prompt that is geared toward the grammar and sentence structure presented in that unit. Students are given five minutes to read the prompt and make a quick writing plan, followed by 25 minutes of actual writing.

Although we have placed this Timed Writing as a final task within a unit, some teachers may prefer to assign this topic as the first task of the unit. In this case, these teachers usually collect students' work and then have them rewrite it at the end of the unit. In this way, students have two opportunities to practice composition while teachers only read and mark papers once.

About the Activities and Practices

Teachers have long noticed that although students do well with grammar in discrete sentences, they have problems with the same grammar when it occurs in a paragraph. Because of this difficulty, most of the activities and practices in *Great Writing 2* work with complete paragraphs. Thus, instead of five unrelated sentences for practice with past tense, we offer a paragraph of five sentences. Our hope is that by practicing the grammatical problem in the target medium, students will produce more accurate writing sooner. The large number of such paragraphs (100) allows a great deal of freedom on the teacher's part in planning this course.

The earliest ESL composition textbooks were merely extensions of ESL grammar classes. The activities in these books did not practice English composition as much as they did ESL grammar points. Later books, on the other hand, tended to focus too much on the composing process. We feel that this focus ignores the important fact that the real goal for English learners is both to produce a presentable product and to understand the composing process. From our years of ESL and other L2 teaching experience, we believe that *Great Writing 2* allows English learners to achieve this goal.

 For the answer key, additional exercises, and other instructor resources, visit the *Great Writing 2* instructor Web site at elt.heinle.com/greatwriting

Additional exercises for each unit are available to students on the *Great Writing 2* student Web site at elt.heinle.com/greatwriting

Acknowledgments

We would like to thank the hundreds of ESL and English composition colleagues who have generously shared their ideas, insights, and feedback on L2 writing, university English course requirements, and textbook design at conferences or in e-mail correspondence since we started writing the first edition of this series. In addition, we would like to thank teachers on two electronic lists, TESL-L and TESLIE-L, who responded to our original queries about their composition classes and thereby helped us write this book.

We would like to thank our editors at Heinle/Cengage Learning, Thomas Jefferies and Yeny Kim. We also remain forever grateful to our previous editors at Houghton Mifflin, Susan Maguire, Kathy Sands-Boehmer, and Kathleen Smith, for their indispensable guidance throughout the birth and growth of this writing project.

Likewise, we are indebted to the following reviewers who offered ideas and suggestions that shaped our revisions:

Don Beck, The University of Findlay, OH
Jodi Brinkley, Florida Community College, FL
Lee Chen, Palomar College, CA
Chip DiMarco, Harvard University, MA
Kathy Flynn, Glendale Community College, CA
Rebecca Ford, Sacramento City College, CA
Linda Forse, University of Texas, Brownsville, TX
Rachel Gader, Georgetown University, Washington, DC
Janet Goldstein, Bramson ORT Technological Institute, NY
Gretchen Hack, Community College of Denver, CO
Kathy Judd, Truman College, IL
Meridith Kemper, University of Central Arkansas, AR
Sarah Mitchell Kim, Miramar College, CA
Tom Kitchens, Texas Intensive English Program, Austin, TX
Chouaib Naamad, Northeastern University, MA
Nelson Rivera Agosto, University of Puerto Rico, Arecibo
Phyllis Ruppert, Coe College, IA
Kim Sanabria, Columbia University, NY
Virginia Scales, San Jose City College, CA
Ken Szok, Mt. San Antonio College, CA
Carol Thurston, Northern Virginia Community College, VA
Colleen Weldele, Palomar College, CA
Sherry Wickham, Brookhaven College, TX

Finally, many thanks go to our students who have taught us what ESL composition ought to be. Without them, this work would have been impossible.

Keith S. Folse
April Muchmore-Vokoun
Elena Vestri Solomon

Guided Tour

 NEW TO THIS EDITION

A new **four-color design** allows for engaging, easy to follow lessons.

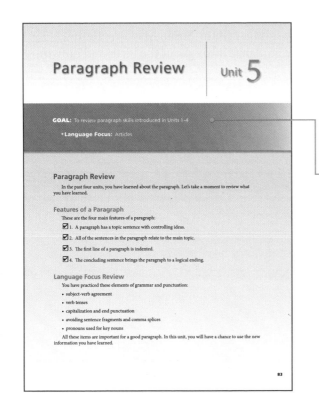

Writing Goals at the beginning of every unit provide a clear road map for the instruction that follows.

Student writing models help students focus on specific writing skills and multiple rhetorical structures.

ACTIVITY 2 Error Correction in a Paragraph

The following paragraph contains errors in indentation, capitalization, and punctuation. Read the paragraph and make corrections. There are 10 mistakes.

EXAMPLE PARAGRAPH 33

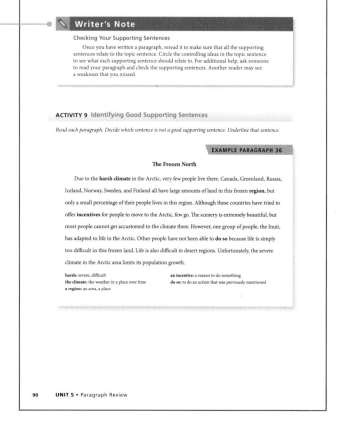

There is a lot to know about the sport of hockey. Hockey is popular in many countries, including canada and the United states. the game is played on Ice, and the players wear skates to move around A hockey player can score a point if he hits a special disk called a Puck into the goal. However, this is not as easy as it seems because each goal is guarded by a special player called a Goalie The goalie's job is to keep the puck away from the goal The next time you see a hockey game on television, perhaps you will be able to follow the action better because you have this information.

ACTIVITY 3 Copying an Edited Paragraph

After you have made the corrections in Activity 2, write the paragraph here. Think of a title and write it on the line above the paragraph.

_____

_____

_____

_____

_____

_____

_____

_____

_____

_____

Guided, structured activities help students to quickly master writing tasks.

✎ **Writer's Note**

Checking Your Supporting Sentences

Once you have written a paragraph, reread it to make sure that all the supporting sentences relate to the topic sentence. Circle the controlling ideas in the topic sentence to see what each supporting sentence should relate to. For additional help, ask someone to read your paragraph and check the supporting sentences. Another reader may see a weakness that you missed.

ACTIVITY 9 Identifying Good Supporting Sentences

Read each paragraph. Decide which sentence is not a good supporting sentence. Underline that sentence.

EXAMPLE PARAGRAPH 36

The Frozen North

Due to the **harsh climate** in the Arctic, very few people live there. Canada, Greenland, Russia, Iceland, Norway, Sweden, and Finland all have large amounts of land in this frozen **region**, but only a small percentage of their people lives in this region. Although these countries have tried to offer **incentives** for people to move to the Arctic, few go. The scenery is extremely beautiful, but most people cannot get accustomed to the climate there. However, one group of people, the Inuit, has adapted to life in the Arctic. Other people have not been able to **do so** because life is simply too difficult in this frozen land. Life is also difficult in desert regions. Unfortunately, the severe climate in the Arctic area limits its population growth.

harsh: severe, difficult
the climate: the weather in a place over time
a region: an area, a place

an incentive: a reason to do something
do so: to do an action that was previously mentioned

Writer's Note sections provide relevant writing-skill instruction that supports the unit's writing goals.

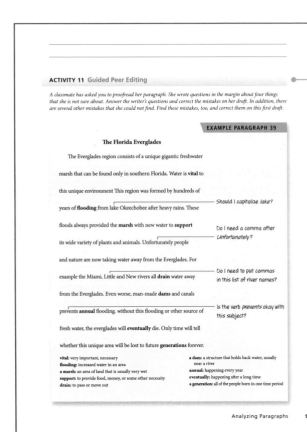

A classmate has asked you to proofread her paragraph. She wrote questions in the margin about four things that she is not sure about. Answer the writer's questions and correct the mistakes on her draft. In addition, there are several other mistakes that she could not find. Find these mistakes, too, and correct them on this first draft.

EXAMPLE PARAGRAPH 39

The Florida Everglades

The Everglades region consists of a unique gigantic freshwater marsh that can be found only in southern Florida. Water is **vital** to this unique environment This region was formed by hundreds of years of **flooding** from lake Okeechobee after heavy rains. These floods always provided the **marsh** with new water to **support** its wide variety of plants and animals. Unfortunately people and nature are now taking water away from the Everglades. For example the Miami, Little and New rivers all **drain** water away from the Everglades. Even worse, man-made **dams** and canals prevents **annual** flooding. without this flooding or other source of fresh water, the everglades will **eventually** die. Only time will tell whether this unique area will be lost to future **generations** forever.

Margin notes:
- Should I capitalize *lake*?
- Do I need a comma after *Unfortunately*?
- Do I need to put commas in this list of river names?
- Is the verb *prevents* okay with this subject?

vital: very important, necessary
flooding: increased water in an area
a marsh: an area of land that is usually very wet
support: to provide food, money, or some other necessity
drain: to pass or move out

a dam: a structure that holds back water, usually near a river
annual: happening every year
eventually: happening after a long time
a generation: all of the people born in one time period

Individual and peer **editing** opportunities in every unit provide focused guidelines for effective editing practice.

Integrated **grammar** lessons teach and practice the grammar necessary to accomplish the writing goals of the unit.

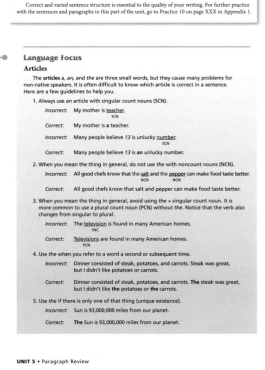

Building Better Sentences

Correct and varied sentence structure is essential to the quality of your writing. For further practice with the sentences and paragraphs in this part of the unit, go to Practice 10 on page XXX in Appendix 1.

Language Focus

Articles

The **articles** *a, an,* and *the* are three small words, but they cause many problems for non-native speakers. It is often difficult to know which article is correct in a sentence. Here are a few guidelines to help you.

1. Always use an article with singular count nouns (SCN).

   Incorrect: My mother is teacher.
                    SCN
   Correct: My mother is a teacher.

   Incorrect: Many people believe *13* is unlucky number.
                    SCN
   Correct: Many people believe *13* is **an** unlucky number.

2. When you mean the thing in general, do not use *the* with noncount nouns (NCN).

   Incorrect: All good chefs know that the salt and the pepper can make food taste better.
                    NCN   NCN
   Correct: All good chefs know that salt and pepper can make food taste better.

3. When you mean the thing in general, avoid using *the* + singular count noun. It is more common to use a plural count noun (PCN) without *the*. Notice that the verb also changes from singular to plural.

   Incorrect: The television is found in many American homes.
                    SNC
   Correct: Televisions are found in many American homes.
                    PCN

4. Use *the* when you refer to a word a second or subsequent time.

   Incorrect: Dinner consisted of steak, potatoes, and carrots. Steak was great, but I didn't like potatoes or carrots.

   Correct: Dinner consisted of steak, potatoes, and carrots. **The** steak was great, but I didn't like **the** potatoes or **the** carrots.

5. Use *the* if there is only one of that thing (unique existence).

   Incorrect: Sun is 93,000,000 miles from our planet.

   Correct: **The** Sun is 93,000,000 miles from our planet.

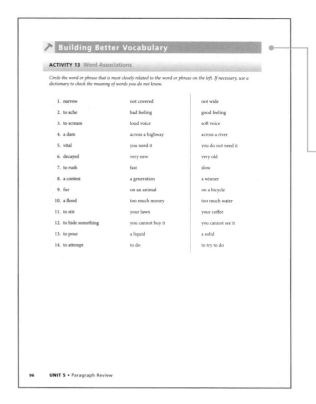

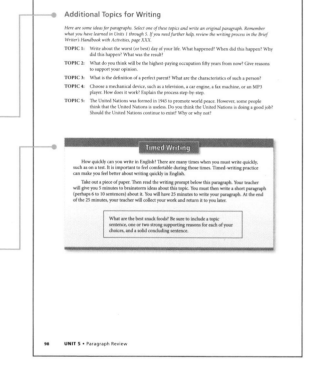

 NEW TO THIS EDITION

Building Better Vocabulary features teach students how to accurately and effectively use written English.

Suggestions for additional writing activities provide the opportunity for even more writing on a variety of topics.

 NEW TO THIS EDITION

Timed Writing activities prepare students for success on standardized tests like the TOEFL®.

Supplements

 NEW TO THIS EDITION

 The **Assessment CD-ROM with** *ExamView*® allows teachers to create tests and quizzes easily.

 NEW TO THIS EDITION

The **Classroom Presentation Tool** makes instruction clearer and learning simpler.

For **Instructor's Resources** like lesson-planning tips, please visit elt.heinle.com/greatwriting.

What Is a Paragraph?

GOAL: To learn the four main features of a paragraph

*Language Focus: Identifying verbs in sentences

What is a **paragraph**? One way to answer this question is to talk about words and sentences.

You know what a word is—a word represents an idea. It is composed of one or more letters. A word alone, however, is usually not enough to express thoughts. To communicate ideas, writers use sentences. A **sentence** is a collection of words that expresses a complete thought. A sentence usually consists of a subject and a verb.

The illustration below shows the relationship of the writing terms *letter, word, sentence, paragraph,* and *essay.* Letters can be combined into a word. Words can be combined into a sentence. Sentences can be combined into a paragraph. Finally, paragraphs can be combined into an essay. In this book, you will study paragraphs.

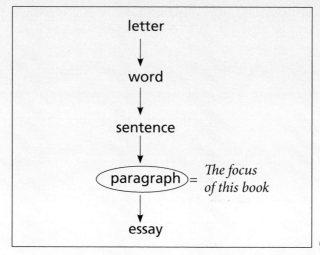

Connections

Example Paragraphs

Another way to learn about paragraphs is to read and study examples. On the next few pages, you will find three paragraphs. Each one is about a different topic and is written in a different style. Each example shows what a good paragraph looks like.

ACTIVITY 1 Studying an Example Paragraph

Read and study this example paragraph. Then answer the questions that follow. The questions will help you understand the content of the paragraph.

This definition paragraph is about a method of written communication for people who cannot see. The words in **bold** are explained below the paragraph.

EXAMPLE PARAGRAPH 1

Braille

Braille is a special system of writing and reading for **blind** people. Braille letters **are made up of dots**, or **bumps**. Blind people read these dots by running their **fingertips** across them to recognize the **pattern** of the dots. Braille uses a special code of sixty-three characters. Each character has one to six dots. These dots are **arranged** in a six-position pattern. For example, in the pattern for the letter *C*, the top two dots are **raised**, but the lower four are not. Braille gets its name from the inventor of this writing system. Louis Braille, a blind science and music teacher, **invented** this special alphabet in France in the 1800s. Today millions of blind people all over the world are able to read and write because of this simple **yet effective** communication system.

blind: not able to see	**arrange:** to put in a special way or order
are made up of: consist of	**raised:** higher than the surrounding area
a dot: a small point	**invent:** to create or make something original
a bump: a small, raised area	**yet:** but
a fingertip: the end of a finger	**effective:** useful, producing a good effect
a pattern: a design, a system	

1. In your own words, what is Braille? Begin your sentence like this: "Braille is . . ."

_____

_____

2. Have you ever seen Braille writing? If so, where?

_____

_____

3. Draw the Braille letters for a simple word. Then exchange books with a classmate to see if he or she can read your Braille word.

A	B	C	D	E	F	G	H	I	J
● ·	● ·	● ●	● ●	● ·	● ●	● ●	● ·	· ●	· ●
· ·	● ·	· ·	· ●	· ●	● ·	● ●	● ●	● ·	● ●
· ·	· ·	· ·	· ·	· ·	· ·	· ·	· ·	· ·	· ·

K	L	M	N	O	P	Q	R	S	T
● ·	● ·	● ●	● ●	● ·	● ●	● ●	● ·	· ●	· ●
· ·	● ·	· ·	· ●	· ●	● ·	● ●	● ●	● ·	● ●
● ·	● ·	● ·	● ·	● ·	● ·	● ·	● ·	● ·	● ·

U	V	W	X	Y	Z	ed	er	ou	ow
● ·	● ·	· ●	● ●	● ●	● ·	● ●	● ●	● ·	· ●
· ·	● ·	● ●	· ·	· ●	· ●	● ·	● ●	● ●	● ·
● ●	● ●	· ●	● ●	● ●	● ●	· ●	· ●	· ●	· ●

ch	gh	sh	th	wh	and	for	of	the	with
● ·	● ·	● ●	● ●	● ·	● ●	● ●	● ·	· ●	· ●
· ·	● ·	· ·	· ●	· ●	● ·	● ●	● ●	● ·	● ●
· ●	· ●	· ●	· ●	· ●	● ●	● ●	● ●	● ●	● ●

_____

_____

✎ Writer's Note

Repetition and Simple Present Tense Verbs

Two common features of paragraphs that explain or describe something are the use of **repetition** and **simple present tense verbs**. The paragraph "Braille" on page 2 explains and describes the Braille system.

Repetition

- How many sentences are there in the paragraph on the Braille system? _____
- Circle the subject of each sentence. (One sentence has two subjects.)
- How many times is the word *Braille* the subject of a sentence? _____

The word *Braille* is repeated often because it is the topic that is being explained and described. Repetition of key nouns is sometimes necessary to avoid confusion.

Simple Present Tense Verbs

- Put two lines under each verb in the paragraph on the Braille system. What tense are most of the verbs? _____

The correct answer is simple present tense. This paragraph explains something that is still true today, so most of the ideas are in the simple present tense.

- One verb is in the simple past tense. Write it here. _____
- Why is this verb in the simple past tense? _____

ACTIVITY 2 Writing Practice

Think of something that is unique about you. It can be about your hobby, language, or family. Write five sentences about that topic. What verb tense will you use?

1. _____

2. _____

3. _____

4. _____

5. _____

ACTIVITY 3 Studying an Example Paragraph

Read and study this example paragraph. Then answer the questions that follow. These questions will help you understand the content and the organization of the paragraph.

This process analysis paragraph tells how to do something. Read it and see if you can follow the steps.

EXAMPLE PARAGRAPH 2

An Easy Sandwich

An egg salad sandwich is one of the easiest and most delicious foods to make for lunch. First, **boil** two eggs for five minutes. Take them out of the water and let them cool off. Next, **peel** away the **shells** and put the eggs into a bowl. Use a fork to **mash** them up very well. After that, add three tablespoons of mayonnaise. Add salt and pepper to taste. Mix these **ingredients** well. Put the egg salad in the refrigerator for **at least** thirty minutes. Just before lunch, **spread** the egg salad on bread and enjoy your creation.

boil: to cook in water at 212°F (100°C)
peel: to take away the outside covering of something
a shell: the outside covering of an egg
mash: to push down and break into small pieces
ingredients: parts that you need to make something

at least: the minimum number or amount of something that is required; that number or more
spread: to move a substance over an area in many directions

1. What is the main purpose of this paragraph? (Why did the author write this paragraph?)

   _____

   _____

   _____

   _____

2. Have you ever made egg salad? If so, is your recipe different? How?

   _____

   _____

   _____

   _____

3. Do you know another easy recipe? Write the main steps of the recipe. Present your information to the class and then listen to your classmates present their recipes.

   _____

   _____

   _____

   _____

   _____

   _____

   _____

   _____

   _____

Imperative Form

Using the Imperative for Giving Directions

An English sentence that begins with a verb is called an **imperative sentence**. Imperative sentences are used to give directions or commands. The purpose of "An Easy Sandwich" on page 4 is to give directions, or steps, in completing a process—making an egg salad sandwich. The writer uses imperative verb forms for most of the verbs in this paragraph.

(NOTE: In spoken language, polite imperatives begin with *please*. For example: "Please wait here for a moment.")

Answer these questions:

How many sentences are there in "An Easy Sandwich"? _____

Circle the main verb or verbs in each sentence.

How many sentences begin with a verb? _____

Sequence

When you give directions, the sequence of the steps is important—the steps should be given in the order that they are to be completed, that is, from first to last. Read "An Easy Sandwich" again. Notice the sequence of the steps that the writer has listed for the recipe.

ACTIVITY 4 Writing Practice

Think of a process that you know how to do. Write four to seven sentences that explain how to complete that process. For example, you can write about food (how to make hummus or how to cook spaghetti) or everyday routines (how to tie a shoe or how to send a text message).

1. _____

   _____

2. _____

   _____

3. _____

   _____

4. _____

   _____

5. _____

   _____

6. _____

_____

7. _____

_____

ACTIVITY 5 Studying an Example Paragraph

Read and study this example paragraph. Then follow the directions on the next page to write three questions. These questions will help you understand the content and organization of the paragraph.

Can you remember a time when you had a strong feeling about something? Perhaps you were happy or sad or angry. In this narrative paragraph, the writer tells about a day when he was afraid. This emotion was so strong that he remembers many details about the event even though it took place in 1972.

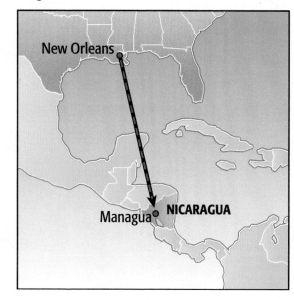

EXAMPLE PARAGRAPH 3

My First Flight

Although the first time I flew on a plane was many years ago, I can still remember how afraid I was that day. All my life, I had **wondered** what it would be like to fly in an airplane. Finally, in March of 1972, I **boarded** my first flight. I flew from New Orleans, Louisiana, to Managua, Nicaragua, on SAHSA Airlines. It was a Boeing 727 jet. There were three seats on each side of the **aisle**. It was **sort of** crowded, and this only made me more nervous. Every time we hit a little **turbulence**, my hands **turned** white. I was so nervous during the **entire** flight that I did not eat the meal they gave me. I would not even go to the bathroom. I cannot tell you how **relieved** I was when the plane finally landed at our **destination**. Since then, I have been on **over** one hundred flights, but I can still remember many small **details** of my first airplane flight.

wonder: to ask yourself about something, to imagine what something is like

board: to get on a plane (or other form of transportation)

an aisle: the row between seats on a plane (or bus or train)

sort of: somewhat, rather

turbulence: rough air during a flight, bumpiness

turn: to change, become

entire: complete, whole

relieved: the feeling when a person no longer feels pressure about something

destination: the final place that you are traveling to

over: more than

a detail: a fact about something

Almost everyone has traveled by plane. Can you remember your first flight? Write three questions to ask a classmate about his or her first flight. Then work in small groups and take turns asking each other your questions. The first question has been written for you.

1. <u>What do you remember about your first flight?</u>

2. _____

3. _____

✎ Writer's Note

Use of *I* and Simple Past Tense

How is "My First Flight" different from "Braille" and "An Easy Sandwich"? "My First Flight" is a narrative paragraph. Writing a story about something that has happened is called narrative writing. Perhaps you already know the word *narrator*. A narrator is the person who tells the story.

Subjects

How many sentences are there in "My First Flight"? _____

Underline all the subjects.

What word is used most often for the subject? _____

"My First Flight" is a narrative in which the narrator (*I*) tells the events of his/her first trip on an airplane.

Simple Past Tense Verbs

Most narrators tell a story about something that happened in the past. Most verbs in narrative writing are in the simple past tense.

Underline all the verbs in "My First Flight."

How many verbs are there? _____

How many of the verbs are in the simple present tense? _____

How many of the verbs are in the simple past tense? _____

(You will learn more about narrative paragraphs in Unit 10.)

Think of something that happened to you, such as a very funny event or a very happy occasion. Write five to ten sentences in which you tell the story.

1. _____

2. _____

3. _____

4. _____

5. _____

6. _____

7. _____

8. _____

9. _____

10. _____

Building Better Sentences

Correct and varied sentence structure is essential to the quality of your writing. For further practice with the sentences and paragraphs in this part of the unit, go to Practice 1 on page 251 in Appendix 1.

Four Features of a Paragraph

These are the four main features of a paragraph:

1. **A paragraph has a topic sentence that states the main idea**. The topic sentence is the foundation for the paragraph. It can be at the beginning, in the middle, or at the end of the paragraph, but it is usually at the beginning. The topic sentence helps the reader understand what the paragraph is about. (Topic sentences will be discussed more in Unit 3.)

2. **All of the sentences in a paragraph are about one topic**. They are connected to the topic sentence. There are no unrelated or extra sentences. How do you know whether something is connected or not? Look at the ideas in the topic sentence, which are sometimes called the *controlling ideas*. All of the other information in the paragraph must be connected to one or more of the controlling ideas in the topic sentence. (You will learn more about this in Unit 3 on page 47.)

3. **The first line of a paragraph is indented**. Indenting is easy to do. Just move the first line to the right about a half of an inch. On a word processor, this is about six spaces or the first tab stop position. This gap, or open space, in the first line is called an indentation.

4. **The last sentence, or concluding sentence, brings the paragraph to a logical conclusion**. For some writers, this is one of the most difficult features of a good paragraph to accomplish. The concluding sentence usually states the main point again or summarizes the main idea of the paragraph. In addition, it can offer a suggestion, an opinion, or a prediction. (Concluding sentences will be discussed more in Unit 4.)

ACTIVITY 7 Analyzing the Features of a Paragraph

Read this paragraph and answer the questions that follow.

EXAMPLE PARAGRAPH 4

Kids and Pets

At some point, most parents have to decide whether or not to **allow** their children to have pets. Some parents believe that pets teach children **a sense of** responsibility because children have to learn how to take care of their pets. In addition, many parents believe that pets can be fun for the family. Pets can also help children become more **compassionate** because children will develop a special **bond** with their pets. **On the other hand**, some parents are afraid that their children might hurt the animals or that these animals might hurt the children. Cats are good pets, but I do not like it when they shed hair on the furniture. Often these parents do not allow their children to have any kind of pet. Other families do not have the extra time or money that pets **require**. In **brief**, although many children want a pet, parents are divided on this issue for **a number of significant** reasons.

allow: to permit, let
a sense of: a feeling of
compassionate: with strong feelings of caring or wanting to help
a bond: a connection, a relationship
on the other hand: an expression used for the second or opposite reason ("on one hand" versus "on the other hand")

require: to need, must have
brief: short
a number of: several
significant: important

1. What is the main idea of the paragraph?

   _____

   _____

2. How many sentences are there in the paragraph? _____

3. How many sentences do NOT relate to the main idea? _____ Draw a line through any unrelated sentences.

4. Draw a line under the topic sentence. (Remember that the topic sentence is the sentence that helps the reader understand the main idea.)

5. How many lines (lines of text, not number of sentences) does this paragraph have? _____

6. What do you call the gap at the beginning of a paragraph? _____

7. Is this paragraph indented? _____

8. Draw two lines under the concluding sentence. How is the information in the concluding sentence related to the information in the topic sentence?

   _____

   _____

ACTIVITY 8 Analyzing the Features of the Example Paragraphs

Look at these three example paragraphs again: "Braille" on page 2, "An Easy Sandwich" on page 4, and "My First Flight" on page 7. Fill in the information about the features of each paragraph.

1. Write the topic sentence of each paragraph.

    "Braille" _____

    _____

    "An Easy Sandwich" _____

    _____

    "My First Flight" _____

    _____

2. What is the general idea of each paragraph?

    "Braille" _____

    "An Easy Sandwich" _____

    "My First Flight" _____

3. Is the first line of each paragraph indented?

    "Braille"   ❏ yes ❏ no

    "An Easy Sandwich"   ❏ yes ❏ no

    "My First Flight"   ❏ yes ❏ no

ACTIVITY 9 Analyzing the Features of Student Paragraphs

Read the following student paragraphs. Then answer the questions regarding the four main features of a paragraph. First, study this example.

Student Use of Computers

Computers are excellent machines to help students. Before computers, students had to do their schoolwork on typewriters. Typewriters did not allow students to make major changes easily, so they had to use special correction **fluid** to **fix** mistakes. Today computers **let** students move information around without retyping it and correct errors with little **effort**. Computers also make research more convenient for students. For example, before computers, students had to go to the library. Many times, they would read for four or five hours in several sources before finding useful information. However, students can now use the Internet from their home to **obtain** the information that they need much more quickly. Some computers are very expensive. My friend bought a computer that cost almost three thousand dollars. Computers have certainly made students' lives much easier.

a fluid: a liquid
fix: to repair
let: to allow, permit

effort: hard work, trying
obtain: to get, take

1. The general topic of the paragraph is how computers help students. Does the paragraph have a topic sentence? If so, write it here.

   <u>Computers are excellent machines to help students.</u>

2. Are all the sentences related to the topic? If not, write the unrelated sentences here.

   <u>Some computers are very expensive.</u>

   <u>My friend bought a computer that cost almost three thousand dollars.</u>

3. Is the first line indented? <u>yes</u>

4. What is the concluding sentence?

   <u>Computers have certainly made students' lives much easier.</u>

Simón Bolívar

Simón Bolívar (1783–1830) was one of South America's greatest generals and one of the most powerful people in world political history. In Spanish, Simón Bolívar is often called *El Libertador*, which means "The Liberator." Spanish is the **main** language in at least twenty-two countries. This **nickname** is a very good one because his planning and military actions helped to gain independence from Spain for six countries: Bolivia (1809), Colombia (1819), Ecuador (1820), Panama (1821), Peru (1821), and Venezuela (1811). In fact, Bolivia is named for Bolívar, making him one of the few people to have a country named for him. These six countries are **approximately** the same size as modern Europe, so the independence of such a large area was an amazing military and political **feat**. **Although** Bolívar's name is not as well-known outside Latin America, people there remember him as perhaps the most important person in their history.

main: principal, the most important
a nickname: a short name that people use in place of a longer name

approximately: about, more or less
a feat: an accomplishment
although: contrast between two ideas; but

1. What is the topic of the paragraph? _____

   Does the paragraph have a topic sentence? If so, write it here. If not, create one here.

   _____

   _____

2. Are all the sentences related to the topic? If not, write the unrelated sentences here. _____

   _____

   _____

3. Is the first line indented? _____

4. Underline the concluding sentence.

The State of South Carolina

First, it is valuable for its industries. South Carolina factories **manufacture textiles** and many chemical products. In addition, two of its most important cash **crops** are **cotton** and **tobacco**. The second reason **involves** American history. Many important **battles** of the American Revolution were **fought** in South Carolina. Almost one hundred years later, on December 20, 1860, it became the first state to leave the Union. Four months later, the Civil War between the North and South began in Charleston, a **port** in South Carolina. The products and history of South Carolina make it **distinct** from the other states.

manufacture: to make, produce
textiles: cloth for clothing
a crop: a plant that is grown for money
cotton: a white fiber that is used to make clothing
tobacco: a plant that is used to make cigarettes and cigars

involve: to have to do with, be connected with
a battle: a fight in a war
fought: past participle form of the verb *fight*
a port: a city on the coast
distinct: different, unique

1. What is the topic of the paragraph? _____

   Does the paragraph have a topic sentence? If so, write it here. If not, create one here.

   _____

   _____

2. Are all the sentences related to the topic? If not, write the unrelated sentences here. _____

   _____

   _____

3. Is the first line indented? _____

4. Underline the concluding sentence.

Jim Thorpe's Final Victory

Jim Thorpe is a controversial sports figure in sports history. He won Olympic gold medals in 1912, but he was not allowed to keep them. In the 1912 Olympics, Thorpe won **both** the pentathlon (five events) and decathlon (ten events). However, a month later, the U.S. Olympic Committee took away his medals because Thorpe had played baseball for money. An athlete who takes money for sports is called a *professional*, and at that time, professional athletes were not allowed to **take part in** any Olympic Games. In 1982, the U.S. Olympic Committee **reversed** this **ruling**. Seventy years after his **achievements**, Thorpe's name was finally returned to the list of 1912 Olympic winners.

both: two
take part in: to participate in
reverse: to change to the opposite position

a ruling: a decision, especially one that is made by a judge or court
an achievement: something special that a person is able to accomplish or do

1. What is the topic of the paragraph? _____

   Does the paragraph have a topic sentence? If so, write it here. If not, create one here.

   _____

   _____

2. Are all the sentences related to the topic? If not, write the unrelated sentences here. _____

   _____

   _____

3. Is the first line indented? _____

4. Underline the concluding sentence. What time phrases in the concluding sentence make the sentence sound like the ending of the paragraph?

   _____

Why I Avoid Breakfast

Like many people, I prefer to **skip** breakfast. I am not a "morning person," so it is very hard for me to wake up and then prepare breakfast. In addition, I do not like to eat breakfast because it makes me feel full the rest of the morning. With this uncomfortable feeling in my stomach, it is difficult for me to do my work well. Finally, I am very **concerned about** my health, so I **avoid** fatty kinds of breakfast foods, **such as** scrambled eggs, buttered toast, or fried sausage. Although others may not agree with my decision, I **choose** to skip breakfast most of the time.

skip: to omit
be concerned about: to be worried about
avoid: to try not to see, be near, or have any contact with

such as: for example
choose: to select

1. What is the topic of the paragraph? _____

   Does the paragraph have a topic sentence? If so, write it here. If not, create one here.

   _____

   _____

2. Are all the sentences related to the topic? If not, write the unrelated sentences here. _____

   _____

   _____

3. Is the first line indented? _____

4. Underline the concluding sentence. Do you think the author might change his opinion about skipping breakfast in the future? Why or why not?

   _____

   _____

My First Class as a Teacher

I can still remember a small **incident** that helped me relax on my first day of teaching many years ago. I was twenty-three years old at the time, and I had just graduated from college. The practice teaching that I had done for six weeks was very different from teaching my own class. When I walked into the room, I was very nervous. I carefully put my books down on the desk. Then I heard a girl say something in Spanish to another classmate. I speak Spanish, so I understood her perfectly when she told her friend to look at my hands. She said, "Look how his hands are **trembling**," and she was right. I was wearing a new watch that day, too. **Neither** of the two girls knew that I could understand Spanish. When I smiled a little, the first girl started to laugh because she realized at that moment that I understood Spanish. It seems like such a **silly** thing now, but the **humor** of the incident really helped me relax on the first day of my **career**.

an incident: a small event, usually not negative
tremble: to shake
neither: not A and not B (used with two choices)

silly: funny, crazy
humor: funny part
a career: what a person does for a living

1. What is the topic of the paragraph? _____

   Does the paragraph have a topic sentence? If so, write it here. If not, create one here.

   _____

   _____

2. Are all the sentences related to the topic? If not, write the unrelated sentences here. _____

   _____

   _____

3. Is the first line indented? _____

4. Underline the concluding sentence.

5. Sometimes key words or phrases appear in both the topic sentence and the concluding sentence. What words are repeated in both the topic sentence and the concluding sentence of this paragraph?

   _____

For more practice with analyzing the features of a paragraph, try Unit 1, Activity 1, Activity 2, Activity 3, and Activity 4 on the *Great Writing 2* Web site: elt.heinle.com/greatwriting

ACTIVITY 10 Capitalization and End Punctuation

In this activity, add correct capitalization and end punctuation to the sentences. See the Brief Writer's Handbook with Activities, pages 228–232, if you need help. The first one has been done for you.

1. the geography of the country of turkey is unique

   The geography of the country of Turkey is unique.

2. most countries are in one continent, but turkey lies in both asia and europe

   _____

3. the asian part is much larger than the european part

   _____

4. the eight countries that share a border with turkey are armenia, azerbaijan, bulgaria, georgia, greece, iran, iraq, and syria

   _____

5. turkey has coasts on the mediterranean sea and the black sea

   _____

6. half of turkey's land is higher than 1,000 meters

_____

7. in fact, two-thirds of turkey's land is higher than 800 meters

_____

8. the unique geography of turkey is one reason that millions of tourists visit this country every year

_____

For more practice with capitalization and end punctuation, try Unit 1, Activity 5 on the *Great Writing 2* Web site: elt.heinle.com/greatwriting

The Title of a Paragraph

What is the title of this textbook? Look on the front cover. Write the title here.

_____

What is the title of Example Paragraph 10 on page 18? Write the title here.

_____

A **title** tells you what you will find in a book, a movie, a story, or a paragraph. A title is not a sentence. A title is usually very short. Sometimes the title is only one word, such as the movie titles *Spiderman, Batman,* and *Titanic.* Can you think of other movie titles in English that are only one or two words long?

A good paragraph title is catchy. It has something that catches the reader's interest, but it does not tell everything about the paragraph. As an example, imagine that you wrote a paragraph about a time when you burned some scrambled eggs. Consider these titles.

Title	Comment
I Burned the Eggs	Poor title. A title should not be a sentence.
Burning the Eggs	Poor title. The meaning is not accurate. This sounds like you will tell how to intentionally burn the eggs.
Cooking Scrambled Eggs	Poor title. The meaning is not accurate. This sounds like you will tell only how to cook scrambled eggs.
A Bad Experience with Scrambled Eggs	A little better, but it is not clear if this is about eating eggs or making eggs.
The Day I Tried to Make Scrambled Eggs	Acceptable if the paragraph tells the events of that day.
A Cooking Disaster	Good title. It sums up the paragraph but does not tell exactly what happened.
A Kitchen Disaster	Good title. It sums up the paragraph but does not tell exactly what happened.
My Mess in the Kitchen	Good title. It sums up the paragraph but does not tell exactly what happened.

Building Better Sentences

Correct and varied sentence structure is essential to the quality of your writing. For further practice with the sentences and paragraphs in this part of the unit, go to Practice 2 on page 252 in Appendix 1.

Working with Paragraphs

In this section, you will begin to learn about the organization and format of a paragraph by copying sentences into paragraphs and then by writing a paragraph of your own.

ACTIVITY 11 Copying a Paragraph

Copy the sentences from Activity 10 in the same order. Make sure your paragraph is indented. Write a title on the top line.

EXAMPLE PARAGRAPH 11

_____

_____

_____

_____

_____

_____

_____

_____

_____

_____

_____

_____

Language Focus

Identifying Verbs in Sentences

Every sentence in English has a verb. Look at the verbs in these examples.

1. Where <u>is</u> the bank?

2. Japan <u>produces</u> many different kinds of cars.

3. Wheat <u>is grown</u> in Argentina.

4. The house on the corner <u>does</u> not <u>have</u> a garage.

5. Two amazing buildings in the United Arab Emirates <u>are</u> the Burj Al-Arab and the Dubai Tower.

Read the same five sentences without the verbs. A sentence without a verb is called a **fragment**. The word *fragment* means a piece of something that has been broken off. You will study more details about fragments in the Language Focus in Unit 3 on pages 56–57.

1. Where the bank?

2. Japan many different kinds of cars.

3. Wheat in Argentina.

4. The house on the corner not a garage.

5. Two amazing buildings in the United Arab Emirates the Burj Al-Arab and the Dubai Tower.

Writer's Note

Checking for the Verb

Although you do not need to worry about every grammar mistake in your writing, one very serious mistake is forgetting the verb.

Remember: Every sentence in English must have a verb. Before you turn in your paper in any class, you should proofread it. To proofread means to read the text carefully to find and correct errors or to make changes so that the writing sounds better. All good writers proofread their work one or two times before submitting it. Some mistakes are difficult to catch, but a sentence without a verb is easy to spot. Always check each sentence to make sure there is a verb!

ACTIVITY 12 Checking Your Grammar

Read each sentence. The subject in each clause is in italics. Underline the verb that goes with each subject. If every subject in the sentence has a verb, write C *for* correct *on the line. If a subject does not have a verb, write* X *on the line and add an appropriate verb in the correct place. (Many different verbs can be used. Use one that you think is appropriate.) The first one has been done for you.*

1. __X__ We <u>know</u> that *languages* <u>vary</u>, but other important communication *methods*~ exist .

2. _____ For example, when two *people* are talking, the appropriate *amount* of space between them varies by culture.

3. _____ In some cultures, *people* near each other when having a conversation.

4. _____ Sometimes these *people* might touch each other during the conversation.

5. _____ *Not standing near the speaker or not touching* might be seen as "cold" or disinterested behavior.

6. _____ In other cultures, *people* stand farther apart.

7. _____ If *one* of the speakers too close, the other *person* might see this as aggressive or strange behavior.

8. _____ The *amount* of personal space from culture to culture.

9. _____ *It* also a form of communication.

10. _____ Just as there is no universal *language*, there is no universal personal *space*.

 For more practice with identifying verbs in sentences and identifying sentences and fragments, try Unit 1, Activity 6 and Activity 7 on the *Great Writing 2* Web site: elt.heinle.com/greatwriting

Copy the sentences with your corrections from Activity 12 in the same order. Make sure your paragraph is indented. On the top line, write an original title for your paragraph.

EXAMPLE PARAGRAPH 12

_____

_____

_____

_____

_____

_____

_____

_____

_____

_____

_____

_____

_____

ACTIVITY 14 Word Associations

Circle the word or phrase that is most closely related to the word or phrase on the left. If necessary, use a dictionary to check the meaning of words you do not know. The first one has been done for you.

1. a destination	(a place)		a time
2. ingredients	for a recipe		for a suitcase
3. a term	a direction		a word
4. to require	to give		to need
5. a detail	a general idea		a specific idea
6. catchy	people like it		people hate it
7. to state	to believe		to say
8. to allow	to let		to put
9. to spread	to move		to stay
10. trembling	afraid, nervous		sleepy, tired
11. to be concerned	to be interested		to be worried
12. blind	cannot hear		cannot see
13. an achievement	something bad		something good
14. a pattern	A1B2C3D4E5		12A3BCD4E5
15. to spot	to see		to run

ACTIVITY 15 Using Collocations

Fill in each blank with the word on the left that most naturally completes the phrase on the right. If necessary, use a dictionary to check the meaning of words you do not know. The first one has been done for you.

1. in / on   _____in_____ brief

2. composed / spread   water is _____ of

3. bright / large   a _____ gap

4. avoid / damage   _____ eating fried foods

5. eye / hand   on the other _____

6. banana / cell phone   to peel a _____

7. almost / major   some _____ changes in (something)

8. damage / issue   a serious _____

9. aisle / though   even _____

10. of / in   consist _____

Original Student Writing

ACTIVITY 16 Original Writing Practice

Now it is your turn to write a simple paragraph. Follow these guidelines:

- Choose a general topic.
- Think of some specific aspect of that topic. Try to be as specific as you can. For example, you might choose "sports" as your first idea. Then you might choose "tennis." Finally, you might choose "how to keep score in tennis."
- Write five to twelve related sentences.
- Include a topic sentence.
- Indent the first line.
- The last sentence should be a good concluding sentence.
- Give your paragraph a title.
- Use at least five of the vocabulary words or phrases presented in Activity 14 and Activity 15. Underline these words and phrases in your paragraph.

You can choose any topic you want. The topics and topic sentences below may help you with ideas. In future units, you will learn how to come up with ideas and then develop them into paragraphs.

Topic	Topic Sentence
Food	The easiest food to prepare is . . .
	The best meal I ever had was . . .
Color	Each color in my country's flag represents something special.
	Colors can affect the way you feel.
Sports	_____ is an excellent _____ (name a sport) player.
	The rules for _____ (name a sport) are not (easy / difficult).
People	_____ has taught me many things about life.
	If I could meet anyone in history, I would like to meet . . .

Introduction to Peer Editing

Many students think that writing a paragraph only once is enough. This is rarely true. Good writers proofread their work and rewrite it several times. Even skilled and professional writers write and edit more than one draft.

Writer's Note

Once Is Never Enough!

Think of the first draft of your paper as your first attempt. Before you rewrite your paper, it is helpful to let someone else read it, offer comments, and ask questions to clarify your meaning. Many writers do not always see their own mistakes, but a reader can help you see where you need to make improvements.

Sometimes you need more than one opinion about your paper. In class, peer editing is an easy way to get opinions about your paper. In this method, other students (your peers) read your paper and make comments using a set of questions and guidelines. (See Peer Editing Sheets in Appendix 2.) You will read someone else's paper, too. Peer editing can help you strengthen any areas in your paragraph that are weak or that appear confusing to the reader.

Writer's Note

Suggestions for Peer Editing

Listen Carefully

In peer editing, you will receive many comments and some suggestions from other students. It is important to listen carefully to comments about your writing. You may think that what you wrote is clear and accurate, but readers can often point out places that need improvement. Remember that the comments are about the writing, not about you!

Make Helpful Comments

When you read your classmates' papers, choose your words and comments carefully so that you do not hurt their feelings. For example, instead of saying "This is bad grammar," or "I can't understand any of your ideas," make helpful comments, such as "You need to make sure that every sentence has a verb," or "What do you mean in this sentence?"

Study an Example of Editing Your Writing

In the Editing Your Writing section of the Brief Writer's Handbook with Activities (page 225), there are examples of edits and comments that a teacher made on a student's first draft. There is also an example of the student's second draft that was written after the teacher offered comments. Look at the examples in Editing Your Writing. Study how the student's second draft was different from the first draft. What kinds of things were changed? What kinds of things were not changed?

Read, Read, Read!

It is important for you to understand why a piece of writing is good or is not good, and the best way to do this is to read, read, and read some more! The more writing styles you become familiar with, the better your writing can become, too.

Exchange papers from Activity 16 with a partner. Read your partner's paper. Then use Peer Editing Sheet 1 on page 267 to help you comment on your partner's paper. Be sure to offer positive suggestions and comments that will help your partner write a better paragraph. Consider your partner's comments as you revise your own paper.

Timed Writing

How quickly can you write in English? There are many times when you must write quickly, such as on a test. It is important to feel comfortable during those times. Timed-writing practice can make you feel better about writing quickly in English.

Take out a piece of paper. Then read the writing prompt below this paragraph. Your teacher will give you 5 minutes to brainstorm ideas about this topic. You must then write a short paragraph (perhaps 6 to 10 sentences) about it. You will have 25 minutes to write your paragraph. At the end of the 25 minutes, your teacher will collect your work and return it to you later.

> Describe the daily life of a police officer. Is being a police officer a good job? Is it easy? What kinds of things does a police officer do every day?

Developing Ideas
for Writing
a Paragraph

GOAL: To learn how to brainstorm ideas for writing

*Language Focus: Subject-verb agreement

Imagine that a man is talking on the phone and suddenly sees thick black smoke coming out from behind a closed door. What should he do?

Make a list of at least three ideas. Work quickly. Do not worry about how good each idea is. For now, do not worry about correct spelling or grammar. Your immediate goal is to create a list of as many ideas as possible in just a few minutes.

1. _____

   _____

2. _____

   _____

3. _____

   _____

Congratulations! You have just finished your first brainstorming session. Now compare your list to your classmates' lists.

Brainstorming

Brainstorming is quickly writing down all the thoughts that come into your head. When you brainstorm, you do not think about whether an idea is good or bad or whether your writing is correct. You simply write to put your ideas on paper. This process is called brainstorming because it feels like there is a storm in your brain—a storm of ideas!

Brainstorm your ideas!

ACTIVITY 1 Brainstorming Practice

Use this topic and situation to practice brainstorming.

Next Saturday is your grandmother's birthday. She is going to be eighty-eight years old. What will you get for her? Make a list of five suitable birthday gifts for her.

1. _____

2. _____

3. _____

4. _____

5. _____

Compare your list to a classmate's list. Can you combine your best ideas with your classmate's best ideas? Sometimes it is helpful to work with other writers and share ideas. Remember that in brainstorming, there are no bad ideas. The purpose of brainstorming is to produce as many ideas as possible and not worry about correct grammar, spelling, or punctuation.

For more practice with brainstorming, try Unit 2, Activity 1, Activity 2, and Activity 3 on the *Great Writing 2* Web site: elt.heinle.com/greatwriting

The Importance of Brainstorming

Brainstorming is like a storm of ideas in your brain. A good writer brainstorms about a topic by completing these two important steps:

- thinking about the topic first, then

- writing down words and ideas.

It is important to remember that the first step in writing a paragraph is not writing—it is <u>thinking</u>.

Consider this example of brainstorming for Example Paragraph 2, "An Easy Sandwich," on page 2. This is the original brainstorming, so there are several ideas that were not included in the final paragraph. In addition, there are a few ideas in the final paragraph that are not in this list.

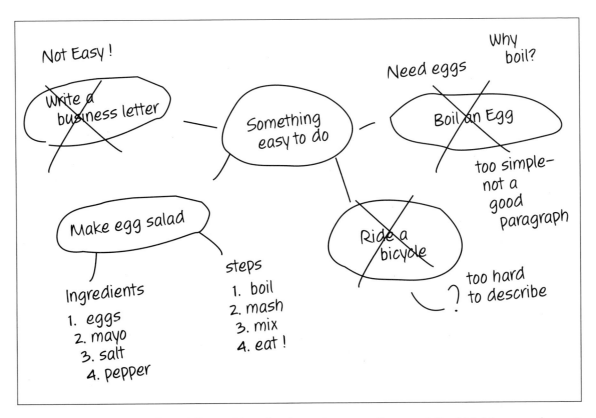

The writer brainstormed four different ideas for the assignment. Can you tell which idea was chosen? Would you have made the same choice?

How Brainstorming Works

From the diagram, you can see that the writer wrote many ideas and crossed out some of them. Brainstorming is not a linear or a consecutive process. Writers do not think of one thing, write it down, then think of something else, write it down, and so on. Instead, brainstorming can be a messy process. Writers move from one idea to another, then back to an earlier idea, then forward again to a new idea, and so on. They cross out words, draw lines to make connections, and change their minds. Brainstorming is a cycle with steps that repeat continually.

Brainstorming involves associating ideas—one idea produces another. Some writers brainstorm in lists. Others cluster or connect their ideas in some other way. Brainstorming can help writers visualize the paragraph.

ACTIVITY 2 Brainstorming Practice

Follow these steps for each of the example topics:

1. Read the topic.

2. Brainstorm about the topic in the box. Make a list of ideas or use the diagram on page 32 as an example of how to connect ideas.

3. Circle the ideas that you think are the best ones to include in a paragraph.

4. Compare and discuss your ideas with a partner. When you compare your notes, be prepared to say why you want to keep some ideas and why you want to take out others. What information will be in the final paragraph?

Topic A: Clothing and fashion

Brainstorm area:

Topic B: Transportation

Brainstorm area:

Topic C: Something valuable

Brainstorm area:

Choose an example paragraph that you read in Unit 1: "Braille," "An Easy Sandwich," or "My First Flight." Brainstorm ideas that are related to the topic of one of these paragraphs. For example, if you choose "My First Flight," you might brainstorm about a frightening experience you have had on an airplane or another experience that was scary.

- Which paragraph did you choose? _____

- Why did you choose this paragraph? _____

_____

Use the space below to brainstorm. If you want, work with another student who chose the same topic. Sometimes when you work with another writer, you get more ideas.

Brainstorm area:

Language Focus

Subject-Verb Agreement

All sentences in English contain a verb. The simple present tense has two forms: the base form and the -s form. The -s form is used when the subject is the third-person singular (*he, she, it*). For example, here are the two forms of the verb *prepare*.

prepare   I prepare   you prepare   we prepare   they prepare

prepares   he prepares   she prepares   it prepares

NOTE: The -s form has two other common spellings that you should learn.

1. When a verb ends in a consonant + -y, the -y changes to -i and you add -es.
   Examples include: *I try → he tries*, *you fly → she flies*, and *we cry → it cries*.

2. When a verb ends in -ch, -sh, -ss, -x, or -zz, add -es.
   Examples include: *I watch → she watches*, *I wash → he washes*, *you miss → it misses*, *they tax → the city taxes*, and *you buzz → it buzzes*.

Common Mistakes

- One of the most common mistakes for non-native writers is to omit the -s with third-person singular subjects in the simple present tense. Another common mistake is to write -s when the verb is not used with a third-person singular subject. This is an error in **subject-verb agreement**. The form of the verb depends on the subject of the sentence. If you first find the subject, then you can write the verb correctly. For example, if you write *we reads*, the subject *we* does not agree with the verb *reads* because *we* is not a third-person singular subject. If you write *she reads*, the subject *she* agrees with the verb *reads*. (*She* is a third-person singular subject.)

- Another common subject-verb agreement mistake involves prepositional phrases. A prepositional phrase includes a preposition, such as *for, at, from, by, with, without, in*, and *of*, and an object of the preposition—the noun or pronoun that follows the preposition.

Example: The owner <u>of these restaurants</u> is Italian.
(PREPOSITION = *of*; OBJECT OF THE PREPOSITION = *restaurants*)

In general, the object of the preposition does not affect the number (singular or plural) of the verb in the sentence. Some students choose the form of the verb by looking at the nearest noun instead of looking at the subject. Remember that the object of the preposition is NEVER the subject of a sentence.

Study the following examples. In each sentence, the subject and the verb are in **bold type**, and the prepositional phrase is <u>underlined</u>. Notice that the verb agrees with the subject even when the object of the preposition comes between the subject and the verb.

Incorrect: The main **product** <u>of Brazil and Colombia</u> **are** coffee.

The main **products** <u>of Brazil</u> **is** coffee and aluminum.

Correct: The main **product** <u>of Brazil</u> **is** coffee.

The main **product** <u>of Brazil and Colombia</u> **is** coffee.

The main **products** <u>of Brazil</u> **are** coffee and aluminum.

Here are 6 incorrect sentences. Can you identify the mistakes and correct them?

1. In my country, most people lives near the coast because the interior is too dry.

2. A pair of scissors are necessary for this project.

3. Laura carry her guitar from class to class every Thursday.

4. The main method of transportation in all of those tropical islands are the public bus system.

5. The trees behind my house is dense.

6. Earth revolve around the Sun.

ACTIVITY 4 Subject–Verb Agreement Practice

Read this student paragraph. It contains several errors in subject-verb agreement. Underline each error and write the correct form above it.

The Hard Work of a Teacher

Some people **may** think that Mimi Robertson has an easy job, but she really do not [*does*]. Mimi is a kindergarten teacher at King Elementary School. She teaches twenty-two very young children. Mimi's class of kindergarten students begin at 8:30 A.M., but she does a lot before then. Every day she arrive at work just after 7:30 A.M. Mimi has to organize her supplies and prepare the room for her students. If one of the parents is there that day to help, then Mimi have [*has*] to explain the lesson plan to the parent. After the students arrive at 8:30, the class begins. Her young students keeps her **extremely** busy for the rest of the day. They play games and learn new things. **However**, there is [*are*] always a few small problems. Mimi's young students does [*do*] not always listen to her, and sometimes they fight or cry. **Every now and then**, one child **shouts**, but Mimi tries to be very patient with all of her students. After school, she **must** attend meetings and create new lessons. Mimi says she loves her job, but it really is **a great deal** of work.

may: possibly, might
extremely: very, to a high degree
however: but
every now and then: sometimes
shout: to speak in a very loud voice, yell, scream

must: to be necessary, have to
a great deal (of): a large amount, a lot (*A lot* is used more in spoken English; *a great deal* sounds more formal and is more common in written English.)

For more practice with subject-verb agreement, try Unit 2, Activities 4–7 on the *Great Writing* 2 Web site: elt.heinle.com/greatwriting

Building Better Sentences

Correct and varied sentence structure is essential to the quality of your writing. For further practice with the sentences and paragraphs in this unit, go to Practice 3 on page 253 in Appendix 1.

ACTIVITY 5 Word Associations

Circle the word or phrase that is most closely related to the word or phrase on the left. If necessary, use a dictionary to check the meaning of words you do not know.

1. frightening	afraid		happy
2. to omit	to forget		to remember
3. interior	inside		outside
4. to revolve	to become		to turn
5. however	and		but
6. to shout	loud voice		soft voice
7. to share	to buy half		to give half
8. the purpose	goal		help
9. suddenly	perhaps		surprise
10. to create	to make		to take
11. a cycle	in a circle		in a line
12. must do	need to do		learn to do
13. kindergarten	adults		children
14. suitable	bad idea		good idea
15. extremely	a little		a lot
16. cluster	alone		together

ACTIVITY 6 Using Collocations

Fill in each blank with the word on the left that most naturally completes the phrase on the right. If necessary, use a dictionary to check the meaning of words you do not know.

1. in / on   depend _____

2. cloud / room   a messy _____

3. at / for   that book is not suitable _____ a child

4. list / storm   make a _____ of (something)

5. and / but   _____ so on

6. in / out   cross _____ an error

7. in / on   talking _____ the phone

8. a page number / a long report   write down _____

9. deal / must   a great _____ of (something)

10. expensive / price   extremely _____

Original Student Writing

ACTIVITY 7 Writing a Paragraph from Brainstorming

Now it is your turn to write a simple paragraph. Choose a topic from Activity 2 on pages 33–35. Use the ideas that you brainstormed about that topic to write a paragraph. Include the four features of a paragraph on pages 9–10. Follow these guidelines:

- Choose a topic from Activity 2 on pages 33–35.

- Use the ideas that you brainstormed about that topic for the sentences for your paragraph.

- Write five to twelve sentences.

- Include the four features of a good paragraph in this checklist from pages 9–10.

  ☐ 1. Does the paragraph have a topic sentence that states the main idea?

  ☐ 2. Are all of the sentences in the paragraph about one topic?

  ☐ 3. Is the first line of the paragraph indented?

  ☐ 4. Is the last sentence a good concluding sentence?

- Give your paragraph a title.

- Be sure to proofread your paragraph for good sentences, vocabulary, and grammar.

- Be especially careful with subject-verb agreement.

- Use at least five of the vocabulary words or phrases presented in Activity 5 and Activity 6. Underline these words and phrases in your paragraph.

Exchange papers from Activity 7 with a partner. Read your partner's writing. Then use Peer Editing Sheet 2 on page 269 to help you comment on your partner's writing. Be sure to offer positive suggestions and comments that will help your partner improve his or her writing. Consider your partner's comments as you revise your own writing.

Timed Writing

How quickly can you write in English? There are many times when you must write quickly, such as on a test. It is important to feel comfortable during those times. Timed-writing practice can make you feel better about writing quickly in English.

Take out a piece of paper. Then read the writing prompt below this paragraph. Your teacher will give you 5 minutes to brainstorm ideas about this topic. You must then write a short paragraph (perhaps 6 to 10 sentences) about it. You will have 25 minutes to write your paragraph. At the end of the 25 minutes, your teacher will collect your work and return it to you later.

In your opinion, is English easy or difficult to learn? Why do you think so? Give two or three strong reasons to support your opinion.

The Topic Sentence

GOAL: To learn how to write a topic sentence

*Language Focus: Sentence fragments and comma splices

In Unit 1, you learned that a good paragraph has these four features:

☑ 1. A paragraph has a topic sentence that states the main idea.

☑ 2. All of the sentences in the paragraph are about one topic.

☑ 3. The first line of a paragraph is indented.

☑ 4. The concluding sentence brings the paragraph to a logical ending.

In this unit, you will learn the answers to these questions about the topic sentence:

- What is the function of a topic sentence?
- What does a good topic sentence look like?
- How can you know whether a sentence is a good topic sentence?
- Where is a topic sentence usually found in a paragraph?

Read and study this example opinion paragraph. Then answer the questions that follow. The questions will help you understand the content of the paragraph and learn about topic sentences.

EXAMPLE PARAGRAPH 14

To Shift or Not to Shift

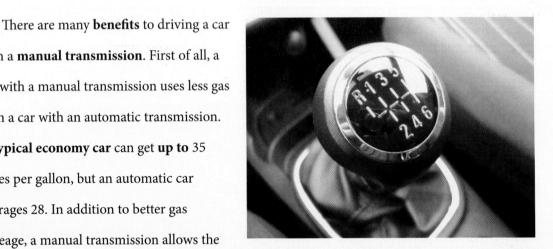

There are many **benefits** to driving a car with a **manual transmission**. First of all, a car with a manual transmission uses less gas than a car with an automatic transmission. A **typical economy car** can get **up to** 35 miles per gallon, but an automatic car averages 28. In addition to better gas mileage, a manual transmission allows the driver to start a car that has a low battery. With a foot on the **clutch**, the driver just needs to put the car in second **gear** and have someone push the car until it gains enough speed. The driver then **releases** the clutch quickly, and the car should start. This is impossible with an automatic transmission. Finally, people with manual transmissions say that they have much more control of their **vehicles**. For example, if the **brakes** suddenly stop working on this **type** of car, the driver can **shift** to a lower gear to slow the car down. In contrast, people who drive automatic transmission cars have to depend on the automatic system. If something **malfunctions**, drivers have no control of their vehicles. **While** automatic cars are more convenient, manual transmission cars certainly offer many more advantages.

benefits: good points, advantages
manual: by hand
a transmission: a device in a vehicle that transfers power from the engine to the axle
typical: usual, average
an economy car: an inexpensive car with good gas mileage
up to: not more than, that number or lower, that amount or lower
a clutch: the left pedal in a manual transmission car that allows shifting of gears

a gear: a toothed machine part that interacts with another part to change speed or direction
release: to let go, allow to escape
a vehicle: a machine for transportation
a brake: the device that stops a vehicle
a type: a kind, a variety
shift: to change or move the gears in a car
malfunction: to stop working, usually suddenly
while: although

1. Which one of these ideas tells the purpose of this paragraph? Put a check mark (✔) next to the correct answer.

   _____ a. to talk about the different kinds of manual transmissions

   _____ b. to explain what a manual transmission is

   _____ c. to tell why a manual transmission is better than an automatic transmission

   _____ d. to describe how a manual transmission interacts with the brakes in a vehicle

2. What is the topic sentence in this paragraph? Underline the topic sentence.

3. If you underlined the first sentence, you are correct. The first sentence states the purpose clearly—to tell about the advantages of having a manual transmission car.

4. A good paragraph has clear organization. This paragraph lists three benefits of a manual transmission. What are they?

   _____

   _____

   _____

5. The following expressions are important to the organization of the paragraph. What does each one mean?

   a. first of all

   _____

   b. in addition to

   _____

   c. finally

   _____

6. Do you prefer driving a vehicle with a manual transmission or one with an automatic transmission? Why?

   _____

   _____

   _____

What do you already know about topic sentences? Read each set of sentences. Write the general topic that the sentences share. Then put a check mark (✔) on the line next to the best topic sentence. Be prepared to explain your answers. The first one has been done for you.

1. General Topic: **winter**

   _____ Winter is a good season.

   _____ Winter weather is cold, and it snows.

   _✔_ The best season for kids is winter.

2. General Topic: _____

   _____ Soccer is popular for many reasons.

   _____ You need a leather ball to play soccer.

   _____ Soccer is a nice game.

3. General Topic: _____

   _____ There are many people in Los Angeles.

   _____ People from many different cultures live in Los Angeles.

   _____ Los Angeles is a big city in California.

4. General Topic: _____

   _____ Monolingual dictionaries have only one language, but bilingual dictionaries have two languages.

   _____ Many language students prefer bilingual dictionaries to monolingual dictionaries.

   _____ Dictionaries that have two languages, such as French and English, are called bilingual dictionaries.

5. General Topic: _____

   _____ French perfumes are expensive for a number of reasons.

   _____ My mother's perfume smells flowery.

   _____ You can purchase perfumes in expensive blue crystal bottles.

6. General Topic: _____

   _____ *An American Education* has 946 pages.

   _____ A woman graduates in *An American Education*.

   _____ *An American Education* is an excellent historical novel.

How did you decide which sentences were the best topic sentences? What were you looking for? Discuss your ideas with your classmates.

 For more practice with recognizing effective topic sentences, try Unit 3, Activity 1 on the *Great Writing 2* Web site: elt.heinle.com/greatwriting

Features of a Good Topic Sentence

A good topic sentence has the following features:

- **It controls or guides the whole paragraph.** When you read the topic sentence, you know what to expect in the paragraph.

- **A good topic sentence is not a general fact that everyone accepts as true.** For example, a bad topic sentence would be, "Libraries have books." The information in this sentence is true, but it is a general fact and is not a good choice for a topic sentence.

- **A good topic sentence is specific.** "Tea is delicious" is not a good topic sentence because the information in the sentence is too general. The reader does not know what to expect in the paragraph. If you want to write a paragraph about tea, make your topic sentence more specific, such as "Green tea has many health benefits."

- However, **a good topic sentence is not too specific.** "This monolingual dictionary contains more than 42,000 words" limits the topic too much—there is nothing else for the writer to say. (Can you imagine what the sentence after this would say? Or the third sentence of the paragraph? No, you cannot because there is really nothing else to add.)

- **A good topic sentence has controlling ideas**—words or phrases that help guide the flow of ideas in the paragraph.

Controlling Ideas

Here are some example topic sentences with controlling ideas. The controlling ideas have been underlined.

1. The <u>best season for kids</u> is winter.

   Explanation: The reader expects the paragraph to give reasons and examples why winter is the best season for children.

2. Soccer is <u>popular for many reasons</u>.

   Explanation: The reader expects the paragraph to give a variety of information about soccer and why it is popular around the world.

3. People from <u>many different cultures</u> live in Los Angeles.

 Explanation: The reader expects the paragraph to include information about various groups of people who make up the population of Los Angeles.

4. Many <u>language students prefer bilingual dictionaries</u> to monolingual dictionaries.

 Explanation: The reader expects the paragraph to explain why this statement is true.

ACTIVITY 3 Recognizing Controlling Ideas in Topic Sentences

Read the following topic sentences. The main idea for each sentence has been circled. Underline the controlling idea. Then explain what information you expect to find in the paragraph.

1. (The SAT Reasoning Test™) contains three distinct sections that deal with three important skills.

 Explanation:

 _____

 _____

2. (The shocking crash of a 747 jumbo jet) off the coast of New York baffled investigators.

 Explanation:

 _____

 _____

3. (Crossword puzzles) are not only educational and fun but also addictive.

 Explanation:

 _____

 _____

4. Recent research has confirmed that (eating dark green, leafy vegetables), such as broccoli and cabbage, may reduce the risk of some types of cancer.

Explanation:

_____

_____

5. Although buying a house may seem appealing, (renting an apartment) has many advantages.

   Explanation:

   _____

   _____

Building Better Sentences

Correct and varied sentence structure is essential to the quality of your writing. For further practice with the sentences and paragraphs in this part of the unit, go to Practice 4 on page 253 in Appendix 1.

ACTIVITY 4 More Practice Recognizing Controlling Ideas

Read the sentences in each item. Put a check mark (✔) next to the best topic sentence. Underline the controlling ideas in that sentence. Be prepared to explain your answers.

1. _____ Most of the girls in the class get higher grades in Spanish than the boys.

   _____ Research has shown that girls are better at languages than boys.

   _____ Many students like languages very much.

2. _____ Cats are better pets than goldfish for many reasons.

   _____ Cats and goldfish are both animals.

   _____ Cats cannot swim very well, but goldfish can.

3. _____ Yesterday I did not have lunch with my coworkers.

   _____ Yesterday I went to work late.

   _____ Yesterday was the worst day of my life.

4. _____ Some people call Paul Cézanne the father of modern art.

_____ Paul Cézanne, the father of modern art, made important contributions to the history of art.

_____ Paul Cézanne's art was not recognized until the end of his career, but he is often called the father of modern art.

5. _____ Many Canadians speak French, and some of them speak Chinese and Japanese.

_____ The current population of Canada is a reflection of the international background of its citizens and immigrants.

_____ A large number of new immigrants live in the western province of British Columbia, but not many of them speak German.

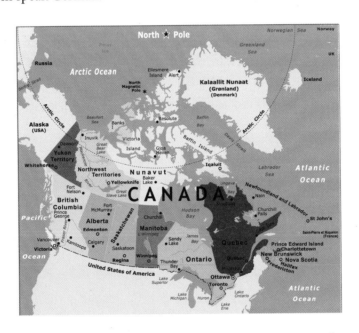

 For more practice with recognizing controlling ideas, try Unit 3, Activity 2 and Activity 3 on the *Great Writing 2* Web site: elt.heinle.com/greatwriting

ACTIVITY 5 More Practice with Controlling Ideas

All of these topic sentences are too general. Rewrite each sentence adding controlling ideas. Compare your sentences with other students' sentences.

Example: Flowers are beautiful.

Flowers are the best gift to receive when you are feeling down.

OR

Only four kinds of flowers grow during the short summers in Alaska.

1. Cats are nice.

_____

_____

2. Paris is the capital of France.

_____

_____

3. The English alphabet has twenty-six letters.

_____

_____

4. Mailing some letters is expensive.

_____

_____

5. Tennis is an enjoyable sport.

_____

_____

_____

For more practice with recognizing good topic sentences, try Unit 3, Activity 4 on the *Great Writing 2* Web site: elt.heinle.com/greatwriting

Working with Topic Sentences

Now it is time to write some topic sentences.

ACTIVITY 6 Writing Topic Sentences

Read each paragraph. Then write a good topic sentence for it. Be sure to end each topic sentence with correct punctuation.

EXAMPLE PARAGRAPH 15

1. _____

_____

Young people tend to buy them because they want to look "cool" to their friends. It is much easier for a young person to impress other people with a fast sports car than with your father's minivan. Wealthy people, however, enjoy sports cars because they want to show others that they have status in their community. I have never seen a doctor or a lawyer driving around in an old station wagon. Finally, sports cars appeal to adventurers. Adventurers are people who like to take risks on the road. Whatever the reasons, I think sports cars are here to stay.

2. _____

_____

One is size. Most modern reptiles are small. Dinosaurs were much, much larger than any reptile that we have on Earth today. Second, the legs of most reptiles today are on the sides of their body. However, dinosaurs' legs were on the bottom of their body. In this way, dinosaurs could stand up on their back legs. Third, today's reptiles use the environment to control their body temperature. In contrast, dinosaurs controlled their own body temperature. They did not depend on their surroundings. While reptiles and dinosaurs may seem very similar, they are actually quite different.

3. _____

_____

First, your body will look better. Exercise is perfect for staying trim and healthy-looking, and it does not have to take a long time. Second, you will actually have more energy. A person who exercises will have fewer problems walking up stairs or climbing hills. In addition, your heart will be healthier. A good, strong heart is necessary for a long, healthy life. Finally, exercise reduces stress and keeps your mind in shape. Therefore, if you want to improve your overall health, exercise is an excellent way to accomplish your goal.

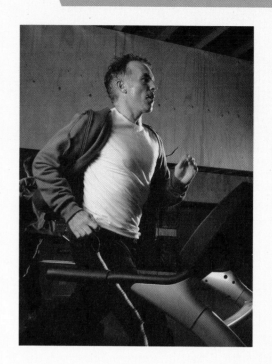

4. _____

_____

It is without a doubt one of the easiest foods to eat. You do not need any special utensils, and it does not have to be served piping hot like some foods do. In addition, with only 20 calories per cup and almost no fat, it is both a filling and a heart-friendly snack. Furthermore, it can be an important source of natural fiber, a substance that has been shown to be important in limiting certain types of cancer. Based on this information, can anyone be surprised that sales of popcorn are soaring in many countries?

(This one is more difficult than the others. Good luck!)

5. _____

_____

In this method, learners form their own sound association between the foreign language word they are trying to learn and any word in their native language. In the second stage, learners form an image link between the target word and the native language word. For example, a Japanese learner of English might look at  the English word *hatchet* and connect it to the Japanese word *hachi*, which means "eight." In this case, the learner might remember that he can use a hatchet eight times to cut down a tree. An English speaker learning Spanish might remember the word *trigo* ("wheat") by using the English words *tree* and *go* because they sound like the Spanish word *trigo*. For some people, this particular method is effective.

  For more practice with writing topic sentences, try Unit 3, Activity 5 and Activity 6 on the *Great Writing 2* Web site: elt.heinle.com/greatwriting

✏ Writer's Note

Keeping a Journal for New Ideas

If you do not have a good topic for your paragraph, then it is very difficult to write a solid, interesting topic sentence. Many students say, "I don't know what to write about." A good source for ideas is a personal journal. A journal is a notebook in which you write ideas about any topic you want. If you do not know what to write, then write what you did today or how you are feeling about an experience. Every now and then, you should read your previous journal entries; you may be surprised to find many good ideas for paragraphs.

Building Better Sentences

Correct and varied sentence structure is essential to the quality of your writing. For further practice with the sentences and paragraphs in this part of the unit, go to Practice 5 on page 254 in Appendix 1.

ACTIVITY 7 Comma Practice

Insert commas in these sentences where necessary. Be prepared to explain your choices. See the Brief Writer's Handbook with Activities (Punctuation Activities, pages 231–238) if you need help. Some sentences are correct.

1. Malaysia and Thailand are two countries in Southeast Asia.

2. Because they are located next to each other we might expect these two nations to share many similarities.

3. To a certain extent this is true.

4. Both countries have temperate climates throughout the year.

5. Thailand's economy is growing and so is Malaysia's.

6. Malaysia has miles of beautiful beaches that attract tourists and Thailand does, too.

7. However there are also many differences.

8. Malaysians and Thais speak completely different languages.

9. The population of Malaysia is about 25 million but the population of Thailand is about 65 million.

10. Thailand has a national king but Malaysia does not.

11. Malaysia was a British colony but Thailand was never a British colony.

12. Thus the fact that two countries are near each other does not always mean they are similar.

Copy the sentences from Activity 7 in the same order. Make sure your paragraph is indented. On the top line, write an original title for your paragraph.

_____

_____

_____

_____

_____

_____

_____

_____

_____

_____

_____

_____

_____

Language Focus

Sentence Fragments and Comma Splices

Two common mistakes in writing are **sentence fragments** and **comma splices**. These mistakes can prevent the reader from understanding the writer's message, so they are serious errors.

Sentence Fragments

A sentence fragment is not a complete sentence. It is usually missing either a subject or a verb. A sentence fragment does not make sense by itself. It is just a piece of the whole idea. The easiest way to correct a fragment is to add the missing part. The missing part is usually a subject or a verb.

Read the sentences and sentence fragments below. (The fragments are underlined.) Notice how the fragments were corrected.

1. I went to Italy last summer. <u>Was a wonderful trip.</u> I want to go again if I can.

   Correction: **It** was a wonderful trip. (Add a subject.)

2. Lázaro Cárdenas was the president of Mexico from 1934 to 1940. His original goal was to become a teacher, but the political situation in Mexico at that time caused him to change his mind. <u>A very difficult decision for Cárdenas.</u>

   Correction: **This was** a very difficult decision for Cárdenas. (Add a subject and a verb.)

3. Only a small number of university students choose to major in art. <u>Because they are concerned about future job possibilities.</u>

   Correction: Only a small number of university students choose to major in **art because** they are concerned about future job possibilities. (Combine two clauses.)

NOTE: You can put the *because*-clause after the main clause, or you can begin the sentence with the *because*-clause. (*Because they are concerned about future job possibilities, only a small number of university students choose to major in art.*) If you put the *because*-clause first, you must separate that clause from the main clause with a comma.

Comma Splices

A comma splice occurs when two or more sentences (independent clauses) are connected with a comma. One way to correct a comma splice is to separate the independent clauses by ending the first one with a period and starting the second one with a capital letter. Another correction is to add a connecting word such as *and, but,* and *or,* after the comma. Finally, a comma splice may be rewritten by combining the most important words from the two sentences (independent clauses) into one sentence.

Read the sentences and comma splices below. (The comma splices are underlined.) Notice how the comma splices were corrected.

1. <u>Last summer I went to Italy, it was a wonderful trip.</u> I want to go again if I can.

   Correction: I went to Italy last summer. **It** was a wonderful trip.

   OR

   My trip to Italy last summer was wonderful.

2. Lázaro Cárdenas was the president of Mexico from 1934 to 1940. <u>His original goal was to become a teacher, the political situation in Mexico at that time caused him to change his mind.</u>

   Correction: His original goal was to become a teacher, **but** the political situation in Mexico at that time caused him to change his mind.

   OR

   Although his original goal was to become a teacher, the political situation in Mexico at that time caused him to change his mind.

3. Only a small number of university students choose to major in art, <u>they are concerned about future job possibilities.</u>

   Correction: Only a small number of university students choose to major in art **because** they are concerned about future job possibilities.

ACTIVITY 9 Correcting Sentence Fragments and Comma Splices

Read each sentence or set of sentences. If it is correct, write C on the line. If there is an error, circle it and indicate the type of error by writing SF for a sentence fragment or CS for a comma splice. Then write the correct sentence(s). More than one correction may be possible. The first one has been done for you.

1. __CS__ A whale is one of the largest animals on the (planet, few) people have seen one in person.

   A whale is one of the largest animals on the planet. Few people have seen one in person.

   OR

   Although the whale is one of the largest animals on the planet, few people have seen

   one in person.

2. __F__ Yesterday's weather caused problems for many travelers. Most of the flights were canceled. Due to the torrential rains and high winds.

   _____

   _____

   _____

3. __CS__ Computer programs can help students learn a foreign language, many students use the language programs in the computer center.

   _____

   Because _____

   _____

4. _ok_ It was definitely a time of nervousness. When the oil embargo was announced, the price of gasoline soared. The government did everything possible to make sure that people did not panic.

_____

_____

_____

5. _CS_ *Our Family* is an internationally known television show, the quality of the acting is not very high.

_____

_____

_____

6. _F_ This magazine won several awards last year. For the content and the style of its stories. The last issue had two superb short stories that were written by distinguished authors.

_____

_____

_____

For more practice with sentence fragments and comma splices, try Unit 3, Activity 7 on the *Great Writing 2* Web site: elt.heinle.com/greatwriting

Building Better Sentences

Correct and varied sentence structure is essential to the quality of your writing. For further practice with the sentences and paragraphs in this part of the unit, go to Practice 6 on page 255 in Appendix 1.

ACTIVITY 10 Word Associations

Circle the word or phrase that is most closely related to the word or phrase on the left. If necessary, use a dictionary to check the meaning of words you do not know.

1. a reptile	animal	disease
2. utensils	people	things
3. distinguished	known	secret
4. brakes	to start	to stop
5. to reduce	to become smaller	to become bigger
6. an axle	wheels	windows
7. a device	a mountain	a thing
8. to purchase	to buy	to sell
9. to baffle	to confuse	to decide
10. up to six things	four or five things	seven or eight things
11. while	after	although
12. an appealing idea	people hate it	people like it
13. a risk	a danger	a product
14. a snack	to allow	to eat
15. the source	place	time

ACTIVITY 11 Using Collocations

Fill in each blank with the word on the left that most naturally completes the phrase on the right. If necessary, use a dictionary to check the meaning of words you do not know.

1. by / with	handicrafts are made _____ hand
2. car / fiber	an economy _____
3. from / with	interact _____
4. first / next	_____ of all

5. bilingual / soaring   _____ prices

6. as / for   vegetables such _____ onions

7. than / that   one thing is easier _____ another

8. by / of   one thing is a reflection _____ another thing

9. never / types   have _____ seen

10. filling / piping   a _____ meal

Original Student Writing

ACTIVITY 12 Brainstorming Ideas for a Paragraph

Choose one of the general topics below and brainstorm your ideas about it in the space provided. When you have finished, circle the ideas that you think are best to include in a paragraph.

Topics:

1. the best type of job
2. foods that are good for your health
3. ways that we can conserve energy
4. how computers are changing society

Brainstorm area:

ACTIVITY 13 Original Writing Practice

Use your brainstorming notes from Activity 12 to write a paragraph.

- *Make sure that your paragraph has the four features explained on pages 9–10.*

- *Use at least five of the vocabulary words or phrases presented in Activity 10 and Activity 11. Underline the words and phrases in your paragraph.*

ACTIVITY 14 Peer Editing

Exchange papers from Activity 13 with a partner. Read your partner's writing. Then use Peer Editing Sheet 3 on page 271 to help you comment on your partner's writing. Be sure to offer positive suggestions and comments that will help your partner improve his or her writing. Consider your partner's comments as you revise your own writing.

Timed Writing

How quickly can you write in English? There are many times when you must write quickly, such as on a test. It is important to feel comfortable during those times. Timed-writing practice can make you feel better about writing quickly in English.

Take out a piece of paper. Then read the writing prompt below this paragraph. Your teacher will give you 5 minutes to brainstorm ideas about this topic. You must then write a short paragraph (perhaps 6 to 10 sentences) about it. You will have 25 minutes to write your paragraph. At the end of the 25 minutes, your teacher will collect your work and return it to you later.

> In your opinion, why do so many people want to learn English?
> Give a few strong examples to support your answer.

Supporting and Concluding Sentences

GOAL: To learn how to write supporting and concluding sentences

*Language Focus: Using pronouns for key nouns

Now that you know how to write a good topic sentence, you will work on another part of the paragraph—supporting sentences. Consider these questions:

- What is a good supporting sentence?

- What are the different kinds of supporting sentences?

- How do the supporting sentences relate to the topic sentence?

Good Supporting Sentences

Good **supporting sentences** are related to the topic sentence and its controlling ideas. Supporting sentences are like the interior walls of a house. If a house does not have interior support, it will collapse. Likewise, if a paragraph does not have good supporting sentences, its meaning will collapse, and readers will not be able to follow the ideas. The paragraph may be confusing or illogical.

Good supporting sentences give information that supports and explains the topic of the paragraph. They answer questions—*who? what? where? when? why?* and *how?*—and give details. Good writers think of these questions when they provide support—that is, write supporting sentences—for the topic sentence.

Read each topic sentence. Circle the main idea. Underline the controlling ideas. Then predict the kind of information you will find in the paragraph.

1. Topic Sentence: One of the best cities to visit on the east coast of the United States is Washington, D.C.

   What kind of information do you think is in this paragraph?

   _____

   _____

   _____

   _____

2. Topic Sentence: If you are searching for an interesting career, think about becoming a flight attendant.

   What kind of information do you think is in this paragraph?

   _____

   _____

   _____

   _____

3. Topic Sentence: One of the people that I most admire is my great-grandmother Carla.

   What kind of information do you think is in this paragraph?

   _____

   _____

   _____

   _____

As you can see, the topic sentences are all very different. The supporting sentences that you write will depend on your topic sentence.

For more practice with predicting paragraph content from controlling ideas, try Unit 4, Activity 1 on the *Great Writing 2* Web site: elt.heinle.com/greatwriting

Read the paragraphs. Notice how the supporting sentences tell you more about the topic sentence. Compare what you wrote in Activity 1 to the information in each paragraph. How well did you predict the content?

A Great Tourist Destination

One of the best cities to visit on the east coast of the United States is Washington, D.C. It has some of the most interesting **landmarks** and tourist **spots** in the country. There are many monuments to visit, such as the Lincoln Memorial, the Jefferson Memorial, and the Washington Monument, which is the tallest building in Washington. For more excitement, the area called Georgetown in northwest Washington is famous for its shopping and restaurants. Finally, there is the White House tour. On this tour, the guide **leads** visitors as they walk through many of the rooms in the White House and **view** the home of the president of the United States. Washington, D.C., might not be as large or as famous as other U.S. cities, but it has an appeal all its own.

a landmark: a historical building, a well-known location
a spot: a place, a location

lead: to show the way, organize
view: to see, look at

A Career in the Sky

If you are **searching for** an interesting career, think about becoming a flight attendant. First of all, flight attendants receive a large amount of training for their job. They learn about interpersonal skills, customer service, and safety. Second, every time flight attendants go to work, their scenery changes. They could be in Korea one day and New York the next. Sometimes they even **get to stay** in a city one or two days before flying home. In addition, flight attendants get **bargain** prices on airline tickets for vacation. Imagine spending no more than a few dollars for a flight anywhere in the world! Finally, flight attendants get to meet a wide variety of people from all over the world. For a truly exciting career, **consider** becoming a flight attendant because the **benefits are worth it**.

search for: to look for
get to (+ verb): to have an opportunity to (do something)
bargain: cheap, inexpensive

consider: to think about
a benefit: an advantage, a good point
be worth it: to be equal to the money, time, or work that something requires

An Immigrant in the Family

One of the people that I most admire is my great-grandmother Carla. She came to the United States from Italy in 1911 as a young woman on a large ship. She had little money and no **property**. Soon after landing at Ellis Island in New York, she began working as a **seamstress** in Brooklyn. She met and married my great-grandfather not long after that. They immediately began their large family. Great-Grandma Carla had eight children—five boys and three girls. In addition to taking care of **such** a large family in a new country, my great-grandmother survived **discrimination** as an **immigrant**, two world wars, the Great Depression, and a long list of illnesses. However, she rarely **complained**, and she was very happy with her new life in America. Whenever I think of my Great-Grandma Carla, I am always filled with **admiration** for her.

property: land or buildings that a person owns
a seamstress: a woman who sews for a living
such: to a great degree, very
discrimination: unfair treatment because of prejudice about some characteristic

an immigrant: a person who comes to live in a new country
complain: to express unhappiness or dissatisfaction about something
admiration: a feeling of approval or pleasure for someone

Notice how each of the supporting sentences in Example Paragraphs 21, 22, and 23 relates directly to the topic sentence. Writing good supporting sentences is an important skill that you will work on in this unit.

Kinds of Supporting Sentences

Good writers use many different kinds of supporting sentences. Good supporting sentences:

- *explain*: The family moved from the village to the capital for economic reasons.
- *describe*: She lived in a lovely, three-story castle surrounded by a forest.
- *give reasons*: Larry finally quit his job because of the stressful working conditions.
- *give facts*: More than ten percent of the university's student population is international.
- *give examples*: Oranges and grapefruits grow in California.
- *define*: My grandmother has a samovar, which is a large copper tea urn.

ACTIVITY 3 Matching Supporting and Topic Sentences

The two topic sentences below talk about two different diets. Read the topic sentences. Then read the list of supporting sentences. Match each supporting sentence with the corresponding topic sentence. Then write the correct topic sentence number on each line beside the supporting sentences. Notice that each sentence is labeled in parentheses with the kind of supporting sentence that it is.

Topic sentences

TS 1: Low-fat diets are an excellent way to stay healthy and trim.

TS 2: High-protein diets are favored by athletes and competitors.

Supporting sentences

a. __2__ These foods help build muscles and increase stamina. (fact)

b. __1__ They are preferred by the general public because they help with weight reduction. (reason)

c. _____ Low-fat diets are recommended by most physicians. (fact)

d. _____ Many athletes eat high-protein foods, such as meat, beans, and nuts. (example)

e. _____ Low-fat foods include fruits, vegetables, and pasta. (example)

f. _____ Because they are easy to find in stores, low-fat foods are convenient. (reason)

g. _____ Athletes generally eat high-protein diets to give them more energy. (reason)

h. _____ Crispy steamed vegetables and grilled fish and chicken are all tasty parts of a low-fat, heart-friendly diet. (description)

For more practice with matching supporting and topic sentences, try Unit 4, Activity 2 on the *Great Writing 2* Web site: elt.heinle.com/greatwriting

Read each topic sentence. What information would you expect the writer to include in the paragraph? Write a question that the supporting sentences should answer. Use a who? what? where? when? why? *or* how? *question. The first one has been done for you.*

1. Smoking should be banned in all public facilities.

   <u>Why should smoking be banned?</u>

2. Texas is home to several kinds of poisonous snakes.

   _____

3. Classrooms without windows have adverse effects on students.

   _____

4. Computer technology will one day eliminate the use of libraries.

   _____

5. Quebec City is a wonderful place to raise children.

   _____

6. I will never forget the day I got married.

   _____

 For more practice with asking questions about topic sentences, try Unit 4, Activity 3 on the *Great Writing 2* Web site: elt.heinle.com/greatwriting

⚒ Building Better Sentences

Correct and varied sentence structure is essential to the quality of your writing. For further practice with the sentences and paragraphs in this part of the unit, go to Practice 7 on page 255 in Appendix 1.

Analyzing and Writing Supporting Sentences

In this section, you will create topic sentences and then analyze and write some supporting sentences.

For each of the general topics in the left column, brainstorm some ideas in the space provided. Then write a topic sentence with controlling ideas in the right column. Underline the controlling ideas. The first one has been done for you.

Brainstorming Topic	Topic Sentence with Controlling Ideas
1. vacation • types (summer, honeymoon) • 5 common destinations (national parks, Caribbean islands) • memories (Why was it special?)	I will <u>never forget</u> my 2007 summer vacation.
2. mathematics	
3. a best friend	
4. restaurants	
5. a (specific) sport	

Choose two of your topic sentences from Activity 5 and write them below. Then write four questions about each topic. Remember to use who? what? where? when? why? *or* how? *questions. If you cannot think of four questions, brainstorm some ideas with a classmate. The first one has been done for you.*

1. Topic Sentence: I will never forget my 2007 summer vacation.

   a. Why was this vacation so memorable?

   b. Where did you go?

   c. What did you do?

   d. How old were you at that time?

2. Topic Sentence: _____

   a. _____

   b. _____

   c. _____

   d. _____

3. Topic Sentence: _____

   a. _____

   b. _____

   c. _____

   d. _____

You now have a lot of ideas about what to include in your supporting sentences. You may not want to write about all of the ideas, but you have many choices. Remember that the supporting sentences must be related to the topic sentence.

For more practice with asking for more information about topic sentences, try Unit 4, Activity 4 on the *Great Writing 2* Web site: elt.heinle.com/greatwriting

Sometimes writers give too much information about the topic. When this happens, the paragraph does not read smoothly, and the reader might get confused about the writer's meaning.

In this activity, do the following for each paragraph:

- *Read the paragraph.*

- *For each of the underlined, numbered sentences, write* good supporting sentence *or* unrelated sentence *on the corresponding lines below the paragraph.*

- *Write reasons for your choices. (One sentence in each paragraph is unrelated to the topic.)*

Remember: All the supporting sentences must be related to the topic sentence. The first paragraph has been done for you.

EXAMPLE PARAGRAPH 24

Rules of Childhood

Fortunately, my parents were very strict with me when I was a child. I think that they were protective because I was an only child. However, at that time, it felt like I was in prison. I had to come straight home after school and immediately do my homework. (1) <u>After I finished my homework, I was allowed to watch only one hour of television.</u> While my friends were playing video games or watching cartoons, I was usually doing chores around the house to help my mother. (2) <u>This included doing some of the laundry and ironing, mowing the lawn, and helping to prepare dinner.</u> (3) <u>My father was an architect, and my mother was a housewife.</u> Looking back, I am not sorry that my parents were strict with me because I benefited from all the hard work.

1. <u>good supporting sentence</u>   It is an example of why the writer felt he or she was in prison.

2. <u>good supporting sentence</u>   It is a list of the chores the writer had to do around the house.

3. <u>unrelated sentence</u>   The writer's parents' occupations are not related to how the writer was treated.
There is no relationship between being an architect and being a strict parent.

Maintaining Your Pool

Swimming pools can be beautiful, but they need to be maintained every day. First, you must check the amount of chlorine in a swimming pool. (1) <u>If there is not enough chlorine, the pool might begin to grow algae.</u> In addition, you must check the pH level, especially after a rainstorm. Certain chemicals can be added to make sure that the pH level of the pool water is balanced. (2) <u>If you accidentally swallow some of these chemicals, you have to go to the doctor at once.</u> (3) <u>Finally, you should remove any leaves and small insects that are in the pool.</u> By doing all these things, you can be certain that your pool will last a very long time.

1. _____ _____

   _____

2. _____ _____

   _____

3. _____ _____

   _____

Sweet Dreams

When people have a hard time falling asleep at night, there are three things that they can do to relax before going to sleep. (1) <u>One of the most pleasant ways to relax is to imagine a beautiful and peaceful place.</u> This requires a creative mind, but it is very effective. Another common method is to practice deep-breathing exercises. These rhythmic exercises are good for getting rid of the tension that causes people to stay awake. (2) <u>A third method is to listen to relaxing music, such as classical or baroque music.</u> (3) <u>Baroque music is also popular because it helps students study better.</u> Some people have developed unique ways to help them fall asleep, but these three methods are extremely effective for the majority of people with sleep problems.

1. _____   _____

   _____

2. _____   _____

   _____

3. _____   _____

   _____

For more practice with identifying supporting sentences, try Unit 4, Activity 5 on the *Great Writing 2* Web site: elt.heinle.com/greatwriting

Analyzing and Writing Supporting Sentences   **73**

Language Focus

Using Pronouns for Key Nouns

Because a paragraph is about one topic, writers often repeat key nouns from the topic sentence in their supporting sentences. However, too much repetition can sound awkward. You can avoid repeating key nouns by replacing them with **pronouns** after the nouns are first introduced. Study these examples:

> One of the best cities to visit on the east coast of the United States is <u>Washington, D.C.</u> <u>It</u> has some of the most interesting landmarks and tourist spots in the country.

> First of all, <u>flight attendants</u> receive a large amount of training for their job. <u>They</u> learn about interpersonal skills, customer service, and safety.

> One of the people that I most admire is <u>my great-grandmother Carla</u>. <u>She</u> came to the United States from Italy in 1911 as a young woman on a large ship.

Consistent Pronoun Use

When you use pronouns, it is important to be consistent. For example, if you use *they* at the beginning of a paragraph, do not switch to *it.* Continue to use the first pronoun throughout the whole paragraph.

Read the following example. The repeated first pronoun and its possessive form are in italics, and the mistakes in pronoun use are underlined.

> Giraffes are among the most interesting of all the animals that live in Africa. *They* are easily recognized by *their* special features. *They* have long necks and long legs, but <u>its</u> neck is longer than <u>its</u> legs. <u>It</u> usually lives in very dry areas. Fortunately, <u>it</u> can survive a long time without drinking any water. In addition, giraffes have thick eyelashes to protect *their* eyes from the dust in *their* dry habitat.

For practice, write the example paragraph on a piece of paper with the correct pronouns and possessive forms.

ACTIVITY 8 Identifying Key Nouns and Replacement Pronouns

Read the following sentences. Write the correct pronoun in each blank. Use it, they, *or* we. *Then underline the key noun that the pronoun refers to. The first one has been done for you.*

1. <u>Tennis rackets</u> have changed tremendously in the last ten years. _____**They**_____ used to be small and heavy, but that is no longer true.

2. Soccer is by far the most widely played sport in the world. _____ is played professionally on nearly every continent.

3. I will never forget my childhood friends Carlos and Juan and what _____ taught me.

4. Not only is text messaging fast, but _____ is also an interesting way to practice English.

5. A bad thing happened to my classmates and me at school yesterday. _____ were late coming to class, so the teacher gave us an extra homework assignment.

6. If you travel to Budapest, Hungary, you will fall in love with the Danube River. _____ separates the city into two parts—Buda and Pest.

 For more practice with identifying key nouns and replacement pronouns, try Unit 4, Activity 6 on the *Great Writing 2* Web site: elt.heinle.com/greatwriting

---

✎ Writer's Note

Staying on Track

As you write a paragraph, always look back at your topic sentence. Do not include any information that is unrelated to the topic sentence. It is very easy to lose track of the main idea if you do not refer to the topic sentence from time to time.

Good Concluding Sentences

Now that you know how to write a good topic sentence and related supporting sentences, it is time to work on another part of the paragraph—the **concluding sentence**. Consider these questions:

- What is a good concluding sentence?
- What are the different kinds of concluding sentences?
- How do the concluding sentences relate to the topic sentence and to the supporting sentences?

The **concluding sentence** is the last sentence of the paragraph. Its job is to bring the paragraph to a logical conclusion. For some writers, coming up with this last sentence is a very difficult task. One helpful practice is to read many examples of good concluding sentences.

Kinds of Concluding Sentences

There are many different kinds of concluding sentences: restatement, suggestion, opinion, prediction.

Restate the Main Idea

Perhaps the easiest concluding sentence to write is one that restates the main idea or summarizes the main points of the paragraph.

Examples:

- (Example Paragraph 4, pages 10–11) "In brief, although many children want a pet, parents are divided on this issue for a number of significant reasons."

  The information in this concluding sentence is very similar to the topic sentence: *At some point, most parents have to decide whether or not to allow their children to have pets.* In addition, the concluding sentence includes the phrase "a number of significant reasons" because the paragraph includes several reasons for allowing or not allowing children to have pets.

- (Example Paragraph 5, page 13) "Computers have certainly made students' lives much easier."

  This concluding sentence also restates the idea of the topic sentence: *Computers are excellent machines to help students.* The examples in the paragraph show how computers help students in their schoolwork, and the concluding sentence emphasizes this fact.

Offer a Suggestion, Give an Opinion, or Make a Prediction

A concluding statement can offer a suggestion, give an opinion, or make a prediction. Sometimes a concluding statement does a combination of these options.

Examples:

- (Example Paragraph 15, page 51) "Whatever the reasons, I think sports cars are here to stay."

  The writer makes a prediction about the topic of the paragraph (sports cars).

- (Example Paragraph 25, page 72) "By doing all these things, you can be certain that your pool will last a very long time."

  In this paragraph, the writer makes a prediction about your pool if you follow the suggestions in the topic sentence—*Swimming pools can be beautiful, but they need to be maintained every day.* Here the writer makes a prediction that is based upon a suggestion.

Analyzing and Writing Concluding Sentences

In this section, you will analyze paragraphs. You will also write concluding sentences and revise them if necessary.

ACTIVITY 9 Paragraph Analysis

In this activity, do the following for each paragraph:

- *Read the paragraph.*
- *Underline the topic sentence and write* TS *above it.*
- *Circle any sentence that is not a good supporting sentence based on the controlling ideas in the topic sentence.*
- *Write a concluding sentence on the lines provided.*

EXAMPLE PARAGRAPH 27

College Adjustments

When I first started going to college, I was surprised at all the studying that was required. In high school, I hardly ever studied, but my grades were fairly good. At the university, it seemed that all my professors gave me mountains of homework every night. They all thought that their class was the most important! I could not watch TV anymore because I had to read pages and pages of information. As a result, my nights out with my friends became limited. In fact, I went out only on Saturday nights. It was a huge change from high school, where I used to go out every other night.

_____

_____

_____

River Turtles

Caring for river turtles is easier than many people think. You do not need a lot of equipment. In fact, all you need is a large aquarium, some rocks, sand, and a little bit of vegetation. After you buy the equipment, arrange all the items inside the aquarium. Remember to make sure that your river turtles have an area for swimming. If you have a large turtle, you will need to construct a small pond in your backyard. _____

_____

_____

_____

Different Ways to Cook Eggs

There are four easy ways to prepare a delicious egg. Some people believe that brown eggs taste better than white eggs. The first and probably the easiest way is to **boil** an egg. Just drop the egg into a pot of water and boil it for five minutes. Another easy way is to **scramble** an egg. All you need is a fork to beat the egg **mixture** before you put it into the hot frying pan. A third way is to fry an egg "over easy." This **involves** breaking the egg into the **skillet** without breaking the **yolk**. After a few moments, take a **spatula** and turn the egg over to cook on the other side. Finally, **poaching** an egg involves cooking the egg in a small dish that is sitting in boiling water. Break the egg into a small metal cup that is sitting in a pan of very hot, **shallow** water. Poaching an egg takes only four to five minutes.

_____

_____

_____

boil: to heat water to 212° Fahrenheit (100° Celsius)

scramble: to mix, blend

a mixture: the ingredients after they have been mixed together

involve: to include or contain as a necessary part of something

a skillet: a frying pan

yolk: the yellow part of an egg

a spatula: a utensil to turn or flip flat items that are being cooked

poach: to cook in hot water or other liquid

shallow: not deep

For more practice with analyzing paragraphs, try Unit 4, Activity 7 on the _Great Writing 2_ Web site: elt.heinle.com/greatwriting

Building Better Sentences

Correct and varied sentence structure is essential to the quality of your writing. For further practice with the sentences and paragraphs in this part of the unit, go to Practice 8 on page 256 in Appendix 1.

Building Better Vocabulary

ACTIVITY 10 Word Associations

Circle the word or phrase that is most closely related to the word or phrase on the left. If necessary, use a dictionary to check the meaning of words you do not know.

1. to eliminate something	it arrives	it leaves
2. to arrange	to put in order	to write many times
3. huge	small	large
4. to scramble	123456789	739245816
5. to get rid of	to add	to subtract
6. used to go	went	will go
7. to view	to hear	to see
8. dust	date	dirt
9. bargain	cheap	expensive
10. property	you own it	you borrow it
11. in brief	a few words	a lot of words
12. likewise	in the same way	very intelligent
13. to remove	to add	to subtract
14. at once	after a little time	right away
15. a spot	a place	a time

Fill in each blank with the word on the left that most naturally completes the phrase on the right. If necessary, use a dictionary to check the meaning of words you do not know.

1. complain / collapse   _____ about something

2. last / straight   _____ a long time

3. insect / reason   a poisonous _____

4. extremely / widely   the most _____ played sport

5. poach / spot   our favorite _____

6. athletes / effects   adverse _____

7. collapsed / logical   a _____ idea

8. do / make   _____ chores

9. careers / vegetables   crispy _____

10. mixture / shallow   a _____ pond

Original Student Writing

ACTIVITY 12 Original Writing Practice

Choose one of the topic sentences that you wrote in Activity 5 on page 69 and write a paragraph about the topic.

- *In your supporting sentences, answer the questions that you wrote in Activity 6. Remember: Write only about ideas that are introduced in the controlling ideas of your topic sentence.*

- *Use the guidelines on pages 75–76 to write a good concluding sentence for your paragraph.*

- *Use at least five of the vocabulary words or phrases presented in Activity 10 and Activity 11. Underline these words and phrases in your paragraph.*

 Writer's Note

Selecting Important Information

What information should you include in your paragraph? What information should you omit? When you write supporting sentences for your paragraph, you as the writer decide what information is important and will help readers understand your topic better.

ACTIVITY 13 Peer Editing

Exchange papers from Activity 12 with a partner. Read your partner's writing. Then use Peer Editing Sheet 4 on page 273 to help you comment on your partner's writing. Be sure to offer positive suggestions and comments that will help your partner improve his or her writing. Consider your partner's comments as you revise your own writing.

Timed Writing

How quickly can you write in English? There are many times when you must write quickly, such as on a test. It is important to feel comfortable during those times. Timed-writing practice can make you feel better about writing quickly in English.

Take out a piece of paper. Then read the writing prompt below this paragraph. Your teacher will give you 5 minutes to brainstorm ideas about this topic. You must then write a short paragraph (perhaps 6 to 10 sentences) about it. You will have 25 minutes to write your paragraph. At the end of the 25 minutes, your teacher will collect your work and return it to you later.

In your opinion, is it a good idea to require all students to wear a school uniform? Give two or three strong reasons to support your opinion. Be sure to include a strong concluding sentence.

Paragraph Review

GOAL: To review paragraph skills introduced in Units 1–4

*Language Focus: Articles

Paragraph Review

In the past four units, you have learned about the paragraph. Let's take a moment to review what you have learned.

Features of a Paragraph

These are the four main features of a paragraph:

☑ 1. A paragraph has a topic sentence with controlling ideas.

☑ 2. All of the sentences in the paragraph relate to the main topic.

☑ 3. The first line of a paragraph is indented.

☑ 4. The concluding sentence brings the paragraph to a logical ending.

Language Focus Review

You have practiced these elements of grammar and punctuation:

- subject-verb agreement
- verb tenses
- capitalization and end punctuation
- avoiding sentence fragments and comma splices
- pronouns used for key nouns

All these items are important for a good paragraph. In this unit, you will have a chance to use the new information you have learned.

Working with the Structure of a Paragraph

If you understand how the parts of a paragraph are arranged, you will be able to write better paragraphs. The activities in this section review the structure of a paragraph.

ACTIVITY 1 Writing Topic Sentences

Read each paragraph and write a suitable topic sentence for each one. Remember: The topic sentence contains the controlling ideas related to the supporting sentences. Be sure to add appropriate end punctuation and remember to indent.

EXAMPLE PARAGRAPH 30

1. *These following steps will make it fast & easy to get into a university*

First, you need to have enough time to request and then submit all the necessary academic records. Often it takes a long time for records, such as transcripts or standardized test scores, to arrive at the university. You must be sure that this paperwork reaches the university before the application deadline. Second, the admissions office must have enough time to look at your academic records and decide whether you will be accepted. Finally, many universities have a quota, or special number, of students who may enter every semester. If you apply too late, there may not be room for you for the semester in which you want to enter. Following these simple steps can help you get into a university quickly and easily.

EXAMPLE PARAGRAPH 31

2. *One of the most incredible bridges is in Canada*

The Capilano Bridge in British Columbia, Canada, is listed in the *Guinness Book of World Records* as the world's longest suspension footbridge. The bridge is 450 feet (137 m) long and rises 230 feet (70 m) above the Capilano River. The original wood and rope bridge was built in 1889 to help loggers cross the steep canyon. However, today only adventure-seeking tourists attempt to cross the narrow, swinging bridge. Unlike the loggers, their goal is not to take trees away from the canyon but simply to enjoy Canadian nature. This bridge is an amazing sight to see.

3. _I will never forget my first rock concert_

I was very young, and it was the first time my parents let me go out in public without them.
I was excited. My friends and I had great seats near the stage. We had to push through crowds
of people to get to our seats. As we sat down, the lights dimmed, and the crowd grew silent.
Then in a flash of light, the band rushed on stage. The guitars blared, and the drums crashed.
The music was deafening! Everyone in the arena screamed and started to dance. My friends and
I did not sit down all night. When I woke up the next morning, my legs ached and my throat
was sore, but I did not care. I thought attending my first rock concert was the most exciting,
grown-up thing I had ever done.

Writer's Note

Proofreading Your Work

Always proofread your work—check it for mistakes.

- Make sure that you have used correct punctuation and capitalization.
- Make sure that you have indented the first line of each paragraph.
- Make sure every sentence has a subject and a verb.

It is a good idea to have someone else proofread your writing for you, too. Sometimes
another reader can see mistakes that you might miss.

ACTIVITY 2 Error Correction in a Paragraph

The following paragraph contains errors in indentation, capitalization, and punctuation. Read the paragraph and make corrections. There are 10 mistakes.

EXAMPLE PARAGRAPH 33

There is a lot to know about the sport of hockey. Hockey is popular in many countries, including canada and the United states. the game is played on Ice, and the players wear skates to move around A hockey player can score a point if he hits a special disk called a Puck into the goal. However, this is not as easy as it seems because each goal is guarded by a special player called a Goalie The goalie's job is to keep the puck away from the goal The next time you see a hockey game on television, perhaps you will be able to follow the action better because you have this information.

ACTIVITY 3 Copying an Edited Paragraph

After you have made the corrections in Activity 2, write the paragraph here. Think of a title and write it on the line above the paragraph.

_____

_____

_____

_____

_____

_____

_____

_____

_____

ACTIVITY 4 Error Correction in a Paragraph

The following paragraph contains errors in indentation, capitalization, and punctuation. Read the paragraph and make corrections. There are 10 mistakes.

EXAMPLE PARAGRAPH 34

Sweet tea is a very easy-to-make drink that is popular in the southern United States. Almost any restaurant in the states of georgia alabama and South carolina will serve this cold beverage To make sweet tea, you must boil a pot of water. once the water boils, add one cup of white sugar to the water. stir the sugar until it **dissolves**. After that, add four tea bags to the pot of water. Let the mixture **brew** for thirty minutes When the tea is ready, **pour** it over ice. This sweet drink will definitely **refresh** you!

once: when, at that time
stir: to move a liquid around with a spoon or similar utensil
dissolve: to break into smaller pieces

brew: to cook something over low heat until it is ready
pour: to move a liquid from one container to another
refresh: to make you feel fresh again

ACTIVITY 5 Copying an Edited Paragraph

After you have made the corrections in Activity 4, write the paragraph here. Think of a title and write it on the line above the paragraph.

_____

_____

_____

_____

_____

_____

_____

For more practice with correcting errors in a paragraph, try Unit 5, Activity 1 and Activity 2 on the *Great Writing 2* Web site: elt.heinle.com/greatwriting

Building Better Sentences

Correct and varied sentence structure is essential to the quality of your writing. For further practice with the sentences and paragraphs in this part of the unit, go to Practice 9 on page 257 in Appendix 1.

ACTIVITY 6 Sequencing Information

These seven sentences make up a paragraph, but they are not in the best order. First, read the sentences and number them from 1 to 5 to indicate the order that they should go in. Then write the kind of sentence that each one is—topic, supporting, *or* concluding.

a. ___2___ During ancient Greek and Roman times, when a new ship was built, a small number of coins were left under the mast of the ship. The shipbuilders did this for a very special reason.

Kind of sentences: _____S_____

b. ___5___ Today scientists find evidence of this long-standing tradition in a variety of locations, from the decayed remains of old Greek ships to the still active frigate USS *Constitution*.

Kind of sentence: _____C_____

c. ___1___ The art of shipbuilding has some odd traditions, and one of the most interesting of all has its roots in Greek and Roman history.

Kind of sentence: _____T_____

d. ___4___ It was believed that sailors without money to cross this river would not be able to take their place in the afterlife.

Kind of sentence: _____S_____

e. ___3___ In case of a disaster at sea, the dead crew needed these coins to pay to get to the afterlife. According to legend, the crew members gave these coins to the ferry master Charon to take them across the river Styx to Hades, the land of the dead.

Kind of sentences: _____S_____

For more practice with sequencing information, try Unit 5, Activity 3 and Activity 4 on the *Great Writing 2* Web site: elt.heinle.com/greatwriting

ACTIVITY 7 Copying a Paragraph

Create a paragraph by copying the sentences from Activity 6 in their new arrangement. On the top line, write a title for the paragraph.

EXAMPLE PARAGRAPH 35

_____

_____

_____

_____

_____

_____

_____

_____

_____

_____

_____

_____

_____

_____

_____

_____

_____

_____

_____

_____

Analyzing Paragraphs

It is important to be able to identify the topic, topic sentence, and writer's purpose in a paragraph.

ACTIVITY 8 Paragraph Analysis

Analyze the content and purpose of the paragraph in Activity 7. Read the paragraph again and answer the following questions.

1. What is the topic? _Odd traditions of shipbuilding_

_____

2. What is the topic sentence? _Sent. C_

_____

3. What is the writer's main purpose for writing this paragraph? _To explain_

_____

4. Do you have any ideas for improving this paragraph? _____

_____

Checking Your Supporting Sentences

   Once you have written a paragraph, reread it to make sure that all the supporting sentences relate to the topic sentence. Circle the controlling ideas in the topic sentence to see what each supporting sentence should relate to. For additional help, ask someone to read your paragraph and check the supporting sentences. Another reader may see a weakness that you missed.

ACTIVITY 9 Identifying Good Supporting Sentences

Read each paragraph. Decide which sentence is not a good supporting sentence. Underline that sentence.

EXAMPLE PARAGRAPH 36

The Frozen North

   Due to the **harsh climate** in the Arctic, very few people live there. Canada, Greenland, Russia, Iceland, Norway, Sweden, and Finland all have large amounts of land in this frozen **region**, but only a small percentage of their people lives in this region. Although these countries have tried to offer **incentives** for people to move to the Arctic, few go. The scenery is extremely beautiful, but most people cannot get accustomed to the climate there. However, one group of people, the Inuit, has adapted to life in the Arctic. Other people have not been able to **do so** because life is simply too difficult in this frozen land. Life is also difficult in desert regions. Unfortunately, the severe climate in the Arctic area limits its population growth.

harsh: severe, difficult
the climate: the weather in a place over time
a region: an area, a place

an incentive: a reason to do something
do so: to do an action that was previously mentioned

Bears of the Arctic

Polar bears have unique bodies that help them live in the harsh weather of the Arctic. They are large animals that weigh up to 1,800 pounds. The body fat from all this weight helps keep them warm. Their heavy white **fur** not only protects them from icy winds but also helps them **hide** in the large **piles** of snow. It snows a lot in the Arctic. The bears have five long sharp **claws** on each **paw**. They use these to walk safely on the ice and to catch their food. Polar bears are truly amazing **creatures**.

fur: hair on an animal's skin
hide: to make invisible or difficult to see
a pile: a small hill (of books, papers, snow, etc.)

claws: fingernails or toenails of animals
a paw: a foot of an animal
a creature: an animal

ACTIVITY 10 Proofreading for Comma Errors

Below is a writing assignment that a student turned in to his teacher. Unfortunately, he did not proofread it, and it has a lot of comma mistakes.

Proofread the paragraph and help the student get a better grade. Correct the comma mistakes and rewrite the paragraph on the lines provided. Hint: *There are 11 comma mistakes. (For help with comma errors, see pages 232–234 in the Brief Writer's Handbook with Activities.)*

A Great Place to Visit in California

When you go to California San Diego is a great spot to visit because of the many exciting things to see and do there. First you should visit the Gaslamp Quarter. In this historic area, you can easily find great food fun and culture. Next, you should visit SeaWorld to see the amazing animal shows. After you visit SeaWorld you

should see a football or baseball game at Qualcomm Stadium. Finally you **ought to** see the animals at the world-famous San Diego Zoo. If you decide to go to the zoo do not forget to see the giant pandas and Hua Mei the only panda cub in the United States. If you visit one two or all of these San Diego **sites** it will certainly be a fun and interesting day!

ought to: should   **a site:** a place, a location

_____

_____

_____

_____

_____

_____

_____

_____

ACTIVITY 11 Guided Peer Editing

A classmate has asked you to proofread her paragraph. She wrote questions in the margin about four things that she is not sure about. Answer the writer's questions and correct the mistakes on her draft. In addition, there are several other mistakes that she could not find. Find these mistakes, too, and correct them on this first draft.

EXAMPLE PARAGRAPH 39

The Florida Everglades

The Everglades region consists of a gigantic freshwater marsh that can be found only in southern Florida. Water is **vital** to this unique environment This region was formed by hundreds of years of **flooding** from lake Okeechobee after heavy rains. These floods always provided the **marsh** with new water to **support** its wide variety of plants and animals. Unfortunately people and nature are now taking water away from the Everglades. For example the Miami, Little and New rivers all **drain** water away from the Everglades. Even worse, man-made **dams** and canals prevents **annual** flooding. without this flooding or other source of fresh water, the everglades will **eventually** die. Only time will tell whether this unique area will be lost to future **generations** forever.

Should I capitalize "lake"?

Do I need a comma after "Unfortunately"?

Do I need to put commas in this list of river names?

Is the verb "prevents" okay with this subject?

vital: very important, necessary
flooding: increased water in an area
a marsh: an area of land that is usually very wet
support: to provide food, money, or some other necessity
drain: to pass or move out

a dam: a structure that holds back water, usually near a river
annual: happening every year
eventually: happening after a long time
a generation: all of the people born in one time period

Building Better Sentences

Correct and varied sentence structure is essential to the quality of your writing. For further practice with the sentences and paragraphs in this part of the unit, go to Practice 10 on page 257 in Appendix 1.

Language Focus

Articles

The **articles** *a, an,* and *the* are three small words, but they cause many problems for non-native speakers. It is often difficult to know which article is correct in a sentence. Here are a few guidelines to help you.

1. Always use an article with singular count nouns (SCN).

   Incorrect: My mother is <u>teacher</u>.
   SCN

   Correct: My mother is **a** teacher.

   Incorrect: Many people believe *13* is unlucky <u>number</u>.
   SCN

   Correct: Many people believe *13* is **an** unlucky number.

2. When you mean the thing in general, do not use *the* with noncount nouns (NCN).

   Incorrect: All good chefs know that **the** <u>salt</u> and **the** <u>pepper</u> can make food taste better.
   NCN   NCN

   Correct: All good chefs know that salt and pepper can make food taste better.

3. When you mean the thing in general, avoid using *the* + singular count noun. It is more common to use a plural count noun (PCN) without *the*. Notice that the verb also changes from singular to plural.

   Incorrect: The <u>television</u> is found in many American homes.
   SNC

   Correct: <u>Televisions</u> are found in many American homes.
   PCN

4. Use *the* when you refer to a word a second or subsequent time.

   Incorrect: Dinner consisted of steak, potatoes, and carrots. Steak was great, but I did not like potatoes or carrots.

   Correct: Dinner consisted of steak, potatoes, and carrots. **The** steak was great, but I did not like **the** potatoes or **the** carrots.

5. Use *the* if there is only one of that thing (unique existence).

   Incorrect: Sun is 93,000,000 miles from our planet.

   Correct: **The** Sun is 93,000,000 miles from our planet.

6. Use *the* when you refer to something specific.

Incorrect: A bank on corner of Fifty-Sixth Street and Fowler Avenue is where Susan works.

Correct: **The** bank on **the** corner of Fifty-Sixth Street and Fowler Avenue is where Susan works.

7. Use *the* when you have a superlative form.

Of all the movies I saw last year, **the** most interesting was *Cry of the Eagle.*

ACTIVITY 12   Correcting Articles

Read this paragraph. Add, delete, or change articles where necessary. Begin with the title.

Best Cook in the World

Beyond a shadow of a doubt, my grandmother Florence Folse is a best cook in world. Many people say that their mother or grandmother can cook a spaghetti, the fried fish, or the beans really well. However, if there were cooking **contest** right now, I am sure that my grandmother would win. My grandmother has cooked for six children, fifteen grandchildren, twenty-four great-grandchildren, and many more relatives. She cooks from experience. Since my family lives in the southern Louisiana, my grandmother knows how to cook the seafood, the red beans and rice, and the gumbo, which is a kind of seafood soup or **stew**. Sometimes she uses cookbook, but most of the time she cooks from memory. If you could eat a plate of her fried chicken or meatballs, I am sure that you would agree with my conclusion about her cooking ability.

beyond a shadow of a doubt: with 100% certainty
a shadow: a dark area

a contest: a competition
stew: a thick soup

For more practice with count nouns and articles, try Unit 5, Activity 5, Activity 6, and Activity 7 on the *Great Writing 2* Web site: elt.heinle.com/greatwriting

ACTIVITY 13 Word Associations

Circle the word or phrase that is most closely related to the word or phrase on the left. If necessary, use a dictionary to check the meaning of words you do not know.

1. narrow	not covered	**not wide**	
2. to ache	**bad feeling**	good feeling	
3. to scream	**loud voice**	soft voice	
4. a dam	across a highway	**across a river**	
5. vital	**you need it**	you do not need it	
6. decayed	very new	**very old**	
7. to rush	**fast**	slow	
8. a contest	a generation	**a winner**	
9. fur	**on an animal**	on a bicycle	
10. a flood	too much money	**too much water**	
11. to stir	your lawn	**your coffee**	
12. to hide something	you cannot buy it	**you cannot see it**	
13. to pour	**a liquid**	a solid	
14. to attempt	to do	**to try to do**	

= *words often used together*

Fill in each blank with the word on the left that most naturally completes the phrase on the right. If necessary, use a dictionary to check the meaning of words you do not know.

1. scream / steep   a ___steep___ canyon

2. for / to   ought ___to___

3. in / on   ___on___ the corner of 41st and Vine Streets

4. pour / seek   to ___seek___ adventure

5. climate / goal   a harsh ___climate___

6. about / odd   an ___odd___ tradition

7. of / to   to find evidence ___of___ a problem

8. building / computer   an ancient ___building___

9. in / of   to consist ___of___

10. doors / lights   then the ___lights___ dimmed

Original Student Writing

ACTIVITY 15 Original Writing Practice

Write a paragraph of five to ten sentences.

- *Choose a general topic and brainstorm a specific idea.*

- *Make sure that you have a topic sentence with controlling ideas.*

- *After you write your paragraph, check to see if all the supporting sentences are related to the controlling ideas in the topic sentence.*

- *Your concluding sentence should restate the topic or make a prediction about it.*

- *Use at least five of the vocabulary words or phrases presented in Activity 13 and Activity 14. Underline these words and phrases in your paragraph.*

ACTIVITY 16 Peer Editing

Exchange papers from Activity 15 with a partner. Read your partner's writing. Then use Peer Editing Sheet 5 on page 275 to help you comment on your partner's writing. Be sure to offer positive suggestions and comments that will help your partner improve his or her writing. Consider your partner's comments as you revise your own writing.

Additional Topics for Writing

Here are some ideas for paragraphs. Select one of these topics and write an original paragraph. Remember what you have learned in Units 1 through 5. If you need further help, review the writing process in the Brief Writer's Handbook with Activities, pages 218–224.

TOPIC 1: Write about the worst (or best) day of your life. What happened? When did this happen? Why did this happen? What was the result?

TOPIC 2: What do you think will be the highest-paying occupation fifty years from now? Give reasons to support your opinion.

TOPIC 3: What is the definition of a perfect parent? What are the characteristics of such a person?

TOPIC 4: Choose a mechanical device, such as a television, a car engine, a fax machine, or an MP3 player. How does it work? Explain the process step-by-step.

TOPIC 5: The United Nations was formed in 1945 to promote world peace. However, some people think that the United Nations is useless. Do you think the United Nations is doing a good job? Should the United Nations continue to exist? Why or why not?

Timed Writing

How quickly can you write in English? There are many times when you must write quickly, such as on a test. It is important to feel comfortable during those times. Timed-writing practice can make you feel better about writing quickly in English.

Take out a piece of paper. Then read the writing prompt below this paragraph. Your teacher will give you 5 minutes to brainstorm ideas about this topic. You must then write a short paragraph (perhaps 6 to 10 sentences) about it. You will have 25 minutes to write your paragraph. At the end of the 25 minutes, your teacher will collect your work and return it to you later.

> What are the best snack foods? Be sure to include a topic sentence, one or two strong supporting reasons for each of your choices, and a solid concluding sentence.

Definition Paragraphs

GOAL: To learn how to write a definition paragraph

***Language Focus:** Simple adjective clauses

Like all forms of writing, paragraphs are written for a specific purpose. The purpose determines what information you include in the paragraph and how you write it. In this unit, you will look at one kind of paragraph—the definition paragraph.

What Is a Definition Paragraph?

A **definition paragraph** defines something. The word *definition* comes from the verb *to define*, which means "to state the meaning of a word or to describe the basic qualities of something." In a definition paragraph, the writer's main purpose is to tell you what something is. For example, a definition paragraph might define the word *gossip* and give examples. Another definition paragraph might define the term *true friendship* and give relevant examples.

If you were writing a whole essay, you might need to include one paragraph early in your essay that defines a specific term. For example, in an essay entitled "Human Progress in My Generation," you might want to first talk about what the word *progress* means to you. Does progress mean making money? Does progress mean change? Does progress mean lack of disease? Can progress be measured, and if so, how?

> A definition paragraph
> - explains what something is.
> - gives facts, details, and examples to make the definition clear to the reader.

The best way to learn what a definition paragraph looks like is to read and study several examples. Even though the three paragraphs that follow are about different topics, each one is an example of a definition paragraph.

Read and study these three examples of definition paragraphs. Answer the questions.

Definition Paragraph 1

This paragraph is about a kind of food that is common in the southern part of Louisiana. You might write a definition paragraph when you need to explain a special dish, a dance, or a custom from your own or another culture.

Before you read the paragraph, discuss these questions with your classmates.

1. What is seafood? Give three examples.

2. What do you know about the people of Louisiana? Do you know anything about the Cajun people? You may need to consult a dictionary, an encyclopedia, or the Internet.

3. Have you ever seen rice growing? What kind of land is good for growing rice?

4. Have you visited or read about New Orleans? What do you know about this city?

Now read the paragraph.

EXAMPLE PARAGRAPH 41

Gumbo

The dictionary definition of *gumbo* does not make it sound as delicious as gumbo really is. The dictionary defines gumbo as a "thick soup made in south Louisiana." However, anyone who has tasted this delicious dish knows that this definition is too **bland** to describe gumbo. It is true that gumbo is a thick soup, but it is much more than that. Gumbo, one of the most popular of all **Cajun** dishes, is made with different kinds of seafood or meat mixed with vegetables, **such as** green peppers and onions. For example, seafood gumbo contains **shrimp** and **crab**. Other kinds of gumbo include chicken, sausage, or **turkey**. **Regardless of** the **ingredients** in gumbo, this **regional delicacy** is a **tasty** dish.

bland: not having much taste (either good or bad)

Cajun: related to people who moved from Acadia (in Canada) to Louisiana in 1755

such as: like, for example

shrimp: a kind of seafood

a crab: a kind of seafood

a turkey: a kind of bird that cannot fly long distances

regardless of: anyway, no matter

an ingredient: a food item in a dish

regional: from a particular area or region

a delicacy: a special food

tasty: delicious, having a good or special taste

1. What is the topic sentence of this paragraph?

   _____

   _____

2. Write one sentence in your own words that defines *gumbo*. Begin your sentence like this: "Gumbo is . . ."

   _____

   _____

3. Notice that the writer quotes a dictionary definition of *gumbo*. Choose one of these food items and write a definition in your own words. Do not look in a dictionary.

sandwich	milk shake	dessert
hamburger	sundae	pie

   _____

   _____

4. Now look in a dictionary for the definition of the word that you chose in number 3. Write a sentence that uses that definition. Use the topic sentence in "Gumbo" as a model.

   _____

   _____

5. Is your original definition in number 3 similar to the dictionary definition? If not, how is it different?

   _____

   _____

Definition Paragraph 2

This paragraph defines something that many people think is wrong, but some people do it anyway.

Before you read the paragraph, discuss these questions with your classmates.

1. What is gossip? Give an example.

2. Is gossip good or bad? Why or why not?

3. Do you think that men gossip less than women do? Explain your answer.

Now read the paragraph.

EXAMPLE PARAGRAPH 42

Gossip

According to *The American Heritage Dictionary*, gossip is a "**trivial rumor** of a personal **nature**," but this definition makes gossip sound harmless when it is really not. At first, gossip might not seem so bad. One person tells a second person something about someone, and that second person tells a third, **and so on**. The information passes from person to person. However, gossip is much more than just information and rumors. As a rumor continues, it grows and changes. People do not know all the facts. They add information. As the gossip goes from one person to the next person, the **damage** continues, and the person who is the **subject** of the gossip cannot do anything to answer or protect himself or herself. Because the **potential** damage may **range** from hurt feelings to a lost career, gossip is much worse than simply a "trivial rumor."

trivial: unimportant
a rumor: information that is passed from person to person
nature: type, kind, characteristics
and so on: etc. (et cetera)

damage: harm, negative effects, injury that reduces the value of something
a subject: a topic or a person
potential: possible but not yet actual
range: to extend (from X to Y)

1. What is the topic sentence of "Gossip"?

_____

_____

_____

2. What is the writer's opinion about gossip? Does the writer think it is wrong? How do you know?

_____

_____

3. Do all the supporting sentences relate to the topic? _____

   Discuss the supporting sentences with a partner.

4. Like the writer of "Gumbo," this writer also quotes a dictionary definition. Read the following sentences. Which ones are easy to read and understand? Which ones are difficult? Rank them from 1 to 4, with 1 being the easiest to read and 4 being the most difficult.

   _____ Paragraph 1: The dictionary defines *gumbo* as a "thick soup made in south Louisiana."

   _____ Paragraph 1: The definition of *gumbo* is a "thick soup made in south Louisiana."

   _____ Paragraph 2: According to *The American Heritage Dictionary*, *gossip* is a "trivial rumor of a personal nature."

   _____ Paragraph 2: *The American Heritage Dictionary* definition of *gossip* is a "trivial rumor of a personal nature."

5. *Gossip* is difficult to define in your own words. Here are some other words that you may find difficult. Choose one, look it up in a dictionary, and write a definition sentence similar to the topic sentence in "Gossip."

   pride   honesty   friendship   luck   fate   patience

   _____

   _____

   _____

   _____

   _____

   _____

Present your sentence to your classmates.

---

fresh|water /frɛʃwɔtər/ ADJ A **freshwater** lake contains water that is not salty, usually in contrast to the sea.

fret /frɛt/ (**frets, fretting, fretted**) V-T/V-I If you **fret** about something, you worry about it. □ *I was constantly fretting about everyone else's problems.* □ *Members of Congress fret that the project will eventually cost billions.*

fric|tion /frɪkʃⁿn/ (**frictions**) **1** N-UNCOUNT **Friction** between people is disagreement and argument between them. □ *Sara sensed that there had been friction between her children.* **2** N-UNCOUNT **Friction** is the force that makes it difficult for things to move freely when they are touching each other.

Fri|day /fraɪdeɪ, -di/ (**Fridays**) N-VAR **Friday** is the day after Thursday and before Saturday.

friend|ly fire N-UNCOUNT If you come under **friendly fire** during a battle, you are accidentally shot at by people on your own side, rather than by your enemy. □ *A high percentage of casualties were caused by friendly fire.*

Word Link	ship ≈ condition or state : censorship, citizenship, friendship

friend|ship /frɛndʃɪp/ (**friendships**) N-VAR A **friendship** is a relationship between two or more friends. □ *She ended our friendship by sending me a hurtful letter.*

fries /fraɪz/ N-PLURAL **Fries** are the same as **French fries**.

frig|ate /frɪgət/ (**frigates**) N-COUNT A **frigate** is a fairly small ship owned by the navy that can move at fast speeds.

Definition Paragraph 3

What is your favorite snack food? This paragraph talks about one kind of popular snack food.

Before you read the paragraph, discuss these questions with your classmates.

1. Write a definition in your own words for *snack*. Compare your definition with your classmates' definitions.

2. Name three examples of popular snacks.

3. Why do you think these three snacks are so popular?

Now read the paragraph.

EXAMPLE PARAGRAPH 43

Pretzels

The **pretzel**, which is a salted and **glazed** biscuit that is shaped like a **knot**, has an interesting history. The first pretzels were made in an Italian **monastery** in A.D. 610. These **twisted strips** of bread were originally called *pretiola*, which means "little **reward**" in Latin. They were given as **treats** to local children. The pretzel rapidly became popular throughout Europe. Today the pretzel is an especially popular snack in Germany, Austria, and the United States.

a pretzel: a snack made of flour
glazed: having a thin, smooth, shiny coating
a knot: a part of a string that is tied in loops
a monastery: a place where members of a
   religious group live

twisted: turned in several directions
a strip: a long, thin piece
a reward: something given for a special service or
   accomplishment
a treat: something special

1. Write the topic sentence of "Pretzels."

_____

_____

2. How is this sentence different from the topic sentences of "Gumbo" and "Gossip"?

_____

3. When you write a definition paragraph, you can include a definition from the dictionary or use an original definition of your own. Here are four items that are difficult to define. Choose one and write your own definition.

giraffe   battery   flag   cell phone

_____

_____

4. Compare your definition with your classmates' definitions. How are they the same? How are they different? Why is yours (or theirs) better?

_____

_____

_____

5. Write an original question about "Pretzels." Your question can be about the content of the paragraph or about the writer's style. Work with another student or in small groups. Take turns asking and answering each other's questions.

Question: _____

_____

Answer: _____

_____

Building Better Sentences

Correct and varied sentence structure is essential to the quality of your writing. For further practice with the sentences and paragraphs in this part of the unit, go to Practice 11 on page 258 in Appendix 1.

Writer's Note

Quotation Marks

When you write, the ideas and the words are usually your own. However, sometimes you might want to borrow someone else's words. When you use another person's words, you must let the reader know that these words are not yours. In English, you do this by putting the borrowed words in **quotation marks**.

For example, if you use a definition that is taken from another source, such as a dictionary, put the definition inside quotation marks. Look at the second sentence of Example Paragraph 41, "Gumbo," and the first sentence of Example Paragraph 42, "Gossip." Both of these sentences include words in quotation marks.

ACTIVITY 2 Adding Quotation Marks

The following sentences are from books and speeches. Add quotation marks where necessary. Sometimes you will have to add a comma and capitalize letters. (Remember that commas, periods, and question marks are placed inside the quotation marks. See pages 235–236 in the Brief Writer's Handbook with Activities for more information.) Items 1 and 6 have been done for you.

Words taken from a book:

1. The dictionary defines *marriage* as "the union of a husband and a wife."

2. According to *The American Heritage Dictionary*, an *errand* is a short trip for a specific purpose, but my trip to the courthouse was certainly not a simple errand.

3. If we believe the dictionary definition of *drug* as a narcotic that is addictive, then surely we must say that cigarettes are used to deliver the drug nicotine.

4. The dictionary definition of *opulent*, extremely wealthy or rich, may sound good, but this word does not have a positive meaning for me.

5. Although the dictionary currently defines *a family* as parents and their children, previous definitions probably included additional family members.

Words that someone spoke:

6. Julie said, "ᴡe really hope the vocabulary exam is not too tough."

7. When all the students were seated, the teacher stood up and announced beginning tomorrow, no student may enter this room wearing any kind of head covering.

8. The taxi driver turned to me and asked where do you want to go?

9. The player stopped the tennis game, approached the net, and calmly asked her opponent are you sure that ball was really out?

10. I cannot wait here any longer the woman said as she walked out the door.

 For more practice with quotations marks, try Unit 6, Activity 1 and Activity 2 on the *Great Writing 2* Web site: elt.heinle.com/greatwriting

Citing Ideas to Avoid Plagiarism

Plagiarism is the improper use of someone else's words. It is using someone else's words as if they were your own words. Simply defined, plagiarism is stealing another person's words. If you want to use another person's words, you must put those words in quotation marks if you have used his or her exact words. If you change most of the words but keep the person's idea, you do not need to use quotation marks because you are not quoting the person's exact words.

Whether you use a person's exact words or not, you must acknowledge that the idea is not yours, but rather, someone else's. You must cite, or show, the source of the idea. Citation methods vary according to academic professions and fields, so you should ask your instructor about the citation system that is required in your course work. You should list all the works, or sources, of the words and ideas you used in the final bibliography, or list of cited works at the end of your paper.

Perhaps the most common way to cite an original source is to use the person's name and the date of the publication where his or her words are found:

According to Solomon (2005), government spending on early education has actually declined to "levels not seen since schools had neither electricity nor running water."

Another common way to cite an original source is to include the person's name and the date of the publication after the borrowed idea. If the same idea is presented in more than one publication, all of these publications should be cited, usually in alphabetical order.

Public perception is that government spending on education is up, but many reports suggest that government spending on early education has actually declined (Brown, 2007; Solomon, 2005; Underhill, 2007).

Because there are so many different ways to cite works, you need to learn the citation system that is required in your academic area.

NOTE: See the Brief Writer's Handbook with Activities, pages 247–248, for more information on using citations in order to avoid plagiarism.

Putting the Paragraph Together: Sequencing

Good writers order their sentences in a way that best conveys the intended meaning of their paragraph.

ACTIVITY 3 Sequencing Sentences

These sentences make up one paragraph. Read the sentences and number them from 1 to 7 to indicate the best order.

a. _____ Similarly, an English speaker learning Malay might remember the word *pintu*, which means "door," by using the English words *pin* and *into*.

b. _____ The learner might remember that he or she can use a hatchet eight times to cut down a tree.

c. _____ The key-word method, which can help foreign language learners remember new vocabulary, is gaining popularity among teachers and students.

d. _____ Through these two simple examples, we can get an idea of how useful this method of remembering vocabulary can be.

e. _____ For example, a Japanese learner of English might look at the English word *hatchet* and connect it to the Japanese word *hachi* ("eight") because they sound alike.

f. _____ In this method, learners first form their own sound association between the foreign language word they are trying to learn and a word in their native language. In the second stage, learners form an image link between the target word and the native language word.

g. _____ He or she can imagine putting a pin into the door to open it.

For more practice with sequencing sentences, try Unit 6, Activity 3 on the *Great Writing 2* Web site: elt.heinle.com/greatwriting

ACTIVITY 4 Copying a Sequenced Paragraph

Now copy the sentences from Activity 3 in paragraph form. The result will be a definition paragraph that describes a method for remembering vocabulary. Give the paragraph an original title.

EXAMPLE PARAGRAPH 44

_____

_____

_____

_____

_____

_____

_____

_____

_____

_____

ACTIVITY 5 Analyzing a Paragraph

The paragraph that you copied in Activity 4 is a definition paragraph. You may want to read it again or refer to it as you complete the answers to these questions.

1. What is the general topic of Example Paragraph 44?

   _____

2. What is the topic sentence? _____

   _____

3. What is the writer's main purpose for writing this paragraph? _____

   _____

4. How many examples are given in the supporting sentences? _____

   Write them here. _____

   _____

   _____

   _____

5. If Example Paragraph 44 did not have any examples, how would that affect your understanding of the information?

   _____

   _____

   _____

6. Can you think of two more examples to further explain the key-word method?

   _____

   _____

   _____

Including Original Examples to Avoid Plagiarism

Good writers include examples, especially when they are writing about a difficult or abstract topic. Be sure to use your own original examples. Copying examples from an existing source without citing the source is plagiarism.

If you use someone else's examples, you can avoid plagiarism by citing the original source of the examples. However, your work will be much better if you can come up with original examples that you know will help your readers connect with your ideas. No one knows your readers better than you do, so you should use original examples that you know will help your readers relate to your writing.

When to Use an Example

How do you know when to use an example? Consider your readers. If you think they already know something about your topic, then you do not have to give many examples, details, or facts. However, if the topic may be new to your readers, it is helpful to include some supporting information. If you think it is necessary to give more than one example of an idea, then put a simple, clear example first and a more complex example second.

Where to Put an Example

Where should you put examples in your paragraph? The best place to put an example is usually just after you have explained an idea. If your paragraph compares two ideas, explain both ideas first. Then provide examples of each idea in the sentences that follow.

How to Begin an Example

How should you begin a sentence that provides an example? You might write, "For example," "For instance," or "An example of this is . . ." You can also write an example sentence without such an introduction. In the following sentences, the example sentence is underlined.

Different cultures have different superstitions, but all cultures have some kind of superstition. People might believe that a certain number is lucky or unlucky. Many North Americans think 13 is an unlucky number, but the Chinese believe 4 is unlucky.

Language Focus

Simple Adjective Clauses

A simple **adjective clause** may consist of a relative pronoun (*that, which,* or *who*) followed by a verb and sometimes an object. It describes the noun that comes before it. Study these examples.

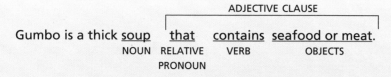

ADJECTIVE CLAUSE

Gumbo is a thick <u>soup</u>   <u>that</u>   <u>contains</u>   <u>seafood or meat</u>.
NOUN   RELATIVE   VERB   OBJECTS
PRONOUN

ADJECTIVE CLAUSE

A goalie is a <u>soccer player</u>   <u>who</u>   <u>protects</u>   <u>his team's goal</u>.
NOUN   RELATIVE   VERB   OBJECT
PRONOUN

Notes:

- Use *that* or *which* for things. (*That* is more common.)

- Use *who* or *that* for people. (*Who* is preferred.)

Let's look at two examples of adjective clauses that writers use to define special terms.

<u>Gumbo</u>   is a thick   <u>soup</u>   <u>that contains seafood or meat</u>.
SPECIFIC NOUN   GENERAL NOUN   ADJECTIVE CLAUSE

<u>Samba</u>   is a rhythmic   <u>dance</u>   <u>that is popular in Brazil</u>.
SPECIFIC NOUN   GENERAL NOUN   ADJECTIVE CLAUSE

In a definition, the specific noun (*gumbo, samba*) is the word you are defining. The general noun (*soup, dance*) is the group that the specific noun belongs to.

ACTIVITY 6 Recognizing Simple Adjective Clauses

Read the next paragraph. Underline all the adjective clauses. Look for the relative pronouns that *and* who. *Circle the noun that each clause modifies or describes. The first one has been done for you.*

Nature's Worst Storm

A hurricane is a dangerous (storm) that features high winds and heavy rains. In addition, areas along the coast may experience a tidal **surge** that can flood whole towns. Hurricanes in the Atlantic Ocean occur mostly between April and November. However, the months that have the most hurricanes are August and September. Modern technology has now made it possible for people who live in a given area to know in advance if there is danger of a hurricane **striking** their region. However, this was not always the case. For example, a hurricane that surprised the residents of Galveston, Texas, in 1900, resulted in thousands of deaths. Although we know much more about hurricanes now and can **keep track of** their movements, hurricanes continue to be one of the most dangerous weather **phenomena**.

a surge: an increase, especially a sudden or unexpected increase

strike: to hit or affect

keep track (of): to have the most recent information about, follow the location of

phenomena: occurrences that we can observe, often something unusual or noteworthy; plural form of *phenomenon*

 For more practice with simple adjective clauses, try Unit 6, Activity 4 and Activity 5 on the *Great Writing 2* Web site: elt.heinle.com/greatwriting

Write a definition for each of the following terms. Include an adjective clause in your definition and underline the clause. The first one has been done for you.

1. turtle

   A turtle is a slow-moving, four-legged animal <u>that goes inside its shell when there is danger.</u>

2. copilot

   _____

   _____

3. skunk

   _____

   _____

4. passport

   _____

   _____

5. submarine

   _____

   _____

6. odd numbers

   _____

   _____

7. William Shakespeare

   _____

   _____

8. plumber

   _____

   _____

9. Pelé

_____

_____

10. the United Nations

_____

_____

Share your sentences with a partner. Did your partner include an adjective clause in each definition?

Writer's Note

Combining Sentences for Variety

One way to improve your writing is to write different kinds of sentences. Many beginning writers use only simple sentences that have a subject, a verb, and an object. For variety, combine two short sentences with a connecting word, such as *and*, *but*, *or*, and *so*.

Simple Sentences:	I studied math for five hours last night. I failed the test.
Combined Sentence:	I studied math for five hours last night, *but* I failed the test.
Simple Sentences:	The scientist forgot to control the temperature. The experiment was not successful.
Combined Sentence:	The scientist forgot to control the temperature, *so* the experiment was not successful.

FANBOYS

You may have studied the acronym *FANBOYS*, which stands for the six connecting words *for, and, nor, but, or, yet,* and *so*. Can you make an example sentence with each of these as a connecting word between two clauses? (NOTE: *For* is usually used in literature, not spoken English.)

Examples of Sentence Variety

In addition to connecting words, good writers use adjectives, adjective clauses, adverbs, adverb clauses, prepositional phrases, and other variations in their sentences. Study these examples. The variations are underlined.

Adjectives

Simple Sentence:	The manager rejected the schedule.
Variation:	The <u>current</u> <u>business</u> manager rejected <u>Mark's</u> <u>revised</u> schedule.

Adjective Clauses

Simple Sentence:	The students liked the suggestion.
Variation:	The students <u>who are in charge of planning the party</u> liked the suggestion <u>that Mark made</u>.

Adverbs

Simple Sentence:	The woman picked up the chain saw.
Variation:	<u>Next</u>, the woman <u>carefully</u> picked up the chain saw.

Adverb Clauses

Simple Sentence:	He asked her to sit down.
Variation:	<u>Before the doctor told the woman the news</u>, he asked her to sit down.

Prepositional Phrases

Simple Sentence:	I did all the homework.
Variation:	I did all the homework <u>on my computer</u> <u>in about three hours</u>.

Reading for Sentence Variety

Read the next two paragraphs. Do you notice any difference in the writing styles? Discuss your impression of each paragraph with a partner.

Example 1: I was walking on Stern Street. I was in front of the bank. I heard a bang. It was loud. It was violent. The front door of the bank opened. This happened suddenly. A man left the bank. He did this hurriedly. He was tall. He was very thin. He had wavy hair. It was brown. He had a gun. It was silver. It was shiny. It was in his right hand. } 17 sentences

Example 2: I was walking in front of the bank on Stern Street. Suddenly I heard a loud, violent bang, and the front door of the bank opened. A tall, very thin man with wavy brown hair hurriedly left the bank. In his right hand, he had a shiny silver gun. } 4 sentences

Perhaps you noted that Example 1 has seventeen sentences and Example 2 has only four sentences. However, both examples include the same information. Example 1 has short, choppy sentences, which make reading uneven and difficult. In Example 2, the writer has combined phrases and ideas to make more complex sentences that sound better and read more smoothly.

Each paragraph is missing a sentence. Create the missing sentence from the sentences below the paragraph. You may want to circle the important information in these sentences. Use all the ideas, but not necessarily all the words. Make one sentence. It should be a good supporting sentence. Write the new sentence on the blank lines in the paragraph.

Patience

Patience means the ability to continue doing something even if you do not see any results **at once**. We can see patience in a teacher who works with young children. She may not be feeling very well that day, but she smiles and does not get angry when a child **misbehaves**. We can see patience in a clerk who is **polite** to a customer even though the clerk has already been at work for seven or eight hours. _____

_____

In our modern society, people often **lack** simple patience. People nowadays expect immediate results all the time. To me, patience is one **mark** of a civilized society.

at once: immediately, right away
misbehave: to act badly or incorrectly
polite: having good manners

drizzle: to rain lightly
lack: to not have
a mark: a sign

We can see patience in a person.
The person is waiting.

The person is at a street corner.
It is beginning to **drizzle**.

Seward's Folly

A folly is a **costly** action that has a bad or an **absurd** result. The purchase of Alaska, which is now the largest oil-producing state in the United States, was once considered a folly. In fact, Alaska was called "Seward's Folly." This name refers to Secretary of State William Seward, who convinced Congress in 1867 that buying Alaska from Russia was a good idea. At that time, many Americans thought that it was a waste of money to

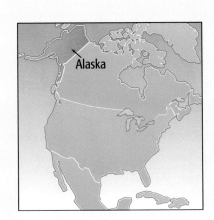

buy a cold, **barren** land for several million dollars. However, they were wrong. _____

_____

Large amounts of gold and other minerals have been found in Alaska. Alaska is an important source of oil for the United States. In addition, thousands of people visit Alaska each year to see the natural beauty of the state. The purchase of Alaska in 1867 may have seemed like a bad decision at the time, but today we know that buying Alaska was certainly not a folly.

costly: expensive
absurd: crazy
barren: empty

Alaska is not a cold place all the time.
Alaska is not a barren place all the time.

It was not a waste of money.

EXAMPLE PARAGRAPH 48

An Unusual Word Relationship

You might never guess that the word *sincere* is related to making pottery. *Sincere* comes from two Latin words: *sin* meaning "without" and *cero* meaning "wax." Thus, *sincere* means "without wax." _____

_____

It took a long time to make this pottery, and occasionally the pottery had cracks in it. Pottery with a crack in it was **worthless** and had to be destroyed. Some potters who did not want to make brand-new pottery would put wax on the crack. To the eye of the **careless** shopper, the pottery looked good. However, people soon realized which potters were good and which were not good. Thus, the most respected potters made pottery that was without wax, or "sincere," and that is how the word *sincere* began.

worthless: having no value
careless: the opposite of careful

People used pottery.
This was in ancient times.
The pottery was made of clay.

The pottery was for plates.
The pottery was for bowls.

Hint: Begin with a time phrase.

 For more practice with sentence combining, try Unit 6, Activity 6 and Activity 7 on the *Great Writing 2* Web site: elt.heinle.com/greatwriting

Building Better Sentences

Correct and varied sentence structure is essential to the quality of your writing. For further practice with the sentences and paragraphs in this part of the unit, go to Practice 12 on page 258 in Appendix 1.

Building Better Vocabulary

ACTIVITY 9 Word Associations

Circle the word or phrase that is most closely related to the word or phrase on the left. If necessary, use a dictionary to check the meaning of words you do not know.

1. plagiarism	to follow	to steal
2. a surge	less	more
3. to reject	to say *no*	to say *yes*
4. to quote	to glaze something	to repeat something
5. bland	tasteless	tasty
6. gossip	ranges	rumors
7. to misbehave	a child	a paragraph
8. to measure	to find a number	to find a person
9. fate	pride	future
10. harmless	safe	dangerous
11. a reward	money	to tell again
12. to strike	to hit	to tell
13. to lack money	poor	rich
14. to rank	$12 \times 8 = 96$	1st, 2nd, 3rd
15. seafood	sausage	shrimp

Fill in each blank with the word on the left that most naturally completes the phrase on the right. If necessary, use a dictionary to check the meaning of words you do not know.

1. of / on   regardless _____

2. costly / quickly   a _____ action

3. area / first   in a given _____

4. from / in   their ages range _____ 18 to 24

5. give / keep   to _____ track of

6. guessed / seemed   it may have _____ difficult

7. lack / polite   a very _____ person

8. concrete / land   barren _____

9. damage / hair   with wavy _____

10. example / turkey   a relevant _____

Original Student Writing: Definition Paragraph

ACTIVITY 11 Original Writing Practice

Write a definition paragraph. Follow these guidelines:

- Choose a topic.
- Brainstorm some information about the topic. What do you want to include? What do your readers know about the topic? What do they want or need to know?
- Write a topic sentence with controlling ideas.
- Write a few supporting sentences that relate to the topic.
- End with a concluding sentence that restates the topic or makes a prediction about it.
- If you use words from another source, put quotation marks around them.
- Use at least five of the vocabulary words or phrases presented in Activity 9 and Activity 10. Underline these words and phrases in your paragraph.
- If you need help, study the example definition paragraphs in this unit. Be sure to refer to the seven steps in the writing process in the Brief Writer's Handbook with Activities on pages 218–224.

Exchange papers from Activity 11 with a partner. Read your partner's writing. Then use Peer Editing Sheet 6 on page 277 to help you comment on your partner's writing. Be sure to offer positive suggestions and comments that will help your partner improve his or her writing. Consider your partner's comments as you revise your own writing.

Additional Topics for Writing

Here are some ideas for definition paragraphs. When you write your paragraph, follow the guidelines in Activity 11.

TOPIC 1: Choose an emotion, such as love or jealousy. How does the dictionary define the emotion? Is it a good emotion or a bad emotion? Who usually feels this emotion and why? Give some examples.

TOPIC 2: Choose a scientific or medical term, such as *gravity, tsunami, molecule, appendix, AIDS,* or *pediatrics.* What is it? Why is it important?

TOPIC 3: Write a paragraph in which you define the word *censorship.* What is it? What is its purpose? Who imposes censorship? Is it acceptable? If so, are there any limitations?

TOPIC 4: Write about a word or phrase that is borrowed from another language. Examples of borrowed words in English are *coup d'état, siesta,* and *sushi.* What is it? What language does the word or phrase come from? What does the word or phrase mean in that language? How long has the word or phrase been widely used in English?

TOPIC 5: What is freedom? Why do people want it? Should there be limitations on freedom? Can there be limitations? Explore the nature of freedom.

Timed Writing

How quickly can you write in English? There are many times when you must write quickly, such as on a test. It is important to feel comfortable during those times. Timed-writing practice can make you feel better about writing quickly in English.

Take out a piece of paper. Then read the writing prompt below this paragraph. Your teacher will give you 5 minutes to brainstorm ideas about this topic. You must then write a short definition paragraph (perhaps 6 to 10 sentences) about it. You will have 25 minutes to write your paragraph. At the end of the 25 minutes, your teacher will collect your work and return it to you later.

> We sometimes hear or read that a certain person showed great courage in doing something. What does the word *courage* mean to you? Give examples to help your readers better understand your definition of *courage.*

Process Analysis Paragraphs

What did you do to get ready for class today? Think about what you did first, then second, and so on. Perhaps you woke up and took a shower. After that, maybe you got dressed and combed your hair. As you prepared yourself to come to class, you completed a process.

The world is full of processes. At times, you are required to describe how to do something or how something works. You can often use a **process analysis paragraph** to convey the information.

What Is a Process Analysis Paragraph?

In a process analysis paragraph, you divide a process into separate steps. Then you list or explain the steps in chronological order—the order of events as they happen over time. Special time words or phrases allow you to tell the reader when a particular step occurs. The process analysis paragraph ends with a specific result—something that happens at the end of the process.

A process analysis paragraph

- explains a sequence or process.
- presents facts and details in chronological order.
- uses time words or phrases.
- ends with a specified result.

The best way to learn what a process analysis paragraph looks like is to read and study several examples. Even though the three paragraphs that follow are about different topics, each one is an example of a process analysis paragraph.

Read and study these example paragraphs. Answer the questions.

Process Analysis Paragraph 1

The topic of this paragraph is a popular Mexican dish. People have to be careful when they eat this food because it can be messy.

Before you read the paragraph, discuss these questions with your classmates.

1. What are some popular Mexican food dishes? Do you know the ingredients? If so, what are they?

2. Are any of these dishes messy when you eat them? If so, what makes them messy?

3. Name a food that you have eaten that was very messy. Why was this particular food messy?

Now read the paragraph.

EXAMPLE PARAGRAPH 49

Eating a <u>Messy</u> Food

Eating a mouthwatering **taco** is not easy— it requires following **specific** directions. First, you must be sure that you are wearing clothes that you do not mind getting dirty. Eating a taco while you are wearing an expensive **silk** blouse is not a smart idea. The next thing that you should do is to decide if you want to eat the taco alone or in front of others. Eating a taco in front of someone you do not know very well can be **embarrassing**. It is important to plan your attack! It is a good idea to pick up the taco gently and then carefully keep it in a **horizontal** position. As you raise the taco, slowly turn your head toward it and position your head at a twenty-degree **angle**. The last step is to put the corner of the taco in your mouth and take a bite. By following these simple directions, eating a taco can be a less messy experience.

messy: not neat
a taco: a Mexican dish consisting of a corn tortilla
    wrapped around a mixture of meat, lettuce, tomato,
    cheese, and sauce
specific: exact
silk: an expensive kind of cloth made from thread
    produced by silkworms

embarrassing: causing a self-conscious
    or uncomfortable feeling
horizontal: across, from side to side
    (opposite of *vertical*)
an angle: where two lines meet

1. What is the topic sentence of this paragraph?

   Eating a taco is not easy — it requires following specific directions

2. This paragraph discusses three things about eating tacos. What are they? The first one has been done for you.

   a. Do not wear expensive clothes because you might spill something on them.

   b. _Decide to eat it alone or w/ others_

   c. _Plan your attack_

3. Do you think that the writer's tone in this paragraph is serious, angry, or humorous?

   _____ Why? _Discusses mess & embarrassment of spilled food_

4. Is there anything that should be added?

   Transition word for 3rd point

Process Analysis Paragraph 2

The next paragraph is about the steps involved in applying to an American university.

Before you read the paragraph, discuss these questions with your classmates.

1. What are the steps in applying to a university?

2. What are the steps in applying to a community college?

3. Have you ever applied to a school online? How does this experience compare with applying to a school on a paper application?

Now read the paragraph on the next page.

Applying to an American University

Although the process for applying to an American university is not **complicated**, it is important to follow each step. The first step is to choose several schools that you are interested in attending. Next, write to these schools to ask for information, **catalogs**, and applications. You may also want to visit the schools' **Web sites**. After you have **researched** several schools, **narrow** your list to between three and five schools. Then mail all the required forms and documents only to your final list of three to five schools. If the school of your choice requires you to take a standardized test, such as the **SAT™**, **ACT**, or **TOEFL®**, be sure to do so early. In addition, ask various school officials and teachers to write letters of recommendation for you if the university requires them. Finally, almost all schools have an application **fee**. This fee should be sent in the form of a check or money order. One last piece of advice is to start early because thousands of high school students are all applying at the same time.

complicated: difficult, complex
a catalog: an information booklet
a Web site: a location of information on the World
   Wide Web ("www")
research: to investigate
narrow: to limit, reduce

the SAT: a college entrance exam used in many American
   colleges and universities
the ACT: American College Test
the TOEFL: Test of English as a Foreign Language
a fee: a required payment

1. What is the topic sentence of this paragraph?

   _____

   _____

2. What is the author's main suggestion for a successful application process?

   Follow each step

   _____

3. Does the paragraph explain the difference between the ACT, the SAT, and the TOEFL? *No*
   Why or why not? *It's not the topic -- just a detail*

   _____

   _____

4. According to the information in this paragraph, how many steps are there in applying to an American university? *8* Which step has two parts? *2* Write them here.

   ① Write to schools to get info
   ② Visit schools' websites

5. Do you think that the writer's tone in this paragraph is serious, angry, or humorous? _serious_

Why? _It explains the process - gives info_

Process Analysis Paragraph 3

Like "Eating a Messy Food," this paragraph is about a kind of food, but it tells how to make the food instead of how to eat it. It describes how to make a Turkish beverage.

Before you read the paragraph, discuss these questions with your classmates.

1. What are some popular beverages? Are they served hot or cold? Are they easy or difficult to prepare?

2. Have you ever visited Turkey? What information do you know about this country?

3. Can you name any popular beverages that come from Turkey?

Now read the paragraph.

EXAMPLE PARAGRAPH 51

A Unique <u>Beverage</u>

Turkish coffee is not easy to make, but the **result** is worth all the work. First, you need a special coffeepot called a *jezve*. This is a long-handled, open **brass** or **copper** pot. Next, pour three small cups of water into the pot. Heat the water until it boils. Then **remove** the pot from the heat. Add three teaspoons of coffee and three teaspoons of sugar to the water. Gently stir the mixture and return it to the heat until you can see **foam** on the top. When the foam appears, take the *jezve* from the heat and hit it lightly with a spoon to make the foam go down. Next, reheat the coffee and tap the pot two more times, making sure to remove it from the heat each time the foam forms. Before you serve the coffee, give everyone a small glass of cold water to drink with the hot, thick coffee.

a beverage: any kind of drink
a result: the product of an action
brass: a gold-colored metal

copper: a reddish-gold metal
remove: to take away
foam: liquid with a lot of tiny air bubbles in it

1. List the first five steps in making Turkish coffee.

   a. _Get the special coffeepot._

   b. _Pour 3 small cups H₂O into pot_

   c. _Heat H₂O to boil._

   d. _Remove pot from heat_

   e. _Add 3 t. coffee & 3 t. sugar_

2. The process of making Turkish coffee includes more than ten small steps. Good writers do not always write one sentence for each small step. Instead, they combine some steps in longer sentences. Write a sentence from the paragraph that has more than one step in it.

Gently stir the mixture & return it to the heat until you can see foam on top

3. Combine these two steps in one sentence: *Next, pour three small cups of water into the pot. Heat the water until it boils.*

4. The author states that Turkish coffee is difficult to make. Find three examples from the paragraph that support this idea.

   a. *Need special pot*

   b. *Takes long time to make*

   c. *Pay attention to each step*

 For more practice with process analysis paragraphs and topics for process analysis paragraphs, try Unit 7, Activity 1 and Activity 2 on the *Great Writing 2* Web site: elt.heinle.com/greatwriting

Building Better Sentences

Correct and varied sentence structure is essential to the quality of your writing. For further practice with the sentences and paragraphs in this part of the unit, go to Practice 13 on page 259 in Appendix 1.

Organizing a Process Analysis Paragraph

The order of steps in a process is important to the success of a process analysis paragraph.

Writer's Note

Using Index Cards to Help You Organize

It is important that all the steps in your process analysis paragraph be in the correct order. A simple way for you to organize the steps is to write each one on a 3-by-5 index card. This organization method will allow you to arrange and rearrange the steps. It will also help point out any steps that may be missing.

Language Focus

Transition Words and Chronological Order

A process analysis paragraph is usually arranged in chronological order. In other words, the steps in the process are listed in the order that they occur in time. The three paragraphs in Activity 1 each describe how to do or make something. The writers use chronological order to show the reader when the steps in the process occur.

Writers use *time phrases*, *time clauses*, and *time words* to show time order in a process. These items are also called **transition words** because they mark the transition from one step to the next.

1. Study the transition words in the following chart. In the right column are examples of how they are used in the paragraphs in Activity 1.

Transition Words	Examples
Then	Then remove the pot . . .
First, (Second, Third, etc.)	First, you must be sure . . . The first step is to choose several schools . . .
Next, (The next step/thing)	The next thing you should do is to decide . . .
The last step (Finally,)	The last step is to put the corner . . .
In addition,	In addition, ask various school officials and teachers to write letters . . .
Before	Before you serve the coffee, . . .
After (When)	When the foam appears, . . .

2. Now turn back to Example Paragraph 50 and circle all the transition words that you can find. Notice that some time phrases and words are followed by a comma when they appear at the beginning of a sentence. Time clauses, such as "After you have researched several schools," are always followed by a comma when they appear at the beginning of a sentence.

For more practice with transition words and chronological order, try Unit 7, Activity 3 on the *Great Writing 2* Web site: elt.heinle.com/greatwriting

ACTIVITY 2 Sequencing Sentences

The following sentences make up a paragraph. Number them from 1 to 8 to indicate the best order. Then underline all the words or phrases that show time order or sequence.

5 a. Hit the ball into the small box on the opposite side of the net.

6 b. After you hit the ball, continue swinging your racket down and across the front of your body.

4 c. Just before the ball reaches its peak, begin to swing your racket forward as high as you can reach.

2 d. First, toss the ball with your left hand about three feet in the air. The best position for the ball is just to the right of your head.

3 e. At the same time, move your racket behind your shoulder with your right hand so that your elbow is pointed toward the sky.

7 f. After you have completed the serve, your racket should be near your left knee.

1 g. Many people think serving in tennis is difficult, but the following steps show that it is quite easy.

8 h. If you are left-handed, you should substitute the words *left* and *right* in the preceding directions.

For more practice with sequencing sentences, try Unit 7, Activity 4 on the *Great Writing 2* Web site: elt.heinle.com/greatwriting

ACTIVITY 3 Sequencing Information in Paragraph Form

Copy the sentences from Activity 2 in paragraph form. The result will be a process analysis paragraph. Give the paragraph an original title.

EXAMPLE PARAGRAPH 52

_____

_____

_____

_____

_____

_____

_____

_____

_____

_____

_____

_____

ACTIVITY 4 Analyzing and Understanding a Paragraph

Read Example Paragraph 52 in Activity 3 again or refer to it as you complete the answers to these questions.

1. What is the general topic of the paragraph?

   Tennis serve

2. What is the topic sentence?

   #1 Many people think ...

3. The main purpose of this paragraph is to explain how to serve a tennis ball. However, the author also expresses an opinion in the topic sentence. Read the topic sentence again. What is that opinion?

   It is quite easy

4. Look at this sentence from the paragraph: "The best position for the ball is just to the right of your head." Unlike the other sentences, this is not a step. What is the purpose of this sentence?

   Supporting detail — gives more info

✎ Writer's Note

Using Technical Terms

Consider your readers when you write a process analysis paragraph. Ask yourself this question: How much do the readers already know about my subject? If they do not know much about your topic, they may not understand the technical terms you have used. You will need to replace the technical terms with simple, clear terms that your readers will understand or provide definitions for the technical terms. In your first draft, underline all the technical terms you use. This step will remind you to rephrase them or write a simple definition when you use them.

Transitional words, phrases, and clauses can show chronological order. Most transitional words and clauses are followed by a comma. (See page 127 for more information if you need help.)

The following sentences make up a paragraph. Number them from 1 to 10 to indicate the best order. In addition, add commas where necessary. Hint: Five sentences need commas.

_____ a. First put the water and the plants in the jar.

_____ b. One week later check the fish.

_____ c. The fact that the fish is still alive shows that oxygen was added. If you look carefully at a plant stem when it is in sunlight, you can see the tiny bubbles of oxygen escaping from the plant.

_____ d. When you do this be sure to leave about an inch of empty space.

_____ e. Keep the jar in a cool place indoors, but be sure that it receives some direct sunlight for a few hours each day.

_____ f. When you are sure that the water in the jar is at room temperature add the fish.

_____ g. Here is a simple science experiment that proves that plants produce oxygen.

_____ h. For this experiment, you will need a clean quart jar with a tight lid, some tape, a goldfish, some water, and a few green plants.

_____ i. Put the lid on as tightly as you can.

_____ j. After that wrap the lid with several layers of tape so that you are sure that no air can pass through it.

For more practice with commas and time phrases, try Unit 7, Activity 5 on the *Great Writing 2* Web site: elt.heinle.com/greatwriting

The sentences in Activity 5 explain the steps of a simple science experiment. After you have added commas and arranged the sentences in the correct order, write the completed process analysis paragraph on the lines below. Create a title for the paragraph.

EXAMPLE PARAGRAPH 53

_____

_____

_____

_____

_____

_____

_____

_____

_____

_____

 ## Writer's Note

Checking Possessive Adjectives

When you write a sentence, you sometimes use possessive adjectives to refer to nouns or pronouns that have already been mentioned. Check to see if these possessive adjectives agree with the noun or pronoun that they refer to. Be careful with singular and plural usage.

Incorrect: **One** of the parent penguins keeps the egg on one of **their** feet at all times.

Correct: **One** of the parent penguins keeps the egg on one of **its** feet at all times.

If you have trouble with possessive adjective reference, circle all the possessive adjectives in your first draft. Underline the nouns or pronouns to which they refer. Check for correct agreement. You may also want to ask a reader to check your draft for correct possessive adjective usage.

 For more practice with checking possessive adjectives, try Unit 7, Activity 6 on the _Great Writing 2_ Web site: elt.heinle.com/greatwriting

Building Better Sentences

Correct and varied sentence structure is essential to the quality of your writing. For further practice with the sentences and paragraphs in this part of the unit, go to Practice 14 on page 260 in Appendix 1.

 # Building Better Vocabulary

ACTIVITY 7 Word Associations

Circle the word or phrase that is most closely related to the word or phrase on the left. If necessary, use a dictionary to check the meaning of words you do not know.

1. a beverage	(a drink)	a food
2. to remove	to add	to subtract
3. a peak	a low point	a high point
4. gently	hard	soft
5. to prove	to show	to try
6. horizontal	left ⟺ right	up ⟺ down
7. copper	a metal	a process
8. to research	to caution	to investigate
9. messy	negative	positive
10. your knee	arm	leg
11. to state	to read	to speak
12. to remind	to release	to remember
13. your shoulder	body	mind
14. a stem	an animal	a plant

Fill in each blank with the word on the left that most naturally completes the phrase on the right. If necessary, use a dictionary to check the meaning of words you do not know.

1. get / put   to ___get___ ready

2. blouse / taco   a silk ___blouse___

3. let / pay   to ___pay___ a fee

4. the Internet / a problem   to point out ___a problem___

5. elbow / remind   my left ___elbow___

6. idea / worm   a smart ___idea___

7. for / of   he reminded me ___of___ my father

8. comma / side   the opposite ___side___

9. tape / tiny   ___tiny___ bubbles

10. angles / information   to convey ___information___

11. lid / plant   a tight ___lid___

12. direct / empty   an inch of ___empty___ space

Original Student Writing: Process Analysis Paragraph

ACTIVITY 9 Original Writing Practice

Write a process analysis paragraph. Follow these guidelines:

- Choose a topic.
- Write some notes about the steps in the process.
- Write a topic sentence with controlling ideas.
- Write supporting sentences that give the steps in chronological order. Use transition words to show that the steps are in the correct order.
- Use at least five of the vocabulary words or phrases presented in Activity 7 and Activity 8. Underline these words and phrases in your paragraph.
- If you need help, study the example process analysis paragraphs in this unit. Be sure to refer to the seven steps in the writing process in the Brief Writer's Handbook with Activities, pages 218–224.

Exchange papers from Activity 9 with a partner. Read your partner's writing. Then use Peer Editing Sheet 7 on page 279 to help you comment on your partner's writing. Be sure to offer positive suggestions and comments that will help your partner improve his or her writing. Consider your partner's comments as you revise your own writing.

Additional Topics for Writing

Here are some ideas for process analysis paragraphs. When you write your paragraph, follow the guidelines in Activity 9.

TOPIC 1:   What do you need to do to get a driver's license?

TOPIC 2:   What are the steps in writing a good paragraph?

TOPIC 3:   What steps does a successful job applicant follow?

TOPIC 4:   How would you ask your boss for a raise?

TOPIC 5:   Describe how to use a search engine to explore a topic on the World Wide Web.

Timed Writing

How quickly can you write in English? There are many times when you must write quickly, such as on a test. It is important to feel comfortable during those times. Timed-writing practice can make you feel better about writing quickly in English.

Take out a piece of paper. Then read the writing prompt below this paragraph. Your teacher will give you 5 minutes to brainstorm ideas about this topic. You must then write a short process analysis paragraph (perhaps 6 to 10 sentences) about it. You will have 25 minutes to write your paragraph. At the end of the 25 minutes, your teacher will collect your work and return it to you later.

> From time to time, a bank or other business sends us a bill or statement that has a mistake. (For example, your credit card bill may have charged you twice for a certain item.) What are the steps in correcting an error on a bill? (If you cannot relate to the above situation, your teacher may assign this option: What should you do if the server at a restaurant has given you your bill with an error on it? How can you rectify this situation?)

Descriptive Paragraphs

GOAL: To learn how to write a descriptive paragraph

*Language Focus: Adjectives; denotation and connotation; prepositions of location

Description is one of the most common purposes of language. You use description every day. You might describe to a family member how you feel or what you had for lunch. You might tell a friend what a room in your house looks likes. You might describe the colors in the paintings in a museum or how the paintings are arranged. When describing, you tell someone what something looks like or how it feels. What descriptions have you used today?

What Is a Descriptive Paragraph?

A **descriptive paragraph** describes how something or someone looks or feels. It gives an impression of something. If, for example, you only wanted to explain to someone what a samovar is, you could write a definition paragraph because a definition paragraph does not include how the writer feels. However, if you wanted to tell about the feelings you had when you drank a cup of Russian tea that was made in a samovar, you would write a descriptive paragraph.

A descriptive paragraph

- describes.

- gives impressions, not definitions.

- "shows" the reader.

- creates a sensory* image in the reader's mind.

*related to the five senses: hearing, taste, touch, sight, and smell

---

Read this example descriptive paragraph.

Samovar Memory

Every time I have a cup of strong Russian tea, I remember my sweet grandma and her magical samovar. When I was a little girl, my grandmother used to make tea for me in this giant, **gleaming** tea **urn**, which is called a samovar. I was **fascinated** by the samovar and its tasty contents. Its copper sides were decorated with beautiful red and black **swirls**. Grandma told me that the **intricate** decorations were painted by **skilled** craftsmen from her **village**. I can still remember the smell of the dark tea that my grandma made using the urn. Its leaves always filled her tiny apartment with an **exotic aroma**, and the rich brew tasted like liquid **velvet**.

gleaming: shining
an urn: a large metal container for serving coffee or other beverages, a vase
fascinated: very curious about or very interested in something
a swirl: a circular design
intricate: complex, having many parts

skilled: having great or special talent
a village: a small, rural town
exotic: unique or special, not usual
an aroma: a good smell from something that is cooking
velvet: a thick cloth that is soft and silky

Describing with the Five Senses

Good writers use words that appeal to some or all of the five senses—sight, taste, touch, hearing, and smell—to help describe a topic. Here is a list of the senses and examples of what they can describe. Add examples of your own under the column labeled "Example 2."

Sense	Example 1	Example 2
sight	a sunset	a flower
taste	a chocolate cake	red wine
touch	silk	dog fur
hearing	a baby's cry	birds chirping
smell	a perfume	fresh basil

ACTIVITY 1 Using Adjectives to Describe Sensory Information

In the left column, write your five examples from your list on page 136. In the right column, write three adjectives that describe each object. Try to use different senses. One has been done for you as an example.

Example	Description
sunset	purple, streaked, majestic
1. flower	yellow, bright, sweet
2. red wine	spicy, smooth, earthy
3. dog fur	soft, relaxing, warm
4. birds chirping	happy, early, musical
5. basil	fresh, spicy, green

For more practice with describing with the five senses, try Unit 8, Activity 1 on the *Great Writing 2* Web site: elt.heinle.com/greatwriting

ACTIVITY 2 Writing Sentences Using Sensory Adjectives

Use the five examples from Activity 1 to write five descriptive sentences. Use each example item as the topic of one of the sentences and include one or more of the adjectives you wrote. Share your sentences with a classmate.

1. _____

2. _____

3. _____

4. _____

5. _____

The best way to learn what descriptive paragraphs look like is to read and study several examples. Even though the three paragraphs that follow are about different topics, each one is an example of a descriptive paragraph.

Read and study these example paragraphs. Answer the questions.

Descriptive Paragraph 1

This first paragraph describes the sights, smells, and sounds of a subway station.

Before you read the paragraph, discuss these questions with your classmates.

1. What is a subway? What is its purpose?

2. Where do you usually find a subway?

3. What kinds of people use the subway?

4. Have you ever been on a subway? How did you feel when you rode on it? Can you recall what you saw, smelled, and heard?

Now read the paragraph.

EXAMPLE PARAGRAPH 55

Underground Events

The subway is an **assault** on your senses. You walk down the steep, **smelly** staircase onto the subway **platform**. On the far right wall, a broken clock shows that the time is four-thirty. You wonder how long it has been broken. A mother and her crying child are standing to your left. She is trying to clean dried chocolate **syrup** off the child's messy face. **Farther** to the left, two old men are **arguing** about the most recent tax increase. You hear a little noise and see some paper trash roll by like a soccer ball. The most interesting thing you see while you are waiting for your subway train is a poster. It reads, "Come to Jamaica." Deep blue skies, a lone palm tree, and **sapphire** waters call you to this exotic place, which is so far from where you actually are.

an assault: an attack
smelly: smelling bad or unpleasant
a platform: a raised area
a syrup: a thick liquid

farther: comparative form of the word *far*
argue: to fight verbally
sapphire: dark blue color like the color
   of a sapphire stone

1. From the information in this paragraph, how do you think the writer feels about the subway?

   Doesn't like them

2. Can you think of other places where people wait for something?

   airport, DMV, train station, bank

3. Which of the five senses does the writer use to describe this place? Give examples from the paragraph to support your answers.

   Smelly staircase - smell
   crying child - sound - 2 men arguing
   dried chocolate syrup - taste, sight
   poster- deep blue skies, sapphire waters - sight

4. What verb tense is used in this paragraph? Why do you think the writer uses that tense?

   present progressive - description

Descriptive Paragraph 2

The following paragraph describes a memory about a dangerous kind of weather.

Before you read the paragraph, discuss these questions with your classmates.

1. What are some dangerous kinds of weather?
2. Have you ever experienced these kinds of weather? How did you feel?
3. When you think of these kinds of weather, what sensory adjectives come to mind?

Now read the paragraph.

Danger from the Sky

The long, **slender tornado** began to **descend** from the **swirling** clouds and started its horrible destruction. When the deadly **funnel** finally touched the ground, pieces of **debris** were **hurled** through the air. The tornado **ripped** the roof from an old house and threw the contents of the home across the neighborhood. The tornado used its power to **uproot** huge trees and toss cars around as if they were toys. Power lines and traffic lights were also victims of its deadly **might**. All the while, the tornado's **ferocious** winds **roared** like a wild beast. It was hard to believe that something that looked so **delicate** could cause so much destruction.

slender: thin, narrow (positive adjective)
a tornado: a rotating column of air that moves at very high speeds
descend: to move downwards
swirling: rotating or spinning
a funnel: a cone-shaped object
debris: broken pieces of something

hurl: to throw with great force
rip: to tear violently and quickly
uproot: to tear a plant up by the roots
might: power
ferocious: very wild and savage
roar: to make a loud, deep, long sound
delicate: fragile

1. What does this paragraph describe?

   tornado's destruction

2. What verb tense does the writer use in this paragraph? _past_

   Choose five verbs and change them to the simple present tense.

   began - begin   started - start   touched - touch
   ripped - rip   used - use

3. Which of the five senses does the writer use to describe this kind of weather? Give some examples to support your answer.

   sight - slender, descend, swirling
   sound - ferocious winds roared liked wild beast

4. One feature of a good descriptive paragraph is the use of adjectives that help the reader feel what it is like to be in the situation. List any five adjectives in "Danger from the Sky." Then write the feelings they describe.

Adjective	Feelings
a. _swirling_	_scary_
b. _ferocious_	_scary_
c. _delicate_	_sight_
d. _slender_	
e. _horrible_	

Descriptive Paragraph 3

The next paragraph describes what the writer's mother did while she worked in her garden. Notice how often the writer appeals to the readers' senses of sight and touch.

Before you read the paragraph, discuss these questions with your classmates.

1. What is a garden? What kinds of gardens can you grow?

2. What is a rose? What does the rose symbolize?

3. What other flowers can you name? Do you think they are as popular as the rose?

4. When you think of a garden, especially a flower garden, what sensory adjectives immediately come to mind?

Now read the paragraph.

My Mother's Special Garden

My father **constantly teased** my mother about the amount of time she spent in her beautiful rose garden. He told her that she treated the garden as if it were a human being, perhaps even her best friend. However, Mom **ignored** his teasing and got up early every morning to take care of her special plants. She **would** walk among the thick green bushes that were covered with huge flowers of every color. While she was walking, she would **rip out** any **weeds** that **threatened** her delicate beauties. She also **trimmed** the old flowers to make room for their bright replacements. Any unwanted **pests** were quickly killed. When she was finished, she always returned from the garden with a wonderful smile and an armful of **fragrant** flowers for us all to enjoy.

constantly: always, without stopping

tease: to make fun of someone or something in a playful or joking manner

ignore: to not pay attention to someone or something

would (+ verb): modal indicating a past event that happened many times

rip out: to take out quickly and violently

a weed: a useless, unwanted plant

threaten: to put in danger, promise to harm

trim: to cut to make something look neat

a pest: an unwanted insect

fragrant: pleasant smelling

1. What does this paragraph describe?

   A rose garden

2. Can any sentences be deleted without changing the paragraph's meaning? If yes, which ones, and why? If no, why not?

   _No_

3. The writer's mother treated the roses as if they were human beings. Find two example sentences from the paragraph that show how she protected her roses.

   a. _She would rip out any weeds that threatened her delicate beauties_

   b. _Unwanted pests were quickly killed_

For more practice with studying descriptive paragraphs, try Unit 8, Activity 2 on the *Great Writing 2* Web site: elt.heinle.com/greatwriting

Writer's Note

Language Focus

Adjectives

Adjectives are important in a descriptive paragraph. They are like spices—they add flavor to your writing. Compare these two sentences. The underlined words in the second sentence are adjectives.

The bride walked down the aisle to meet her groom.

The <u>tall</u> <u>graceful</u> bride in her <u>white</u> dress walked down the <u>long</u> aisle to meet her <u>proud</u> groom.

Which sentence is more descriptive? The second sentence gives you more sensory information—in this case, the sense of sight. The writer gives a more detailed impression in the second sentence.

What Is an Adjective?

An **adjective** is a part of speech that describes a noun. An adjective usually answers one or more of the following questions: *Which one? What kind? How many?* or *How much?* In descriptive writing, an adjective is the most powerful kind of word that you can use in your work.

Which one?	*this, that, these, those*
What kind?	*big, old, yellow, crumpled*
How many?	*some, few, many, two*
How much?	*enough, bountiful, less, more*

For practice with identifying and studying adjectives, try Unit 8, Activity 3 and Activity 4 on the *Great Writing 2* Web site: elt.heinle.com/greatwriting

Using Adjectives in the Correct Place

It is important to remember that in English, an adjective never follows the noun it modifies or describes. Generally, adjectives come before the nouns they modify. In these examples, the adjectives are underlined, and the arrows point to the nouns the adjectives modify.

Angry customers have complained about poor service in the new restaurant.

Blue skies ensured that bronzed sun worshipers could improve their golden tans.

When you proofread your first draft, circle all of the adjectives and draw an arrow to the nouns they modify. This will help you notice misplaced adjectives.

Incorrect: The samovar's shiny sides are decorated with beautiful swirls red.

Correct: The samovar's shiny sides are decorated with beautiful **red** swirls.

Adjectives sometimes appear after a linking verb. See the following Grammar Note for a more detailed explanation.

Grammar Note about Verbs and Adjectives

When an adjective occurs after a linking verb, it is called a **predicate adjective**. The predicate adjective's job is to modify the subject and complete the meaning of the linking verb. The predicate adjective must *immediately* follow the linking verb.

Read the following common linking verbs:

be	become	seem	feel	taste
sound	appear	remain	keep	look

Examples: The teacher is intelligent and kind.

The soup tastes good.

Mr. Cioffi feels ill.

The decorations at the dance looked horrid!

ACTIVITY 4 Correcting Adjectives

Read each sentence. Circle all the adjectives. Are the adjectives placed correctly? If the sentence is correct, write C on the line. If you find an adjective error, draw an arrow from the adjective to its correct location in the sentence. The first one has been done for you.

1. _____ John's puppy chewed on his shoes (new).

2. __C__ A yellow piece of paper is on the floor.

3. _____ The teacher wrote our assignment on the blackboard old.

4. _____ My best friend wrote a letter long.

5. __C__ The five black dogs chased the police car.

6. _____ Colorado is a place great to go skiing when it is cold.

7. __C__ My neighbor found a large wallet stuffed with new one-dollar bills.

8. __C__ The gourmet chef created a slightly spicy but delicious meal.

9. __C__ The clock on the rough stucco wall of the busy railway station was antique.

10. _____ Egyptian pyramids are an example excellent of ancient architecture.

ACTIVITY 5 Adding Adjectives

Read each sentence. Write adjectives in the blanks to create a more vivid description. You may write more than one adjective in each blank. The first one has been done for you.

1. The ___tired___ teacher walked into the ___noisy___ room.

2. The ___happy___ couple watched a ___golden___ sunset.

3. My ___new___ coworker is a ___terrific___ athlete.

4. The ___antique___ samovar sat on an ___old___ table.

5. That ___huge___ spider scared my ___younger___ sister.

6. The ___sports___ car raced down the ___curvy___ road.

7. My ___tired___ feet ached from walking on the ___uneven___ sidewalk.

8. Barbara wore a ___red___ dress to the ___dance___ party last night.

9. The ___brown___ cow ate ___green___ grass in the ___large___ field.

10. A ___young___ boy sat on the ___hard___ ground and played with some ___used___ toys.

For more practice with using adjectives to enhance descriptive writing, try Unit 8, Activity 5 on the *Great Writing 2* Web site: elt.heinle.com/greatwriting

Describing with the Five Senses **145**

Read each set of nouns. Using the nouns, write an original sentence with at least two adjectives. Circle the adjectives. The first one has been done for you.

1. vacation / California

   People who want the (perfect) vacation should visit (sunny) California.

2. students / computers

   The (1500) students used the (outdated) computers

3. dictionaries / libraries

   There are (German) dictionaries in (college) libraries

4. trees / forest

   The (green) trees thrive in the (old-growth) forest

5. skyscraper / city

   The (gigantic) skyscraper highlights the (bustling) city

🔨 Building Better Sentences

Correct and varied sentence structure is essential to the quality of your writing. For further practice with the sentences and paragraphs in this part of the unit, go to Practice 15 on page 260 in Appendix 1.

✎ Writer's Note

Using a Bilingual Dictionary

Most English learners own a bilingual dictionary. A bilingual dictionary is divided into two parts. One part lists words in English with their foreign-language equivalent(s), and the other part lists words in a foreign language with their English equivalent(s).

Check the Meanings

A bilingual dictionary is especially helpful when you are first learning English. However, be careful when you use this kind of dictionary. It is easy to choose the wrong word listed in the entry. In fact, the most common error is to choose the first word that you find. You should always read all of the possible translations to find the best word that accurately fits in your sentence.

After you find a translation, you should always double-check the meaning of the word that you have selected by checking its equivalent in the other section of your dictionary. This will help make sure that you choose the appropriate word.

Practice with a Word

Practice double-checking meanings by looking up the English word *nice* in your bilingual dictionary. How many meanings are listed? Think of two words that mean *nice* in your language. Look them up in the other part of the dictionary. Was there a change in meaning? Were you surprised by what you found?

Using Denotation and Connotation to Describe

Good writers learn to distinguish between the **denotation**, which is the dictionary definition of a word, and the **connotation** of a word, which is its emotional or associated meaning. This distinction can help your writing convey your specific meaning.

Language Focus

Denotation and Connotation

When you write, it is important to use words that have the precise meaning that you want. Sometimes words have more than one meaning. The *denotation* of a word is its actual, or dictionary, meaning. The *connotation* of a word is its emotional meaning, or the meaning beyond the basic definition. Many words can cause an emotional reaction—either good or bad—in the reader. If you choose a word with the incorrect connotation, you may give your reader the wrong idea.

The <u>thrifty</u> old man saved all his money for his retirement.

The <u>stingy</u> old man saved all his money for his retirement.

Look up *thrifty* and *stingy* in your dictionary. The denotative meanings for these words are similar—they both describe someone who is careful with money. However, there is a big difference in their connotative meanings. The *thrifty* person is wise and economical with money, but the *stingy* person is greedy and does not want to spend or share money.

Consider the adjectives *skinny*, *slender*, and *thin*. The word *thin* has a neutral connotation because it simply states a fact. However, *skinny* has a negative connotation, and *slender* has a positive connotation. For example, a *skinny* tiger needs more food, but a *slender* tiger appears to be healthy and perhaps ready for physical activity.

Words that leave a good emotional impression have a positive connotation. Words that leave a bad emotional impression have a negative connotation. Not all words have a separate connotative meaning. Always check both meanings of new words.

The two descriptive paragraphs below are about the same topic. Read the paragraphs and underline the adjectives. There are 13 descriptive adjectives in Example Paragraph 58 and 12 descriptive adjectives in Example Paragraph 59. The first adjective in each paragraph has been underlined for you.

The Blue River is an <u>important</u> part of the forest, and the quality of the river shapes the environment around it. The fresh, clear water is home to a wide variety of fish and plants. Colorful trout compete with perch for the abundant supply of insects near the beautiful river. The tall trees that line the banks are green and healthy. Wild deer come to drink the sweet water and rest in the shadows cast on the grassy banks of the river.

The Blue River is an <u>important</u> part of the forest, and the quality of the river shapes the environment around it. The sluggish brown water does not contain fish or plants. Scrawny trout struggle with perch to catch the limited number of insects that live near the dirty river. The old trees near the river are gray and brittle. They do not provide adequate protection for the wild animals that come to drink from the polluted river.

1. Briefly, what is being described in each paragraph?

   Example Paragraph 58 _____ *healthy river* _____

   Example Paragraph 59 _____ *dirty river* _____

2. What is your impression of the topic in Example Paragraph 58? What words helped you form this opinion?

   _____ *positive adjectives* _____

   _____

   _____

   _____

3. What is your impression of the topic in Example Paragraph 59? What words helped you form this opinion?

   _____ *negative adjectives* _____

   _____

   _____

   _____

4. Can you find an adjective in one paragraph that has the opposite meaning of an adjective in the other paragraph? For example, we can say that *clear* in Example Paragraph 58 is opposite in meaning to *brown* in Example Paragraph 59. Can you find other examples?

   _____ *fresh - sluggish* _____

   _____ *abundant - limited* _____

   _____ *beautiful - dirty* _____

   _____

   _____

For more practice with positive and negative connotation in a paragraph, try Unit 8, Activity 6 on the *Great Writing 2* Web site: elt.heinle.com/greatwriting

ACTIVITY 8 Positive and Negative Connotations of Adjectives

Think of adjectives that can describe the nouns listed below. In the first blank, write one or more adjectives with a positive connotation. In the second blank, write adjectives with a negative connotation. Remember: The purpose of this activity is to increase your vocabulary, so do not use simple or general words, such as nice or bad. Use your dictionary to find the precise vocabulary to express your ideas. The first one has been done for you.

Noun	Positive Connotation	Negative Connotation
1. cheese	creamy, buttery, light	rancid, smelly, stinky
2. rock		
3. painting		
4. laughter		
5. flavor		
6. smell		
7. music		
8. texture		

For more practice with positive and negative connotations, try Unit 8, Activity 7 on the *Great Writing 2* Web site: elt.heinle.com/greatwriting

ACTIVITY 9 Changing Meaning with Connotation

The paragraph below describes a man walking into a room. Many of the adjectives have been deleted. Fill in each blank with an adjective and create your own paragraph.

The _____ man entered the _____ room. He had _____,

_____ hair. He wore a(n) _____ suit with _____ shoes. The man

was very _____. Everyone in the room was _____ when they saw him. He was

such a(n) _____ man! They could not believe that he was in the room with them.

Next, rewrite your paragraph in the space below. Be sure to indent. Then switch books with a partner and compare paragraphs. What impression do you have of the man in your partner's paragraph? Is it positive or negative? Add an original title.

_____

_____

_____

_____

_____

_____

_____

_____

_____

_____

Using Prepositions of Location to Describe

To be precise in description, writers often need to indicate where something or someone is, particularly in relation to something or someone else. You can use **prepositions of location** to help you place people and things in description.

Language Focus

Prepositions of Location

A common way to describe something is to describe the parts of the item and where they are. For example, if you are describing a room, you can describe what is on the right side, what is on the left side, what is on the ceiling, and what is on the floor. If you are describing a sports car, you might talk about what is in the front seat, what is in the back, what is on the hood, and what is under the hood. If you are describing a person, you can talk about what he is wearing on his head (a hat or cap) or what he has on his wrist (a shiny watch).

When you tell the location of something, it is important to use the correct preposition of location, followed by a noun. This noun after a preposition is called the **object of the preposition**. This preposition and noun combination is called a **prepositional phrase** (e.g., *in the kitchen*). Study these examples (the prepositional phrases are underlined).

The new bank is <u>on Wilson Road</u> <u>near the park</u>.

<u>Next to the river</u>, there is a grassy field that goes <u>from Wilson Road</u> <u>to the corner of Maple Street and Lee Road</u>.

<u>On the left</u>, there is an old sofa. <u>On the right</u>, there are two wooden chairs.

Good descriptive writers use many adjectives and prepositional phrases to help readers visualize the thing or person that is being described.

Common Prepositions of Location

above	before	far from	on top of
across	behind	from	opposite
after	below	in	outside
against	beneath	in back of	over
ahead of	beside	in front of	past
along	between	inside	throughout
among	beyond	near	under
around	by	next to	
at	close to	on	

ACTIVITY 10 Using Prepositions of Location to Describe a Place

Write five true sentences about the location of things or people in your classroom. Circle the prepositions and underline the objects of the preposition. The first one has been done for you.

1. The teacher's desk is (in front of) the whiteboard.

2. _____

3. _____

4. _____

5. _____

6. _____

ACTIVITY 11 Studying Example Paragraphs with Prepositions of Location

Read and study each example paragraph. Then answer the questions.

Paragraph with Prepositions of Location 1

The following paragraph describes a room in a house. Notice how often the writer appeals to the reader's sense of sight by describing the location of the things in the room.

Before you read, discuss these questions with your classmates.

1. What are three things that most people expect to find in a living room?

2. Is your living room always neat? Usually neat? Almost never neat?

3. What is in the middle of your living room? On the left side? On the right side?

Now read the paragraph.

A Great Living Room

My living room may be small, but it is **tidy** and well organized. On the right, there is a wooden bookcase with four **shelves**. On top of the bookcase is a small lamp with a blue **base** and a **matching** lampshade. The first and third shelves are filled with carefully arranged books. On the second shelf, there is an **antique** clock with **faded** numbers on its face. The bottom shelf has a few newspapers. On the opposite side of the room is a television set with nothing on top of it. Between the television and the bookcase is a large sofa. A fat, **striped** cat with long **whiskers** is **curled up** in a ball on the right side of the sofa. Lying to the left of my cat is a single sock that the cat probably brought from another room. Directly in front of the sofa, there is a long coffee table with short legs. On the right side of this table lie two magazines. They are stacked one on top of the other. Perhaps the most **striking item** in the room is the beautiful beach painting above the sofa. This **extraordinary** painting shows a **peaceful** beach scene with a sailboat on the right, far from the beach. Although it is a small room, everything in my living room is in its place.

tidy: neat, clean, arranged, organized
a shelf: a flat surface inside a bookcase
a base: the bottom part, the foundation of something
matching: going together well, similar
antique: old, from earlier days
faded: difficult to see
striped: with stripes or lines

whiskers: the hairs on a cat's face
curled up: in a circle, not in a line
striking: exceptional, very noticeable
an item: a thing
extraordinary: not usual, very special
peaceful: quiet, serene

1. Why did the writer write this paragraph?

    _____ a. to define a living room

    ___✓___ b. to describe a living room

    _____ c. to explain the process of creating a good living room

2. What is the sequence of describing the room?

    ___✓___ a. from right to left to middle

    _____ b. from left to right to middle

    _____ c. from right to middle to left

    _____ d. from left to middle to right

3. How many prepositional phrases are there? Count carefully! __32__

4. In the topic sentence, the writer says that the room is tidy. Can you find words or phrases that paint this image for the reader?

    carefully arranged books, a few newspapers,
    an old tv w/ nothing on top of it, magazines stacked,
    everything is in its place.

5. Can you think of one part of the room that was not described well enough? Use your imagination to write a sentence for that area of the room. Use prepositions of location.

    _____

    _____

    _____

Paragraph with Prepositions of Location 2

This paragraph describes a famous monument in New York Harbor. Notice how often the writer appeals to the reader's sense of sight by describing different parts of the monument.

Before you read, discuss these questions with your classmates.

1. If you have visited the Statue of Liberty, what was the experience like? What, if anything, was different from what you expected?

2. How high do you think the Statue of Liberty is? What does the Statue of Liberty symbolize?

3. When you think of the Statue of Liberty, what adjectives come to mind?

EXAMPLE PARAGRAPH 62

The Statue of Liberty

The Statue of Liberty, an internationally known **symbol** of freedom that was completed in 1886, is certainly an **impressive** structure. The statue is of a woman who is wearing long, **flowing** robes. On her head, she has a **crown** of seven **spikes** that **symbolize** the seven oceans and the seven continents. The statue weighs 450,000 pounds and is 152 feet high. The statue appears much larger, however, because it stands on a **pedestal** that is about 150 feet high. In her raised right hand, the woman holds a **torch**. In her left hand, she carries a **tablet** with the date "July 4, 1776" written on the cover. At her feet lie broken **chains**, which symbolize an escape to freedom. The Statue of Liberty is an amazing monument.

a symbol: a figure, a representation
impressive: outstanding, special, making an impression
flowing: moving easily
a crown: a decoration for the head to show high position, often worn by kings and queens
a spike: a point
symbolize: to represent

a pedestal: a base
a torch: an instrument for carrying fire as light
a tablet: an item that you can write on, somewhat similar to a notepad or notebook
chains: circular, connected links, usually metal, that can be used to prevent someone from moving or escaping

1. What is the writer's purpose for writing this paragraph?

    _____ a. to inform the reader of the history of the Statue of Liberty

    _____ b. to explain why the Statue of Liberty was built

    _____ c. to tell the steps in the construction of the Statue of Liberty

    __✓__ d. to describe the Statue of Liberty

2. What is the sequence of describing the Statue?

    __✓__ a. body — head — base — right hand — left hand — feet

    _____ b. body — head — base — left hand — right hand — feet

    _____ c. body — right hand — left hand — head — base — feet

    _____ d. body — left hand — right hand — head — base — feet

3. The writer organizes the description of parts of the statue by location. To help you understand this organization better, answer these three questions.

    a. Where is the tablet? _____it's in her left hand_____

    b. Is the statue on the ground? If not, what is it on? _____On a 150ft pedestal_____

    c. Where is the torch? _____in her raised right hand_____

✎ Writer's Note

Word Order with Prepositions of Location

Prepositional phrases of location usually occur at the end of a sentence.

The room was a mess. There were many papers <u>on the floor</u>. A fat, fluffy cat was sleeping <u>on top of the television</u>. An empty pizza box was <u>under the sofa</u>.

However, for sentence variety, these same prepositional phrases can also occur at the beginning of a sentence. In this case, we usually use a comma between the prepositional phrase and the rest of the sentence.

<u>On the floor</u>, there were many papers.

<u>On top of the television</u>, a fat, fluffy cat was sleeping.

If you want to move a prepositional phrase of location to the beginning of a sentence with the verb *be*, you must invert the subject and the verb and drop the comma after the prepositional phrase.

		SUBJECT	VERB	
Correct:		An empty pizza box	was	<u>under the sofa</u>.

	VERB	SUBJECT	
Correct:	<u>Under the sofa</u>	was	an empty pizza box. (No comma)

Incorrect: <u>Under the sofa</u>, an empty pizza box was.

When a *there is / there are* sentence begins with a prepositional phrase of location, writers sometimes drop *there* and the comma after the prepositional phrase.

Study the examples. Both sentences are correct. Note that the first one is common in speaking and writing, and the second one is more common in writing.

Correct:	On the floor, there are many papers.	(Comma)
Correct:	On the floor are many papers.	(No comma)

ACTIVITY 12 Identifying Objects of Prepositions

Read the paragraph. Look at the 16 underlined prepositions. Circle the object of each preposition. Then correct the three comma errors.

EXAMPLE PARAGRAPH 63

Josh

One of the most interesting people that I know is Josh Curren, a legal assistant in my lawyer's office. Josh has curly hair and big blue eyes that seem to shine. Even on the difficult work days that we all have Josh is always smiling. He is always ready to help the clients by listening to their perplexing legal questions. Around his neck, is a thin chain that fastens to his eyeglasses so that he does not lose them among the piles of thick folders on his cluttered desk. On the right side of his crisp white cotton shirt he wears an I.D. tag that indicates his name and his position at the law firm. Josh always wears a unique tie that he collects from his business trips around the globe. Everyone agrees that Josh Curren is one of a kind.

⚒ Building Better Sentences

Correct and varied sentence structure is essential to the quality of your writing. For further practice with the sentences and paragraphs in this part of the unit, go to Practice 16 on page 261 in Appendix 1.

ACTIVITY 13 Word Associations

Circle the word or phrase that is most closely related to the word or phrase on the left. If necessary, use a dictionary to check the meaning of words you do not know.

1.	a village	**a town**	a city
2.	delicate	**can break easily**	will never break
3.	to recall	**to remember**	to understand
4.	a skyscraper	**high**	low
5.	an assault	**negative**	positive
6.	to descend	10, 11, 12, 13	**13, 12, 11, 10**
7.	to rip	to send	**to tear**
8.	a swirl	**a circle**	a line
9.	constantly	**always**	never
10.	a syrup	**a liquid**	a solid
11.	to argue	**negative**	positive
12.	to tease	**to make fun of**	to argue with
13.	precise	approximate	**exact**
14.	a crown	your feet	**your head**
15.	to roar	**loud**	soft

Fill in each blank with the word on the left that most naturally completes the phrase on the right. If necessary, use a dictionary to check the meaning of words you do not know.

1. storm / worker   a skilled __worker__

2. of / to   a symbol __of__ freedom

3. colorful / wonderful   a __wonderful__ aroma

4. bank / body   a slender __body__

5. come / go   to __come__ to mind

6. fish / photo   a faded __photo__

7. drink / plan   an intricate __plan__

8. dress / office   a tidy __office__

9. hair / voice   curly __hair__

10. of / with   stuffed __with__ feathers

11. broken / written   __broken__ chains

12. of / under   the connotation __of__ a word

Original Student Writing: Descriptive Paragraph

ACTIVITY 15 Original Writing Practice

Write a paragraph that describes something. Your goal is to give the reader an impression of what you are describing. Follow these guidelines:

- Choose a topic.

- Brainstorm some sensory adjectives (sight, hearing, smell, taste, touch).

- Write a topic sentence with controlling ideas.

- Write supporting sentences that relate to the topic.

- Make sure the adjectives mean precisely what you want them to mean—check both the denotation and the connotation.

- Use prepositional phrases of location in your paragraph. Be sure to vary the placement of the phrases. Put some at the beginning of sentences and some at the end of sentences. Remember that good writers use sentence variety.

- Make sure your concluding sentence restates the topic.
- Use at least five of the vocabulary words or phrases presented in Activity 13 and Activity 14. Underline these words and phrases in your paragraph.

If you need help, study the example descriptive paragraphs in this unit. Be sure to refer to the seven steps in the writing process in the Brief Writer's Handbook with Activities, pages 218–224.

ACTIVITY 16 Peer Editing

Exchange papers from Activity 15 with a partner. Read your partner's writing. Then use Peer Editing Sheet 8 on page 281 to help you comment on your partner's writing. Be sure to offer positive suggestions and comments that will help your partner improve his or her writing. Consider your partner's comments as you revise your own writing.

Additional Topics for Writing

Here are some ideas for descriptive paragraphs. When you write, follow the guidelines in Activity 15.

TOPIC 1: Describe a national monument that is important to you. What does it look like? What feelings does the monument inspire in you?

TOPIC 2: Describe a family tradition. When do you follow the tradition? Why is the tradition important to you and your family?

TOPIC 3: Describe your favorite or least favorite meal. Be sure to tell how the food tastes, smells, and looks.

TOPIC 4: Describe something that makes you happy, sad, nervous, or afraid.

TOPIC 5: Describe a person you know. What is this person like? What are some of his or her characteristics? Make sure that the description would allow your reader to identify the person in a crowd.

Timed Writing

How quickly can you write in English? There are many times when you must write quickly, such as on a test. It is important to feel comfortable during those times. Timed-writing practice can make you feel better about writing quickly in English.

Take out a piece of paper. Then read the writing prompt below this paragraph. Your teacher will give you 5 minutes to brainstorm ideas about this topic. You must then write a short descriptive paragraph (perhaps 6 to 10 sentences) about it. You will have 25 minutes to write your paragraph. At the end of the 25 minutes, your teacher will collect your work and return it to you later.

> In your opinion, what is the ideal teacher? Describe your ideal teacher. Which characteristics make this kind of teacher ideal to you? (Do not use names of current teachers, but you should use their characteristics that you consider ideal.)

Opinion Paragraphs

GOAL: To learn how to write an opinion paragraph

*Language Focus: Word forms

What do you think of this book? What do you think of your current English proficiency? How do you like the weather in your area? Your answers to all of these questions are your opinions. A paragraph that concentrates on the writer's opinions is called an **opinion paragraph**. In an opinion paragraph, writers attempt to persuade their audience about a certain point of view. In other words, they present an argument for or against something. This kind of writing is also referred to as persuasive or argumentative writing.

What Is an Opinion Paragraph?

An opinion paragraph expresses the writer's opinion. A good writer will include not only opinions but also facts to support his or her opinions. For example, if a writer says, "Smoking should not be allowed anywhere," the writer must give reasons for this opinion. One reason could be a fact, such as, "Thirty thousand people died in the United States and Canada last year because of lung cancer—a known result of smoking." This fact supports the writer's opinion.

> A good opinion paragraph
>
> - gives the writer's opinion or opinions about a topic.
>
> - interprets or explains facts.
>
> - is often about a controversial issue.
>
> - causes the reader to think about an issue seriously, perhaps even causing the reader to reconsider his or her own opinion about the issue.
>
> - considers both sides of an argument (although it gives more attention to the writer's side of the issue).

Working with Opinions

It helps to know how you feel about a topic before you read an opinion paragraph. Sometimes the writer may try to persuade you to agree with her or him.

ACTIVITY 1 Example Opinion Paragraphs

Read and study these example paragraphs. Answer the questions.

Opinion Paragraph 1

This paragraph is about cell phone use while driving, which has been a topic of much interest and debate in many countries for some time.

Before you read, discuss these questions with your classmates.

1. Do you think that using a cell phone while driving is acceptable? Why or why not?

2. Should there be a law banning the use of cell phones while driving? Why or why not?

Now read the paragraph.

EXAMPLE PARAGRAPH 64

Driving and Cell Phones

Because cell phones and driving are a **deadly** mix, I am in favor of a ban on cell phone use by drivers. The most **obvious** reason for this ban is to save lives. Each year, thousands of drivers are killed because they are talking on cell phones instead of watching the road while they are driving. This first reason should be enough to support a ban on cell phones when driving, but I have two other reasons. My second reason is that these drivers cause accidents that kill other people. Sometimes these drivers kill other drivers; sometimes they kill passengers or even pedestrians. These drivers certainly do not have the right to **endanger** others' lives! Finally, even in cases where there are no injuries or deaths, damage to cars from these accidents costs us millions of dollars as well as countless hours of lost work. To me, banning cell phones while driving is **common sense**. In fact, a **wide range of** countries has already put this ban into effect, including Australia, Brazil, Japan, Russia, and Turkey. Driving a car is a privilege, not a right. We must all be careful drivers, and talking on a cell phone when driving is not safe.

deadly: dangerous, able to cause death
obvious: evident, clear
endanger: to cause to be in a dangerous situation

common sense: so obvious that everyone knows it
a (wide) range of: a (great) number of

1. What is the topic sentence of the paragraph? _____

_____

2. What is the author's opinion on cell phone usage by drivers? _____

_____

3. List three reasons that the writer favors a ban on cell phones while driving.

   a. _____

   b. _____

   c. _____

4. What is your reaction to this paragraph? Do you agree or disagree with the author's opinion? Why or why not?

_____

_____

_____

Opinion Paragraph 2

This paragraph is about a less serious topic than the topic that Example Paragraph 64 deals with. The subject of this paragraph is the question, "Which is better—calling or texting?"

Before you read, discuss these questions with your classmates.

1. How many phone calls do you make each day?

2. How many text messages do you send each day?

3. Do you prefer to call or text someone when you need to tell that person something? Why?

Read the following paragraph and see how the writer feels about calling and texting.

EXAMPLE PARAGRAPH 65

The Best Way to Communicate

No matter how much my friends try to convince me that I should **text** them more often, I prefer calling to texting. Yes, some people might say that using a telephone to make a call is **old-fashioned**, but I do not care. Texting is certainly very common now because it is convenient and fast. However, I really like to call my friends because I want to hear my friends' voices and interact with them. **Without a doubt**, calling is my preferred **mode** of communication.

no matter: it does not matter or make a difference
text: to communicate by text message
old-fashioned: old style, not modern

without a doubt: 100%, certainly
a mode: a method, manner

1. What is the topic sentence of this paragraph? _____

   _____

2. What phrases from the paragraph show the reader that the writer is giving an opinion and not a fact?

   _____

   _____

3. Do you agree with the supporting statements that the writer makes about texting and calling? Why or why not?

   _____

   _____

   _____

4. Can you think of two other topics that could be compared in a similar way?

   _____

   _____

Opinion Paragraph 3

This paragraph deals with a current controversial issue—school uniforms.

Before you read, discuss these questions with your classmates.

1. Have you ever worn a school uniform?

2. Do you think wearing uniforms is a good idea or a bad idea?

3. What is the best type of uniform for female students? For male students?

Read how the writer feels about this topic.

An A+ for School Uniforms

School uniforms should be **mandatory** for all students for a number of reasons. First of all, uniforms make everyone equal. In this way, the "rich" kids are on the same level as the poor ones. In addition, getting ready for school can be much faster and easier. Many kids waste time choosing what to wear to school, and they and

their parents are often unhappy with their final choices. Most important, some **studies** show that school uniforms make students **perform** better in school. Many people might say that uniforms take away from personal freedom, but I believe the benefits are stronger than the **drawbacks**.

mandatory: obligatory, something that must be done
a study: a research report

perform: to produce work
a drawback: a disadvantage

1. What is the author's opinion about school uniforms?

   _____

   _____

2. The author gives three reasons to support the opinion. Write them here.

   _____

   _____

   _____

3. The paragraph states that some people do not think that school uniforms should be required. What is their main reason?

   _____

   _____

For more practice with identifying opinions, try Unit 9, Activity 1 on the *Great Writing 2* Web site: elt.heinle.com/greatwriting

Writer's Note

Including an Opposing Opinion

In argumentative writing, an effective technique is to include at least one sentence with an opposing opinion (an opinion that disagrees with your point of view). At first, this might not seem like a good idea, but it is common to state one point of view that disagrees with your own point of view. This is called a **counterargument**. This counterargument is then followed by a statement that refutes or diminishes the counterargument. This is called a **refutation** because you refute the counterargument.

In a good opinion paragraph, the writer

- states an opinion about a topic.

- provides supporting sentences with factual information.

- briefly mentions one opposing point of view (the counterargument).

- refutes the counterargument in one or two sentences (the refutation).

- finishes the paragraph with a concluding sentence that restates the topic sentence and/ or offers a solution.

Remember: Most of your supporting sentences will agree with your opinion of the topic. However, it is a good idea to include one opposing point in the paragraph. You should acknowledge this other opinion, but you should downplay, or minimize, it. One way to do this is to use weak words, such as *some, may,* and *might,* as we can see in the following examples:

Some teenagers might say that uniforms are boring, but wearing a school uniform is a sign of pride in your school and your education.

ACTIVITY 2 Recognizing Good Topic Sentences for Opinion Paragraphs

Read the following sentences. Which ones are good topic sentences for opinion paragraphs? Put a check (✔) next to those sentences.

1. _____ A hospital volunteer usually has many duties.

2. _____ Soccer is a much more interesting game to play and watch than golf.

3. _____ The largest and best-known city in all of France is Paris.

4. _____ Eating a vegetarian diet is the best way to stay healthy.

5. _____ Hawaii is the best place for a vacation.

6. _____ The U.S. government uses a system of checks and balances.

7. _____ The Nile River splits into the White Nile and Blue Nile in Sudan.

8. _____ Security alarms are the most effective way to protect homes from burglaries.

For more practice with recognizing good topic sentences for opinion paragraphs, try Unit 9, Activity 2 on the *Great Writing 2* Web site: elt.heinle.com/greatwriting

Facts and Opinions

A **fact** is information that can be verified or proved. A fact is always true. An **opinion** is what someone thinks or believes to be true. An opinion may be true or false.

Example of writing with facts:

I live in Orlando, Florida. Orlando is located in central Florida. Orlando is home to several large theme parks as well as the University of Central Florida. The average annual temperature is 73°F.

Example of writing with opinions:

I live in Orlando, Florida. Orlando is a great city for people of all ages. There are many fun places to visit. The University of Central Florida is an excellent university. I like the weather in Orlando very much.

It is rare to write a paragraph that is made up entirely of facts or entirely of opinions. When you are trying to write an opinion paragraph, it is very important to include facts. If you choose helpful supporting facts with examples that the reader can clearly relate to, your opinion paragraph will be stronger. You might even convince readers to agree with you, and that is often the goal of this kind of writing. The reason for writing an opinion paragraph is to explain your opinion in the most convincing way. You are trying to persuade the reader that the issue is important and that your view or your solution is the best one.

In persuasive writing, you can include opinions, but facts will convince more people about a topic rather than just opinions. Include many facts and be sure to give examples when you can. Readers will remember good related supporting examples, so be sure to give time and effort to creating the most convincing examples.

ACTIVITY 3 Identifying Facts and Opinions

Read the following statements and decide if they are facts or opinions. Write F for fact and O for opinion. The first two have been done for you.

__O__ 1. Soccer is a much more interesting game to play and watch than golf.

__F__ 2. The Nile River splits into the White Nile and Blue Nile in Sudan.

_____ 3. The most beautiful city in the world is Paris.

_____ 4. Citrus fruits include oranges, lemons, and grapefruit.

_____ 5. Hawaii is the best place for a vacation.

_____ 6. The capital of Thailand is Bangkok.

_____ 7. Security alarms are the most effective way to protect homes from burglaries.

_____ 8. School uniforms should be mandatory for all students.

_____ 9. A glass of milk has more calcium in it than a glass of apple juice.

_____ 10. Apple juice tastes better than milk.

Reread Example Paragraph 64 about cell phone use while driving. It contains some information that is factual and some that is the writer's opinion. Find two examples of facts and two examples of opinions in the paragraph and write them on the lines below.

Fact

1. _____

   _____

2. _____

   _____

Opinion

1. _____

   _____

2. _____

   _____

 For more practice with identifying facts and opinions, try Unit 9, Activity 3 on the *Great Writing 2* Web site: elt.heinle.com/greatwriting

Building Better Sentences

Correct and varied sentence structure is essential to the quality of your writing. For further practice with the sentences and paragraphs in this part of the unit, go to Practice 17 on page 262 in Appendix 1.

ACTIVITY 5 Sequencing Sentences in a Paragraph

The following sentences make up a paragraph. Read the sentences and number them from 1 to 6 to indicate the correct order. Then write O or F on the line after each sentence to indicate whether the sentence contains an opinion or a fact.

a. _____ The damage of these rays may not be seen immediately in children, but adults who spent a lot of time in the sun when they were children have a much higher chance of developing skin cancer than adults who did not spend time in the sun. _____

b. _____ Too much time in the sun can cause severe skin damage, especially in young children. _____

c. _____ This disease, which can be deadly if it is not treated quickly, is a direct result of the sun's harmful ultraviolet rays. _____

d. _____ In conclusion, the information in this paragraph is enough evidence to persuade parents not to let their children play outside in the sun without sunscreen. _____

e. _____ Although many people enjoy playing in the sun, parents should make sure that their children put on sunscreen before going outside. _____

f. _____ The most serious example of this is skin cancer. _____

For more practice with sequencing sentences in a paragraph, try Unit 9, Activity 4 on the *Great Writing 2* Web site: elt.heinle.com/greatwriting

ACTIVITY 6 Copying a Paragraph

Now copy the sentences from Activity 5 in the best order to create a good opinion paragraph. Add a title of your choice.

_____

_____

_____

_____

_____

_____

_____

_____

_____

_____

Language Focus

Word Forms

Many English words have different forms for different parts of speech—**noun, verb, adjective,** or **adverb**. Always check your writing for the correct word forms.

Study these four parts of speech: noun, verb, adjective, and adverb.

A **noun** names a person or thing.	_growth, driver, uniform_
A **verb** shows action or being.	_desire, equalize_
An **adjective** describes or modifies a noun.	_financial, unique_
An **adverb** modifies a verb, adjective, or another adverb.	_sweetly, illegally_

Some parts of speech have endings that indicate the part of speech. For example, words that end in _–tion_ or _–ment_ are usually nouns: _vacation, entertainment_. Words that end in _–ish_ or _–ial_ are usually adjectives: _greenish, financial_.

Sometimes a word can function as different parts of speech without any change in ending. For example, the word _paint_ can be a noun (_Where is the paint?_) or a verb (_Let's paint the kitchen._). The word _hard_ can be an adjective (_The candy is hard._) or an adverb (_She studied hard._).

ACTIVITY 7 Identifying Word Forms

Each item below contains a group of related words. Identify the word form of the words in each group. Write N (noun), V (verb), ADJ (adjective), or ADV (adverb) on the line. (Some items will not have all four forms.) Use a dictionary if necessary. The first one has been done for you.

1. increasingly   ADV
   increase   N
   increasing   ADJ
   increase   V

2. believe   _____
   belief   _____
   believable   _____

3. illegality   _____
   illegal   _____
   illegally   _____

4. logically   _____
   logic   _____
   logical   _____

5. finance   _____
   financially   _____
   finance   _____
   financial   _____

6. sweetly   _____
   sweetness   _____
   sweet   _____
   sweeten   _____

7. simplicity   _____
   simply   _____
   simple   _____
   simplify   _____

8. equality   _____
   equal   _____
   equalize   _____
   equally   _____

9. benefit   _____
   beneficial   _____
   beneficially   _____
   benefit   _____

10. freedom   _____
    freely   _____
    free   _____
    free   _____

For more practice with word forms, try Unit 9, Activity 5 on the *Great Writing 2* Web site: elt.heinle.com/greatwriting

ACTIVITY 8 Correcting Word Forms

Some of these sentences contain word form errors. Read each sentence. If the sentence is correct, write C on the line. If it contains an error, write X on the line and correct the word form error.

1. _____ Many people did not belief the world was round until after Christopher Columbus's voyages.

2. _____ She parked her car illegally and got a $30 ticket.

3. _____ Taking multivitamins can be benefit to your health.

4. _____ Students in this class are allowed to speak freedom.

5. _____ During civil rights demonstrations, protesters fought for equality.

6. _____ Babies often speak using simply words and phrases.

7. _____ My sister is a very sweetly girl.

8. _____ Mathematicians must use their logical to solve difficult problems.

9. _____ Taxpayers do not want the government to increase taxes.

10. _____ Mary and Bob's financial situation has improved this year.

 For more practice with correcting word forms, try Unit 9, Activity 6 on the *Great Writing 2* Web site: elt.heinle.com/greatwriting

Choosing a Topic for an Opinion Paragraph

In Unit 2, you learned about developing ideas for writing paragraphs. This work includes talking about topics and brainstorming. One good source for topics for opinion paragraphs is the newspaper. Most front-page stories in newspapers can become good opinion topics. The editorial section may also help you with ideas.

Two kinds of brainstorming work well for opinion paragraphs. One kind is to brainstorm using the clusters that you did in Unit 2. This will help you think of ideas and supporting information for a topic. It will also help you eliminate unnecessary or unrelated ideas. A second kind of brainstorming is to make two columns about your topic. On one side, list the negative ideas about the topic; on the other side, list the positive ideas.

Here is an example of how to set up a negative-positive brainstorm design.

TOPIC:	
Negative Points	**Positive Points**

Remember: Whichever argument organization you choose, include at least one sentence that disagrees with your point of view. If you look at the example paragraphs in this unit, you will find a sentence in each one that goes against the main opinion of the writer (the counterargument). However, the writer states this contrasting point of view and gives facts to refute the idea (the refutation).

 For practice with positive-negative brainstorming, try Unit 9, Activity 7 on the *Great Writing 2* Web site: elt.heinle.com/greatwriting.

Building Better Sentences

Correct and varied sentence structure is essential to the quality of your writing. For further practice with the sentences and paragraphs in this part of the unit, go to Practice 18 on page 262 in Appendix 1.

ACTIVITY 9 Word Associations

Circle the word or phrase that is most closely related to the word or phrase on the left. If necessary, use a dictionary to check the meaning of words you do not know.

1.	obvious	serious	evident
2.	mandatory	possible	required
3.	a burglary	to give	to take
4.	to set up	to design, plan	to change, alter
5.	a point of view	an opinion	permission
6.	to split	to combine	to divide
7.	to ban	to prohibit	to transport
8.	severe	negative	positive
9.	without a doubt	it is certain	it is possible
10.	a drawback	a problem	a solution
11.	to downplay	to maximize	to minimize
12.	duties	fun	work
13.	entirely	annually	completely
14.	a voyage	a trip	a subject
15.	to convince	to persuade	to restate

ACTIVITY 10 Using Collocations

Fill in each blank with the word or phrase on the left that most naturally completes the phrase on the right. If necessary, use a dictionary to check the meaning of words you do not know.

1.	but also / for example	not only X, _____ Y
2.	for / from	to protect your home _____ burglaries
3.	all / no	first of _____

4. agree / offer   to _____ a solution

5. in / on   to spend money _____ food

6. may / than   rather _____

7. communication / effort a mode of _____

8. damage / evidence   to cause _____

9. fact / issue   a controversial _____

10. doing / to do   to waste time _____ something

Original Student Writing: Opinion Paragraph

ACTIVITY 11 Original Writing Practice

Develop a paragraph about a strong opinion that you have. Include facts to support your opinion. Follow these guidelines:

- Choose a topic.
- Brainstorm your topic. If you want, use the newspaper for ideas.
- Write a topic sentence with controlling ideas.
- Write supporting sentences with facts that support your opinions.
- Check for incorrect word forms.
- Use at least five of the vocabulary words or phrases presented in Activity 9 and Activity 10. Underline these words and phrases in your paragraph.

If you need help, study the example opinion paragraphs in this unit. Be sure to refer to the seven steps in the writing process in the Brief Writer's Handbook with Activities, pages 218–224.

ACTIVITY 12 Peer Editing

Exchange papers from Activity 11 with a partner. Read your partner's writing. Then use Peer Editing Sheet 9 on page 283 to help you comment on your partner's writing. Be sure to offer positive suggestions and comments that will help your partner improve his or her writing. Consider your partner's comments as you revise your own writing.

Additional Topics for Writing

Here are some ideas for opinion paragraphs. When you write, follow the guidelines in Activity 11.

TOPIC 1: Do you think professional athletes receive too much money? Why or why not?

TOPIC 2: Do you think it is necessary to take an entrance exam to enter a college or university? Why or why not?

TOPIC 3: Should women be allowed in combat positions in the military? Why or why not?

TOPIC 4: When should a person be considered an adult?

TOPIC 5: Which type of music do you prefer—classical music or pop music? Why is one better than the other?

Timed Writing

How quickly can you write in English? There are many times when you must write quickly, such as on a test. It is important to feel comfortable during those times. Timed-writing practice can make you feel better about writing quickly in English.

Take out a piece of paper. Then read the writing prompt below this paragraph. Your teacher will give you 5 minutes to brainstorm ideas about this topic. You must then write a short opinion paragraph (perhaps 6 to 10 sentences) about it. You will have 25 minutes to write your paragraph. At the end of the 25 minutes, your teacher will collect your work and return it to you later.

> In many places, the minimum age necessary to obtain a driver's license is 16 or 17. Many people say this minimum age should be increased to 21. In your opinion, what minimum age should be required to get a driver's license?

Narrative Paragraphs

GOAL: To learn how to write a narrative paragraph

*Language Focus: Verb tense consistency

Have you read a good story lately? What did you like about it? Readers enjoy a good story when it is told well. When you write **a narrative paragraph**, you tell a story. The information in this unit will help you write a good narrative paragraph.

What Is a Narrative Paragraph?

A narrative paragraph can be fun to write because you tell a story or depict an event. Narratives have a beginning, a middle, and an end to their stories. Any time you go to a movie or read a fiction book, you are being exposed to a narrative. A narrative paragraph often describes an event from the writer's life.

A narrative paragraph

- tells a story.

- gives background information in the opening sentence or sentences.

- has a clear beginning, a middle, and an end.

- entertains and informs.

- uses vivid, descriptive language that paints a picture that is so real that the reader can almost feel that he or she is witnessing the event live.

Writer's Note

Including Background Information

The topic sentence of a narrative paragraph—usually the first sentence—gives background information about the action that is going to happen in the story. The background sentence is not usually the beginning of the story—it sets up the story. Try to think of what information you need to give your reader so that the story flows smoothly.

Beginning, Middle, and End

Every narrative paragraph has a beginning, a middle, and an end. Read this example paragraph from a student whose fear of public speaking causes her great grief in her speech class. Then read the explanation of the parts of the narrative paragraph that follows.

EXAMPLE PARAGRAPH 68

Background of story (topic sentence) → I never thought I could do it, but I finally conquered my fear of public speaking.

Beginning of story — At the beginning of the semester, my English teacher assigned us the daunting task of speaking in front of the class for three minutes, and I worried about it for the next two months. I have always been afraid of making a speech in public. I wrote all of my ideas on note cards. I practiced my speech with my notes in front of a mirror, in front of my cat, and in front of my husband. Would I be able to make my speech in front of my class?

Middle of story — When the day of my speech came, I was ready. As I reached the podium, I looked at my audience and smiled. Then I looked down at my note cards. At that moment, I realized that I had the wrong information. These were the notes for my biology test, not the information about my speech! I closed my eyes and took a deep breath. Without further hesitation, I began the speech. To my surprise, the words flowed from my mouth.

End of story — Three minutes later, it was over. Everyone applauded my speech that day, and I left the podium feeling like a winner.

The Topic Sentence

The first sentence in the paragraph—the topic sentence—gives background information about the story. The writer introduces the main character—the writer herself—and prepares her readers for the action that will come. The reader can guess from this first sentence that the story will probably be about what the writer did or what happened that made her less afraid of public speaking.

The Beginning of the Story

The topic sentence is the beginning of the paragraph, but it is not usually the beginning of the story. The main action begins after the topic sentence. Not all narratives contain action. They may be about a problem or a conflict. In this paragraph, the writer has a problem—she has to make a speech in front of the class, but she is afraid of public speaking.

The Middle of the Story

After the beginning part, you will find the middle part of the story. The middle part is where the main action or problem occurs. In this paragraph, the main action or problem is the speech. When the writer stood in front of the class, she discovered that she had biology notes instead of speech notes.

The End of the Story

The end of the story gives the final action or result. If there is a problem or conflict in the story, the solution is presented here. In this paragraph, the story has a happy ending. Because the writer had practiced the speech so many times, she remembered it without her notes. The writer learned that she had the ability to make a speech in front of a group.

ACTIVITY 1 Analyzing Example Narrative Paragraphs

Read and study these example paragraphs. Answer the questions.

Narrative Paragraph 1

The following paragraph is a personal story about a time when the writer was scared.

Before you read the paragraph, discuss these questions with your classmates.

1. Have you ever felt really scared? Describe the situation.

2. What was going on around you during the scary event? Give some sensory adjectives that describe the surroundings.

3. How did the situation end?

Now read the paragraph.

My Department Store Nightmare

I will never forget the first time I got lost in New York City. I was traveling with my parents during summer vacation. We were in an incredibly large department store, and I was so excited to see such a huge place. Suddenly I turned around to ask my mom something, but she was gone! I began crying and screaming **at the top of my lungs**. A salesclerk came up to me and asked if I was OK. She got on the public address system and **notified** the customers that a little boy with blue jeans and a red cap was lost. Two minutes later, my mom and dad came running toward me. We all cried and hugged each other. This story took place over twenty years ago, but every time that I see a department store, I am reminded of that terrified little boy.

at the top of my lungs: very loudly   **notify:** to give information

1. What is the topic sentence of this paragraph? _I will never forget..._

_____

2. Where does the story take place? _NYC Dept Store_

3. How old do you think the boy was at the time of the story? _5 - 6_

4. What is the beginning of the story? (*Circle one.*)

   (a.) He was in a large New York department store.   b. He got separated from his parents.

5. What is the middle of the story? (*Circle one.*)

   a. He screamed and cried.   b. (He) got separated from his parents.

6. What is the end of the story? (*Circle one.*)

   (a.) His parents found him.   b. The size of the store excited him.

7. What is the writer's purpose for writing this paragraph? _Describe the memory_
   of a time when he was scared

Narrative Paragraph 2

The following paragraph deals with an embarrassing moment in the writer's life.

Before you read the paragraph, discuss these questions with your classmates.

1. Think of an embarrassing moment in your life. What happened? What was the result?

2. Imagine that you are a waiter or waitress in a restaurant. What do you think is the most embarrassing thing that could happen to you in this job?

Now read the paragraph.

Friday Night <u>Disaster</u>

My most embarrassing moment happened when I was working in a Mexican restaurant. I was a **hostess** working on a busy Friday night. As usual, I was wearing a blouse and a long Mexican skirt. While I was taking some menus to a table, one of the waiters **accidentally** stepped on the **hem** of my skirt. This made my skirt come off. However, I did not feel it fall off, and I walked through the whole dining room in my **slip**. Almost every customer in the restaurant saw me without my skirt on! I was so embarrassed by the event that I had a hard time **showing my face** there the next day.

a disaster: a complete failure
a hostess: the person who takes you to your table in a restaurant
accidentally: not intentionally or on purpose
a hem: the sewn edge of clothing

a slip: a loose undergarment that functions as a lining for a skirt or dress
show (my, your, etc.) face: to be seen by someone, to show up in public

1. What is the topic sentence? _My most embarrassing moment..._

2. Why was the writer embarrassed? _Her skirt came off & she walked through the restaurant in her slip w/o realizing it_

3. What is the beginning of the story? (*Circle one.*)

    a. She was embarrassed.   b. She was working in a restaurant.

4. What is the middle of the story? (*Circle one.*)

    a. Her skirt fell off.   b. She was working in a restaurant.

5. What is the end of the story? (*Circle one.*)

    a. She was embarrassed because the customers saw her without a skirt.   b. She quit her job.

6. What is the writer's purpose for writing this story? _To tell about her embarrassing experience_

Narrative Paragraph 3

This example narrative paragraph tells about a time in a boy's life when he was unhappy. He learned an important lesson from his unhappiness.

Before you read the paragraph, discuss these questions with your classmates.

1. Think of your best friend. How long have you been best friends?

2. What are the most important qualities in a friend?

3. Have you ever moved away and had to make new friends? Describe the situation. Was it easy? If not, how did you overcome this situation?

Now read the paragraph.

A Lesson in Friendship

I learned the hard way how to make friends in a new school. At my old school in Toronto, I was on the football and track teams, so I was very popular and had lots of friends. Everything changed when I was sixteen years old because my parents decided to move to Florida. Going to a new school was not easy for me. The first few days in my new school were extremely difficult. The class schedule was different, and the teachers were more informal than in my old school. All the students dressed **casually** in shorts and T-shirts instead of a school uniform. Some kids tried to be nice to me, but I did not want to talk to them. To me, they looked and acted **funny**!

casually: informally

funny: strange

After a few weeks, I realized that no one even tried to talk to me anymore. I began to feel lonely.

Two months passed before I **swallowed my pride** and got the courage to talk to a few classmates.

Finally, I realized that they were normal people, just like me. I began to develop some **relationships** and eventually some good friendships. I learned a **valuable** lesson about making friends that year.

swallow my pride: to put self-respect aside and accepted the situation

a relationship: a friendship
valuable: important

1. What is the general topic of this paragraph? _A lesson learned about how to make friends_

2. What is the topic sentence? _I learned the hard way..._

3. In your own words, what is the beginning of the story?
He had many friends, but then his family moved to FL

4. In your own words, what is the middle of the story?
Some kids tried to be nice to him, but he ignored them. Then he got lonely

5. In your own words, what is the end of the story?
2 months later, he realized that even though the other ss looked & acted differently, they were normal people. He began to be nice to them & made some friends

6. What lesson did the writer learn from this experience?

Different ≠ bad or wrong.
Accept friendship.
Make an effort to be nice to others

For more practice with analyzing the features of a narrative paragraph, try Unit 10, Activity 1 on the *Great Writing 2* Web site: elt.heinle.com/greatwriting

Working with Ideas for Narrative Paragraphs

You can find stories from your own memories and experiences. Many times, the best narrative stories are about real events that actually happened to someone. In fact, we have an expression "truth is stranger than fiction," which means that it is sometimes more difficult to invent a story ("fiction") than to tell about something that actually happened ("truth").

ACTIVITY 2 Recognizing Topics for Narrative Paragraphs

Read the following paragraph titles. Put a check (✓) next to the titles that you think would make good narrative paragraphs. Be prepared to exp

_____ My Best Friend, Luke

_____ How to Become a Doctor

_____ The Day I Almost Died

Compare your choices with a classmate. I .... arrative paragraphs? Explain why or why not.

For more practice with topics for n .... t Writing 2 Web site: elt.heinle.com/greatwriti

Writer's Note

Using Vivid Language to Help Readers "See" Your Story

In narrative writing, you want the readers to be able to imagine that they are actually in the story with you. In order to accomplish this goal, you need to describe your setting as carefully as possible. Use vivid language to help your readers imagine that they are actually there with you at the event. Your goal is to make your readers understand why this event is so special or significant for you.

These sentences form a narrative of a personal experience with death. Read the sentences and number them from 1 to 7 to indicate the best order.

_____ a. At 7:18 the next morning, a severe earthquake measuring 8.1 on the Richter scale hit Mexico City. I was asleep, but the violent side-to-side movement of my bed woke me up. Then I could hear the rumble of the building as it was shaking.

_____ b. As I was trying to stand up, I could hear the stucco walls of the building cracking. I was on the third floor of a six-story building, and I thought the building was going to collapse. I really believed that I was going to die.

_____ c. I flew to Mexico City on September 17. The first two days were uneventful.

_____ d. My trip to Mexico City in September 1985 was not my first visit there, but this unforgettable trip helped me realize something about life.

_____ e. I visited a few friends and did a little sightseeing. On the evening of the eighteenth, I had a late dinner with some friends that I had not seen in several years. After a very peaceful evening, I returned to my hotel and quickly fell asleep.

_____ f. In the end, approximately 5,000 people died in this terrible tragedy, but I was lucky enough not to be among them. This unexpected disaster taught me that life can be over at any minute, so it is important for us to live every day as if it is our last.

_____ g. When I looked at my room, I could see that the floor was moving up and down like water in the ocean. Because the doorway is often the strongest part of a building, I tried to stand up in the doorway of the bathroom.

For more practice with sequencing sentences in a paragraph, try Unit 10, Activity 3 on the *Great Writing 2* Web site: elt.heinle.com/greatwriting

ACTIVITY 4 Copying a Paragraph

Now copy the sentences from Activity 3 in the best order for a narrative paragraph. Add a title of your choice.

_____

*Background
information
(topic sentence)*
_____

_____

_____

Beginning of story
_____

_____

_____

_____

_____

Middle of story
_____

_____

_____

_____

_____

_____

_____

_____

_____

End of story
_____

_____

_____

_____

_____

Correct and varied sentence structure is essential to the quality of your writing. For further practice with the sentences and paragraphs in this part of the unit, go to Practice 19 on page 263 in Appendix 1.

Language Focus

Verb Tense Consistency

When writers tell a story, they usually use the simple past tense and perhaps the past progressive tense. Consistency in verb tense means that all the verbs are in the same tense. For example, if your story begins with the simple past tense, do not suddenly switch to the simple present tense and then go back to the simple past tense. Be careful to keep the verb tense consistent.

ACTIVITY 5 Identifying Verb Tenses

Read this narrative paragraph. Circle the verbs. The verbs in the first two sentences have been done for you. Then answer the questions that follow.

EXAMPLE PARAGRAPH 73

Mihai's Surprise

Mihai (knew) how difficult it (was) to get a student
visa for the United States. However, he (gathered)
all the important paperwork, including his I-20
document, passport, bank statements, and even a
letter from his doctor. On the cold morning of his
interview, he jumped on a bus to the capital. For
five long hours, he rode in silence, looked out the

window at the gray landscape, and wondered about the interview. When he arrived at the embassy,
he saw a line of more than one hundred people. He patiently waited until a guard gave him a
number to enter the warm building. The faces of the embassy personnel frightened him, except

for an older woman who reminded him of his grandmother. She was working at window number 4. He hoped that she would be the one to look at his paperwork. When it was his turn, he looked up quickly. A baby-faced worker at window number 3 was calling him to come up. Mihai stepped up to the window and gave all his documents to the young embassy employee. He glanced at "Grandma" and thought his chance was gone. Then he heard her message to another man, "You will not get a visa in a thousand years! Next in line, please." Mihai was shocked. He turned to the embassy worker in front of him. The worker said, "Here you are, sir. Your student visa is valid for one year." Mihai could not believe it. The impossible had happened. Happily, he took his passport and left the building.

1. What tense are most of the verbs in this paragraph in? _____

2. A few of the verbs are not in this tense. Can you explain why this is? _____

_____

_____

_____

_____

For more practice with verb tense consistency, try Unit 10, Activity 4 on the *Great Writing 2* Web site: elt.heinle.com/greatwriting

Read the following narrative paragraph. Circle all the verbs. Then make corrections so that all the verbs are in a tense that expresses past time—either the simple past tense or the past progressive tense.

EXAMPLE PARAGRAPH 74

My First Job

The happiest day of my life is when I get my first job last year. After college, I try and try for six months to get work with an advertising firm, but my luck is bad. Finally, one day while I am eating a sandwich in a downtown coffee shop, my luck will begin to change. A young woman who is sitting next to me asks if she could read my newspaper. I say OK, and we start talking. She begins to tell me that she is an executive in a huge advertising company and is looking for an assistant. I will tell her that I am very interested in mass communications and study it for four years at the university. She gives me her business card, and within one week, I am her administrative assistant. It is the best lunch of my life!

 For more practice with choosing verb tenses, try Unit 10, Activity 5 on the *Great Writing 2* Web site: elt.heinle.com/greatwriting

Read the teacher's comments and the narrative paragraphs. Match each teacher comment to the correction needed in each paragraph. Write the number on the line at the end of the paragraph.

Teacher Comments

1. Your first sentence is too specific to be a topic sentence. Who is "her"? Your topic sentence should tell the reader what the paragraph is going to be about.

2. Be careful with verbs. The verbs you used jump from the simple present to the simple past tense.

3. Your paragraph is excellent! The topic sentence sets up the rest of the paragraph very nicely. You also use good supporting sentences and correct verbs.

4. Your paragraph is good. However, you didn't indent the first line of your paragraph. Be careful with correct paragraph form.

5. This isn't a narrative paragraph—it is a descriptive one. Follow directions more carefully.

EXAMPLE PARAGRAPH 75

An Unfortunate Family Dinner

My family and I went to her house almost every Sunday, but this one time her food almost made me sick. When I sat down at the table, she put some food on my plate. It looked like an old fishing net. I asked her what kind of food it was, but she just said that it was healthy and tasty. I looked around the table and saw that everyone else was eating, even my little brother. Without thinking about it, I put some of the reddish brown food in my mouth. Two seconds later I ran into the bathroom and spit everything out. It was the most terrible stuff I had ever eaten! Later that night, my grandmother told me what the food was—fried tripe and cow tongue.

Teacher Comment: _____

Brandy's Luck

I will never forget an awful experience that almost took my favorite dog Brandy's life. I always played with Brandy in our front yard every day after school. One day while we were playing, Brandy saw a cat on the other side of the street. She did what any normal dog would do; she started to run across the street to get the cat. I screamed for her to come back, but she did not listen. Suddenly a car appeared and hit her. The driver of the car was very nice and immediately took Brandy to the neighborhood veterinarian. The vet had to operate on Brandy's leg and ended up putting her leg in a cast. When my dog finally returned home, she was almost as good as new. From that day, she never left our front yard again.

Teacher Comment: _____

My Favorite Place

My bedroom is small but comfortable. The walls are covered with posters and banners of my favorite sports teams. On the left side, there is a twin bed that I have had since I was ten years old. Next to the bed is my dresser. It is blue and white with gold knobs. Beside the dresser is my bookshelf, which holds most of my schoolbooks, dictionaries, and Kurt Vonnegut novels. Across from the bookshelf, you can see my closet. It is too small to hold all my clothes, so some of my stuff has **permanent residence** on my chair. The clothes get wrinkled there, but I do not mind. My mom does not like it that my room is so messy, so one of these days I am going to clean it up and make her happy.

permanent: always, not temporary   **a residence:** where someone or something lives

Teacher Comment: _____

A Travel Nightmare

When I decided to travel across Europe with a backpack, I did not think I would meet the local police. My best friend and I were sitting in Frankfurt on a train bound for Paris when the nightmare began. A young man comes to the window of the train and asks me what time the train leaves. It took us only ten seconds to open the window and answer him. When we turned away from the window and sat down in our seats, we noticed that our backpacks were missing. Quickly, we got off the train and went to the police headquarters inside the station. We explained what happened. The police officers did not look surprised. They say it is a common way of stealing bags. One person stays outside the train and asks a passenger for help or information. While the passenger is talking to this person, someone else comes quietly into the train car and steals bags, purses, or other valuables. The team players are so good at it that they can steal what they want in less than three seconds. The police officers tell us that there is really nothing we can do, but they suggest that we look through the garbage cans and hope that the robbers took only our money and threw our passports and bags away. We looked and looked, but we never found our bags. The next morning, we were not in Paris; we were at our embassy in Frankfurt, waiting for duplicate passports.

Teacher Comment: _____

The Trick That Failed

Twin brothers Freddie and Felix often played tricks at school, but one day they went too far. On that day, they decided to try to cheat on a French exam. Freddie was very good at learning languages and was always the best student in both Spanish and French. Felix, however, excelled in mathematics. He was not interested in languages at all. When Felix discovered that he had to take a standardized exam in French, he asked his brother for help. The day of Felix's test, they met in the boys' restroom during lunch and switched clothes. Freddie went to his brother's French class and took the test for him. Meanwhile, Felix followed Freddie's schedule. After school, the twins laughed about their trick and headed home. As they entered the house, their mother called them into the kitchen. She was furious! She had received a phone call from the school principal. The French teacher had found out about the trick! "How did he know?" cried Felix. "Easily," replied his mother. "Everyone at the school knows that one obvious difference between you and your brother is that you are right-handed and Freddie is left-handed. While the French teacher was grading the tests, he noticed that the check marks on the test were made by a left-handed person." Felix and Freddie got into a lot of trouble that day, but they learned a valuable lesson—and they never cheated again.

Teacher Comment: _____

For more practice with editing narrative paragraphs, try Unit 10, Activity 6 and Activity 7 on the *Great Writing* 2 Web site: elt.heinle.com/greatwriting

Building Better Sentences

Correct and varied sentence structure is essential to the quality of your writing. For further practice with the sentences and paragraphs in this part of the unit, go to Practice 20 on page 264 in Appendix 1.

ACTIVITY 8 Word Associations

Circle the word or phrase that is most closely related to the word or phrase on the left. If necessary, use a dictionary to check the meaning of words you do not know.

1.	to depict	to find	to show
2.	valuable	important	not important
3.	grief	negative	positive
4.	a rumble	a noise	a smell
5.	to flow	to move	to seem
6.	applauded	negative	positive
7.	came up to me	approached me	persuaded me
8.	to switch	to appreciate	to change
9.	a hem	clothing	vehicles
10.	to witness	to see	to think
11.	to collapse	to cancel	to fall
12.	scary	afraid	necessary
13.	casually	formal	not formal
14.	a tragedy	a bad event	a good event
15.	to hug	to embrace	to prosper

ACTIVITY 9 Using Collocations

Fill in each blank with the word on the left that most naturally completes the phrase on the right. If necessary, use a dictionary to check the meaning of words you do not know.

1. life / task   a daunting _____

2. at / up   to set _____

3. deep / hard   to take a _____ breath

4. lesson / nightmare   a valuable _____

5. of / on   What's going _____?

6. pride / reality   to swallow my _____

7. natural / tense   a _____ disaster

8. shirt / truck   a wrinkled _____

9. ears / lungs   screamed at the top of her _____

10. against / without   _____ any hesitation at all

Original Writing Practice: Narrative Paragraph

ACTIVITY 10 Original Writing Practice

Write a narrative paragraph about an experience that you have had. Follow these guidelines:

- Choose a topic.
- Brainstorm the events in your story.
- Write a topic sentence with controlling ideas.
- Give enough background information to help your readers understand the setting.
- Write supporting sentences for the middle of your narrative.
- Check for consistency in simple past and past progressive verbs.
- Write the end of the story.
- Use at least five of the vocabulary words or phrases presented in Activity 8 and Activity 9. Underline these words and phrases in your paragraph.

If you need help, study the example narrative paragraphs in this unit. Be sure to refer to the seven steps in the writing process in the Brief Writer's Handbook with Activities, pages 218–224.

Exchange papers from Activity 10 with a partner. Read your partner's writing. Then use Peer Editing Sheet 10 on page 285 to help you comment on your partner's writing. Be sure to offer positive suggestions and comments that will help your partner improve his or her writing. Consider your partner's comments as you revise your own writing.

Additional Topics for Writing

Here are some ideas for narrative paragraphs. When you write your paragraph, follow the guidelines in Activity 10.

TOPIC 1:   Write about the most memorable movie you have seen. Briefly explain the plot (story) of the film.

TOPIC 2:   Create a short fable using an animal as the main character. What happens to this animal?

TOPIC 3:   Write about how someone you know got out of trouble.

TOPIC 4:   Write about an important lesson that you have learned.

TOPIC 5:   Write about the most frightening (or happy or difficult) experience you have ever had.

Timed Writing

How quickly can you write in English? There are many times when you must write quickly, such as on a test. It is important to feel comfortable during those times. Timed-writing practice can make you feel better about writing quickly in English.

Take out a piece of paper. Then read the writing prompt below this paragraph. Your teacher will give you 5 minutes to brainstorm ideas about this topic. You must then write a short narrative paragraph (perhaps 6 to 10 sentences) about it. You will have 25 minutes to write your paragraph. At the end of the 25 minutes, your teacher will collect your work and return it to you later.

> Choose a specific event from your childhood that you consider special or significant. Why do you still remember this event? You might decide to write about your first day of school, a particularly difficult class or exam, a time when you were called to the principal's office for something you had done, or one of your early birthday parties. Describe the people and places that are related to the event. Use vivid language to help your readers imagine that they were actually there with you at the event. Your goal is to make your readers clearly understand why this event is so special or significant to you.

Paragraphs in an Essay: Putting It All Together

GOALS: To understand how paragraphs and essays are related; to understand the basic steps in composing an essay.

In Unit 1, we learned what a paragraph is. We saw that a letter becomes a word, a word becomes a sentence, a sentence becomes a paragraph, and a paragraph becomes an essay.

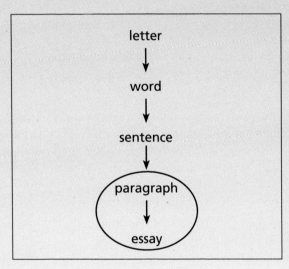

The focus of this unit: How paragraphs form an essay

In this book, the emphasis is on writing a paragraph. You have studied many different aspects of writing a good paragraph, including the four features of a good paragraph:

TOPIC SENTENCE	1. A paragraph has a topic sentence that states the main idea.
ONLY ONE TOPIC	2. All of the sentences in the paragraph are about one topic.
INDENTED LINE	3. The first line of a paragraph is indented.
CONCLUDING SENTENCE	4. The last sentence, or concluding sentence, brings the paragraph to a logical conclusion.

The steps in the process of writing a paragraph are

- developing ideas (brainstorming).

- creating the topic sentence (narrowing the topic).

- writing supporting sentences (developing the ideas).

- writing concluding sentences (ending the paragraph).

Now that you have reviewed some facts about paragraphs, it is time to study how paragraphs work together to form an essay. First, let's find out what you already know about essays.

ACTIVITY 1 What Do You Know about Essays?

Answer these questions. Then work in small groups to compare answers.

1. What do you think an essay is?

   A collection of TSs about 1 main idea

2. Have you ever written an essay? _____ If yes, what was the topic of the essay?

   How long was the essay? _____

3. What do you think the differences are between a paragraph and an essay?

   Essay = longer

Getting to Know Essays

What Is an Essay?

An **essay** is a collection of paragraphs that presents facts, opinions, and ideas on a topic. An essay can be as short as three or four paragraphs or as long as ten or more typed pages that include many paragraphs. Perhaps you have heard of a research paper, which is a special paper that answers a research question. A research paper is actually a kind of essay.

Why Do People Write Essays?

There are many possible reasons.

- As you may know, an essay is a common assignment for students in an English composition class. Students write essays on various topics to practice their writing skills.

- Students also write essays for other classes, such as literature, history, or science classes. In these classes, the essays are about topics in the subject matter of the course.

- Another occasion for essays is the Test of English as a Foreign Language (TOEFL®). For students whose native language is not English, it is often necessary to take this test to be able to enter a college or university. The current TOEFL requires all test takers to complete two writing tasks: (1) a short writing task based on material that you read and listen to and (2) a short writing task to support your opinion on a topic.

- Articles in magazines and other publications are considered essays.

- Some authors collect essays about a topic or theme, such as traveling or nature, and compile them in books.

How Are Essays and Paragraphs Similar?

Essays are similar to paragraphs in a number of ways.

- They both discuss one topic.

- They both use similar organizational elements to help the reader understand the information.

- Essays have supporting and concluding paragraphs, just as paragraphs have supporting and concluding sentences.

- Both paragraphs and essays have an introduction (or topic sentence), a body (supporting information), and a conclusion.

The following chart shows the main elements that paragraphs and essays have in common.

Comparison of Paragraphs and Essays		
Purpose of Parts	**Paragraph**	**Essay**
Introduction • Gets readers interested. • Gives the main idea.	Topic sentence	Hook Thesis statement
Body • Organize the main points. • Give supporting information.	Supporting sentences	Supporting paragraphs Topic sentences
Conclusion • Signals the end of the writing.	Concluding sentence	Concluding paragraph

How Are Essays and Paragraphs Different?

The main difference between an essay and a paragraph is the length and, therefore, the scope of the information. Remember that the length depends on the topic and on the purpose of the writing. Imagine that your teacher gives you the general topic of university education. You are asked to write a paragraph about something related to university education. A paragraph usually has five to ten sentences, so you must narrow down your subject to include the most important information in these few sentences. Your paragraph topic could be the tuition costs at the university.

On the other hand, your teacher might ask you to write an essay about university education. Your essay will need to include several paragraphs about a larger topic, such as a comparison of university and community college education. In general, a paragraph topic is very specific while the essay topic must cover a wider scope.

 For practice with identifying similarities in essays and paragraphs, try Unit 11, Activity 1 on the *Great Writing 2* Web site: elt.heinle.com/greatwriting

Each pair of sentences is about one topic. Decide which sentence is the topic sentence for a paragraph (P)
and which is the thesis statement for an essay (E). (Hint: The thesis statements cover more information.)

1. Topic: Japanese customs

   A. _____E_____ If you travel to Japan, you should first find out about Japanese customs, taboos,
   and people.

   B. _____P_____ The worst mistake that a foreigner can make with Japanese customs is standing up
   chopsticks in a bowl of rice.

2. Topic: Education in Taiwan and the United States

   A. _____P_____ One difference between the educational systems in Taiwan and the United States
   is the role of sports programs in the curriculum.

   B. _____E_____ Because I have studied in both countries, I have seen several areas in which education
   in Taiwan and education in the United States are different.

3. Topic: Household chores

   A. _____P_____ Ironing clothes is a dreaded household task because it cannot be completed quickly
   or thoughtlessly.

   B. _____E_____ The three *most feared* most dreaded household tasks include ironing clothes, washing dishes,
   and cleaning the bathroom.

4. Topic: School uniforms

   A. _____E_____ Wearing school uniforms is a good choice for public school students for a number
   of reasons.

   B. _____P_____ Wearing school uniforms would make students' morning routines much simpler.

5. Topic: Capital punishment

   A. _____E_____ Some people say that the government does not have the right to end someone's life,
   but the following reasons will show why capital punishment is appropriate.

   B. _____P_____ One reason that capital punishment is appropriate is financial; it is cheaper to execute
   someone than to support him or her in prison.

For more practice with topics for paragraphs and essays, try Unit 11, Activity 2 on the *Great Writing 2*
Web site: elt.heinle.com/greatwriting

What Does an Essay Look Like?

There are many different kinds of essays just as there are many different kinds of paragraphs. The following example essay is simple, clearly organized, and easy to understand. It was written by a student in an English composition class. This was the assignment:

> Many inventions in the past one hundred years have changed people's lives. In your opinion, which invention has been the most important and why? Use specific examples and details in your essay.

As you read the essay, notice the thesis statement that states the main idea of the essay, the topic sentence in each paragraph, and the transition words that help connect ideas.

EXAMPLE ESSAY 1

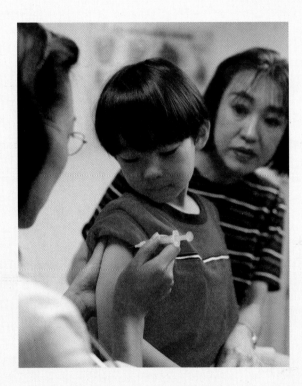

The Most Important Invention in the Past Century

General ideas on topic

1   When you woke up today, you turned on the lights, ran the hot water in the shower, put on mass-produced clothing, watched television, drove to work in your car, and spoke on the telephone. Every day we are surrounded by thousands of useful things that were invented only a relatively short time ago. *In fact,* we depend on these things for the good quality of life that we have now. **All of these inventions have been very important to humans, but the one that has been the most important in improving people's health over the centuries is the discovery of antibiotics.**

Transition ➡ Phrase

Thesis ➡ Statement

2 <u>The bubonic plague, which killed millions of Europeans six hundred years ago, was nothing more than bacteria.</u> It was spread by **rodents** and **fleas**, which were very common during that time. This disease was also called the Black Death because when a person **contracted** the disease, his or her neck and face would swell up and turn black. Back then, no one was aware that this plague could have easily been treated with penicillin. The Black Plague eventually retreated, but people were still in danger of dying from simple bacteria.

← Topic Sentence

3 <u>Even as recently as one hundred years ago, medical knowledge was much more limited than it is now.</u> Something as **trivial** as a simple cut could sometimes result in an **amputation** or even death if it became **infected**. Medical professionals knew what was happening; *however,* there was simply no way to stop the infection from spreading or causing more harm. The discovery of penicillin in the early part of the twentieth century changed all of that. Antibiotics finally allowed humans to maintain their good health and continue their lives for many more years.

← Topic Sentence

← Transition Word

Transition Phrase →

4 *In fact,* <u>antibiotics are an inexpensive and effective treatment for a number of ailments.</u> When we have an infection nowadays, we do not think about it too much. We go to the doctor, who will prescribe some kind of medicine. We take this medicine as directed, and *then,* after a few days,

← Topic Sentence

Transition Phrase →

we are healthy again. The medicine is probably a form of antibiotics. *In addition,* these antibiotics are painless and fast acting. Without them, countless people would suffer through painful and life-threatening ailments.

← Transition Word

5 When people think of the most important invention in the past one hundred years, most people think about electricity, cars, airplanes, or computers. <u>While all of these are certainly extremely important, the invention of antibiotics promoted good health and longer lives.</u> People tend to take antibiotics and other medicine for granted, but they should not do this. If antibiotics had not been invented in the past century, millions of people would have died much earlier, and human beings would not be able to enjoy the quality of life that we have today.

← Restated Thesis

a rodent: a small, often disease-carrying animal, such as a rat or mouse

a flea: a small insect that lives on cats and dogs; it jumps very quickly

contract: to get something, such as a disease

trivial: not important

an amputation: the removal of an exterior body part, such as a leg or an arm

be infected: to have disease-producing bacteria (or similar substances) in the body

an ailment: a sickness, an illness

An Essay Outline

The steps in writing a paragraph are similar to the steps in writing a good essay. After you brainstorm a suitable topic for an essay or paragraph, you think about an introduction, supporting ideas, and a conclusion. For an essay, an important step is to make an **outline**. Here is an outline of "The Most Important Invention in the Past Century" that you just read. Reread the essay before you read the outline. Then compare the essay information with the outline to help you understand its organization better.

I. Introduction (Paragraph 1)—Many important things have been invented in the past century, but the most important was the discovery of antibiotics.

II. Body (Paragraph 2)—Hundreds of years ago, millions of Europeans died from bubonic plague.

III. Body (Paragraph 3)—Medicine was limited until the invention of penicillin in the early twentieth century.

IV. Body (Paragraph 4)—Antibiotics are currently used for a variety of ailments.

V. Conclusion (Paragraph 5)—The invention of antibiotics promoted good health and longer lives.

 Writer's Note

Varying Your Vocabulary

Vocabulary is a key part of good writing. The level of vocabulary that you use is an indication of your English proficiency. Better vocabulary often favorably influences the reader's opinion of your writing.

Note that the vocabulary in the outline is not always the same as the vocabulary in the essay. VARIETY is important! In your essays, try to use synonyms, phrases, and sometimes whole sentences to say the same information in a different way. Avoid repeating the same vocabulary.

 For more practice with varying your vocabulary, try Unit 11, Activity 3 on the *Great Writing 2* Web site: elt.heinle.com/greatwriting

The Thesis Statement

We learned that the most important part of any paragraph is the topic sentence. The first paragraph of an essay has a similar sentence that is called a **thesis statement**. It tells the reader what the essay is about. The thesis statement also indicates what the organization of the essay will be. The thesis statement is usually the last sentence in the introduction paragraph. Find and reread the thesis statement in "The Most Important Invention in the Past Century." (Answer: "All of these inventions have been very important to humans, but the one that has been the most important in improving people's health over the centuries is the discovery of antibiotics.")

Now read these examples of thesis statements.

1. Three things make traveling to Southeast Asia an unforgettable experience.

2. Serving in the military offers not only professional advantages but also personal benefits.

3. Computer literacy is one of the fastest growing needs for young adults.

4. The person I most respect and admire is my aunt Josephine.

As you can see, the topics for the essays with these thesis statements range from serious subjects to personal stories. The thesis statement that you write will depend on the assignment that your teacher gives you.

 For practice with thesis statements, try Unit 11, Activity 4 on the *Great Writing 2* Web site: elt.heinle.com/greatwriting

Supporting Ideas

Essays need **supporting ideas** just like paragraphs. Writers should have two or three ideas that support the thesis statement. Each of these ideas will eventually become a separate paragraph. Asking a question about the thesis statement is a good way to come up with material for supporting paragraphs. Remember that it is important to provide specific examples and details within the paragraph.

Here are some questions to ask and ideas to develop about the thesis statements you read above.

1. Three things make traveling to Southeast Asia an unforgettable experience.

   Question: Why is it an unforgettable experience?

   Ideas to develop: The people are very friendly; there are beautiful places to see; the food is incredibly delicious.

2. Serving in the military offers not only professional advantages but also personal benefits.

   Question: What are these advantages and benefits?

   Ideas to develop: Professional advantages: a full-time job with good benefits, vocational training. Personal benefits: a sense of pride in serving your country, developing maturity

3. Computer literacy is one of the fastest growing needs for young adults.

   Question: Why is the need for computer literacy so important?

   Ideas to develop: Computer literacy is essential for advanced studies (college or university), for the workplace, and for life in general (banking, buying and selling, etc.).

4. The person I most respect and admire is my aunt Josephine.

   Question: Why do you admire her so much?

   Ideas to develop: She taught me about hard work; she loved me unconditionally; she always gave me excellent advice.

 For practice with supporting ideas, try Unit 11, Activity 5 on the *Great Writing 2* Web site: elt.heinle.com/greatwriting

Different Kinds of Essay Organization

Once you write a thesis statement, you can develop your essay in different ways. In the following activity, you will work with some possibilities for essay organization.

ACTIVITY 3 Working with Essay Organization

Read the thesis statements of five essays and the outlines of the first three essays. For the last two, write a brief outline that shows how you might organize the essay. Follow the first three examples. Note: Essays usually have four to ten paragraphs.

1. Thesis Statement: Prisoner rehabilitation has succeeded by providing various programs that help inmates function in the real world when they are released.

   I. Introduction (Paragraph 1)

   II. Body (Paragraph 2): rehabilitation program 1

   III. Body (Paragraph 3): rehabilitation program 2

   IV. Body (Paragraph 4): rehabilitation program 3

   V. Body (Paragraph 5): example of a prison that uses all three of these rehabilitation programs

   VI. Conclusion (Paragraph 6)

2. Thesis Statement: Three things make traveling to Southeast Asia an unforgettable experience.

   I. Introduction (Paragraph 1)

   II. Body (Paragraph 2): friendly people

   III. Body (Paragraph 3): beautiful sights

   IV. Body (Paragraph 4): incredibly tasty food

   V. Conclusion (Paragraph 5)

3. Thesis Statement: Serving in the military offers not only professional advantages but also personal benefits.

   I. Introduction (Paragraph 1)

   II. Body (Paragraph 2): professional advantages (full-time job and vocational training)

   III. Body (Paragraph 3): personal benefits (pride and maturity)

   IV. Conclusion (Paragraph 4)

4. Thesis Statement: Computer literacy is important for young adults for many reasons.

   I. Introduction (¶ 1)

   II. Body (¶ 2) Advanced Studies

   III. Body (¶ 3) Workplace

   IV. Body (¶ 4) Life in general

   V. Conclusion (¶ 5)

5. Thesis Statement: The person I most respect and admire is my aunt Josephine.

I. Intro (¶1)
II. Body (¶2): taught me about hard work
III. Body (¶3): loved me unconditionally
IV. Body (¶4): gave excellent advice
V. Conclusion (¶5)

 For more practice with working with an essay outline and essay organization, try Unit 11, Activity 6 and Activity 7 on the *Great Writing 2* Web site: elt.heinle.com/greatwriting

ACTIVITY 4 Comparing Outlines

Now work in groups to compare your outlines from Activity 3. Discuss how you would develop the ideas in the essays in items 4 and 5, based on your outline.

ACTIVITY 5 Working with a Sample Essay

Read and study the following essay. Then work with a partner to answer the questions that follow.

EXAMPLE ESSAY 2

The Benefits of Being Bilingual

1   The Vieira family moved to the United States in 1981. At that time, they made a decision. They decided to stop speaking Portuguese at home and only communicate in English. They were, in fact, living in an English-speaking country. The Vieira children are adults now, and from time to time they travel to Portugal to visit old family and friends. There is a problem however. Mr. and Mrs. Vieira's children cannot communicate with their relatives. This particular event happens frequently all over the world. When people immigrate to new lands, many of them begin disregarding not only their cultural traditions but also their native language. This disregard for the native language is a mistake because there are many benefits to being bilingual.

2   One of the most basic advantages of being bilingual is a purely linguistic one. People who can speak more than one language can communicate with more people around the world. They

do not have to rely on another person to automatically know their own language or resort to an interpreter to get their message across. These bilingual people are independent and self-reliant. Their message can be heard and understood without the aid of others. In contrast, people who are monolingual must put all their trust in others in order to make communication happen. Bilinguals are masters of their own words and ideas.

3   In addition to linguistic advantages, speaking a second language also allows people to experience another culture. Even if these people have never visited another country, bilingualism enhances cultural and social awareness of another group of people. Idiomatic expressions, vocabulary, and even jokes can have a powerful impact on a person's understanding of another culture. For example, a person who speaks American English knows the expression "to put your John Hancock*" on something, which means to sign something. However, only people who know about John Hancock's role in the signing of the Declaration of Independence can fully understand the literal meaning and historical significance of this expression. Thus, becoming bilingual clearly increases knowledge of a new culture.

4   Finally, widespread bilingualism can contribute to global awareness. If everyone in the world spoke a second or third language, different areas of the world could become more closely entwined. Countries could better communicate and perhaps have a better global understanding of others' ideas, values, and behaviors. Being able to speak another country's language makes people more sympathetic to the problems and situations in that country. Conversely, not knowing the language of a potential enemy (country) can only increase miscommunication and suspicion.

5   The benefits of bilingualism are clear. In fact, there is no single disadvantage to speaking more than one language. The real tragedy, however, is not that people do not make the effort to study and learn a second language. It is that people who already have the gift of speaking another tongue let themselves forget it and become a part of the muted majority as a result.

*Cultural Note: This expression has a much larger historical context. When the American colonists wrote the Declaration of Independence, some people were afraid to sign their name because this action put their lives in danger. However, John Hancock was not afraid and wrote his name first on the list and in very big letters so the king would have no trouble seeing it. From this part of American history and culture, we have the modern expression "to put your John Hancock" on a document.

Answer the questions with a partner. Circle the best answer.

1. How does the essay begin?

   a. a fact b. an opinion c. a story *(circled)*

2. Reread the concluding paragraph. Which word best describes it?

   a. suggestion b. opinion *(circled)* c. prediction

3. Which paragraph discusses the cultural benefits of speaking a second language?

   a. Paragraph 1 b. Paragraph 3 *(circled)* c. Paragraph 5

4. Which paragraph discusses the global benefits of bilingualism?

   a. Paragraph 1 b. Paragraph 2 *(circled/scratched out)* c. Paragraph 4 *(circled)*

5. Which paragraph gives the author's opinion about people who have lost a language?

   a. Paragraph 2 b. Paragraph 3 c. Paragraph 5 *(circled)*

ACTIVITY 6 Working with an Outline

Reread "The Benefits of Being Bilingual" and complete the outline.

I. Introduction (Paragraph 1)
   A. Hook: Story of Vieira children
   B. Thesis Statement: _____ ... many benefits to being bilingual_____

II. Body
   A. Paragraph 2: Topic Sentence: _One of ... linguistic one_____

      1. Supporting Idea: They can communicate with more people.

      2. Supporting Idea: They do not need an interpreter.

      3. Supporting Idea: They are in charge of their own ideas.

      4. Supporting Idea: Monolingual people cannot speak on their own.

   B. Paragraph 3: Topic Sentence: Speaking a second language also allows people to experience another culture.

      1. Supporting Idea: Bilinguals have more cultural and social awareness of another group of people.

      2. Supporting Idea: Idiomatic expressions, vocabulary, and jokes help people understand a different culture.

      3. Supporting Idea (example): _John Hancock - signature_____

C. Paragraph 4: Topic Sentence: _Finally, ... global awareness_

    1. Supporting Idea: Countries could become closer.

    2. Supporting Idea: _Countries communicate better & better global understanding_

    3. Supporting Idea: Not knowing an enemy country's language can increase miscommunication.

III. Concluding paragraph (Paragraph 5)

    A. Restatement of Thesis: Bilingualism has only positive effects.

    B. Opinion: _Prob. is ppl who let themselves forget native language_

Putting an Essay Together

Now that you have learned some of the basics of an essay, it is time to practice writing one. In the following activities, you will work with your classmates to produce an essay.

ACTIVITY 7 Brainstorming

In this activity, you will brainstorm ideas for an essay that you will write in Activity 8. Read the following essay topic. Then follow the steps below to brainstorm ideas about this topic.

Topic: Living in a big city is better than living in a small town.

1. Form three groups. Each group must brainstorm and come up with as many reasons as possible why living in a large city is better than living in a small town.

    Your group's reasons: _____

    _____

    _____

    _____

2. Write all your ideas on the board. As a class, vote for the three best reasons. (These reasons will become the topic sentences for the essay you will write in Activity 8.) Each group will brainstorm examples for one reason. Decide which reason each group will be responsible for. Write them below.

    Group 1 reason: _____

    _____

    Group 2 reason: _____

    _____

Group 3 reason: _____

_____

3. Brainstorm some examples that support your topic sentence (reason).

_____

_____

_____

_____

4. Share your group's examples with the rest of the class. Fill in the list below.

Group 1 reason: _____

Examples: _____

_____

Group 2 reason: _____

Examples: _____

_____

Group 3 reason: _____

Examples: _____

_____

ACTIVITY 8 Writing an Essay Draft

You are now ready to complete an essay. Read the following partial essay and fill in the blanks with the information you gathered. Use additional paper if necessary.

EXAMPLE ESSAY 3

The Advantages of City Life

1   The population of Small Hills is 2,500. Everyone knows everyone else. The mayor of the city is also the owner of the sporting goods store. There is only one school in Small Hills, and all the students know each other, from age six to age eighteen. On weekends, many residents of Small Hills go to the only restaurant in town, and perhaps after dinner, they go to the only cinema. This routine continues. On the other hand, the population of Los Angeles is approximately 4 million. It is a city that is so culturally diverse that at any given time one can go to any type of restaurant, watch any

type of film, and see countless exhibits and museums. Which type of life is better? It seems obvious that living in a large city full of diversity is much better than living in a small, rural community.

2   First, living in a large city is better because ___Choices_____

_____

_____

_____

_____

_____

3   In addition, city life can ___Culture_____

_____

_____

_____

_____

_____

_____

4   Finally, large cities give people the opportunity to ___relax_____

_____

_____

_____

_____

_____

_____

5   In conclusion, there are many benefits to living in a large city. While some people might be afraid of existing among such a large and often chaotic group of people, the benefits that a large city can afford its citizens are well worth it. Besides, there is always a place to find tranquility, even in busy metropolitan areas.

ACTIVITY 9 Peer Editing

Exchange books with a partner and look at Activity 8. Read your partner's writing. Then use Peer Editing Sheet 11 on page 287 to help you comment on your partner's writing. Be sure to offer positive suggestions and comments that will help your partner improve his or her writing. Consider your partner's comments as you revise your own writing.

 # Building Better Vocabulary

ACTIVITY 10 Word Associations

Circle the word or phrase that is most closely related to the word or phrase on the left. If necessary, use a dictionary to check the meaning of words you do not know.

1. to narrow down	to become general	(to become specific)
2. aware	(you realize)	you do not realize
3. threatening	(negative)	positive
4. entwined	(connected)	not connected
5. widespread	(common)	rare
6. dreaded	(negative)	positive
7. the mayor	(one person)	most people
8. literacy	technology	(knowledge)
9. a routine	(usual)	unusual
10. muted	serious	(silent)
11. removal	addition	(subtraction)
12. an appropriate action	(a correct action)	a brief action
13. chaotic	(crazy)	quiet
14. countless	a few	(a lot)
15. an infection	a health benefit	(a health problem)

Fill in each blank with the word on the left that most naturally completes the phrase on the right. If necessary, use a dictionary to check the meaning of words you do not know.

1. of / on   the scope _____of_____ a report

2. make / take   to _____take_____ something for granted

3. come / know   to _____come_____ up with a good example

4. car / job   a full-time _____job_____

5. of / on   the role _____of_____ education

6. friendly / specific   a _____specific_____ example

7. give / show   to _____give_____ a person some advice

8. to / with   to resort _____to_____ a different plan

9. on / to   X has an impact _____on_____ Y

10. danger / tragedy   to put their lives in great _____danger_____

Next Steps

In this unit, we have presented an introduction to writing an essay. We have pointed out the similarities between writing a paragraph and writing an essay. If you understand the components of a paragraph and the steps in the process of writing a paragraph, then writing an essay should be a relatively easy next step for you.

To complete any essay assignment, be sure to follow the steps of the writing process in the Brief Writer's Handbook with Activities (see Understanding the Writing Process: The Seven Steps). The most important steps for both paragraphs and essays are (1) choosing a good topic, (2) brainstorming ideas, (3) outlining/organizing ideas, (4) writing the first draft, (5) getting feedback from a peer, (6) revising, and (7) proofreading the final draft.

The companion books *Great Writing 3: From Great Paragraphs to Great Essays, Great Writing 4: Great Essays,* and *Great Writing 5: Greater Essays* can lead you further into the process of writing essays. These books present essay writing in more detail and with many more activities and opportunities for writing practice. In learning to write both paragraphs and essays, it is important to write a lot—practice, practice, practice!

Original Student Writing: Essay

Write an essay about one of the topics in this list. Use at least five of the vocabulary words or phrases presented in Activity 10 and Activity 11. Underline these words and phrases in your essay.

Narrative Essay: Tell a story about a time in your life when you learned a lesson.

Comparison Essay: What are the differences between being an entrepreneur and working for a company?

Cause-Effect Essay: Why do some people prefer to take classes online rather than in a traditional classroom setting?

Argumentative Essay: Should high schools include physical education in their curriculum or devote their time to teaching only academic subjects?

Timed Writing

In many classes, you will be asked to write short essays within a limited amount of time. Good writers use their time wisely by reading the writing prompt two or three times, spending a few minutes brainstorming the topic, and outlining their ideas before they begin writing their draft. By doing these steps, they often have time to review their writing before they turn it in. In this assignment, your instructor will give you a time limit for writing a basic essay in class.

Read the essay guidelines and writing prompt below. On a piece of paper, write a basic outline for this writing prompt (include the thesis statement and your three main points). When you have completed your outline (try to use no more than 5 minutes), write a five-paragraph essay.

Essay Guidelines

- Remember to give your essay a title.

- Double-space your writing.

- Write as legibly as possible (if you are not using a computer).

- Include a short introduction (with a thesis statement), three body paragraphs, and a conclusion.

> What should happen to students who are caught cheating on an exam? Why?

Brief Writer's Handbook
with Activities

Understanding the Writing Process: The Seven Steps 218

    The Assignment 218

    Steps in the Writing Process 219

        Step 1: Choose a Topic 219

        Step 2: Brainstorm 220

        Step 3: Outline 220

        Step 4: Write the First Draft 221

        Step 5: Get Feedback from a Peer 221

        Step 6: Revise the First Draft 224

        Step 7: Proofread the Final Draft 224

Editing Your Writing 225

Capitalization Activities 228

    Basic Capitalization Rules 228

    Capitalization Activities 229

Punctuation Activities 231

    End Punctuation 231

    Commas 232

    Apostrophes 234

    Quotation Marks 235

    Semicolons 236

    Editing for Errors 237

Additional Grammar Activities 238

    Verb Tense 238

    Articles 241

    Editing for Errors 244

Citations and Plagiarism 247

Understanding the Writing Process: The Seven Steps

This section can be studied at any time during the course. You will want to refer to the seven steps many times as you write your paragraphs.

The Assignment

Imagine that you have been given the following assignment: *Write a definition paragraph about an everyday item*.

What should you do first? What should you do second, third, and so on? There are many ways to write, but most good writers follow certain general steps in the writing process.

Look at this list of steps. Which ones do you usually do? Which ones have you never done?

STEP 1: Choose a topic.

STEP 2: Brainstorm.

STEP 3: Outline.

STEP 4: Write the first draft.

STEP 5: Get feedback from a peer.

STEP 6: Revise the first draft.

STEP 7: Proofread the final draft.

Now you will see how one student went through all the steps to do the assignment. First, read the final paragraph that Susan gave her teacher. Read the teacher's comments as well.

EXAMPLE PARAGRAPH 41

Gumbo

The dictionary definition of *gumbo* does not make it sound as delicious as gumbo really is. The dictionary defines gumbo as a "thick soup made in south Louisiana." However, anyone who has tasted this delicious dish knows that this definition is too bland to describe gumbo. It is true that gumbo is a thick soup, but it is much more than that. Gumbo, one of the most popular of all Cajun dishes, is made with different kinds of seafood or meat mixed with vegetables, such as green peppers and onions. For example, seafood gumbo contains shrimp and crab. Other kinds of gumbo include chicken, sausage, or turkey. Regardless of the ingredients in gumbo, this regional delicacy is a tasty dish.

Teacher comments:

100/A⁺   Excellent paragraph!
I enjoyed reading about gumbo. Your paragraph is very well written. All the sentences relate to one single topic. I really like the fact that you used so many connectors—however, such as.

Now look at the steps that Susan went through to compose the paragraph that you just read.

Steps in the Writing Process
Step 1: Choose a Topic

Susan chose gumbo as her topic. This is what she wrote about her choice.

○ *When I first saw the assignment, I did not know what to write about. I did not think I was going to be able to find a good topic.*

First, I tried to think of something that I could define. It could not be something that was really simple like television or a car. Everyone already knows what they are. I thought that I should choose something that most people might not know.

I tried to think of general areas like sports, machines, and inventions. However, I chose food as my general area. Everyone likes food.

○ *Then I had to find one kind of food that not everyone knows. For me, that was not too difficult. My family is from Louisiana, and the food in Louisiana is special. It is not the usual food that most Americans eat. One of the dishes we eat a lot in Louisiana is gumbo, which is a kind of thick soup. I thought gumbo would be a good topic for a definition paragraph because not many people know it, and it is sort of easy for me to write a definition for this food.*

Another reason that gumbo is a good choice for a definition paragraph is that I know a lot about this kind of food. I know how to make it, I know what the ingredients are, and I know what it tastes like. It is much easier to write about something that I know than about something that I do not know about.

○ *After I was sure that gumbo was going to be my topic, I went on to the next step, which is brainstorming.*

Susan's notes about choosing her topic

Step 2: Brainstorm

The next step for Susan was to brainstorm ideas about her topic.

In this step, you write down every idea that pops into your head about your topic. Some of these ideas will be good, and some will be bad—write them all down. The main purpose of brainstorming is to write down as many ideas as you can think of. If one idea looks especially good, you might circle that idea or put a check mark next to it. If you write down an idea and you know right away that you are not going to use it, you can cross it out.

Look at Susan's brainstorming diagram on the topic of gumbo.

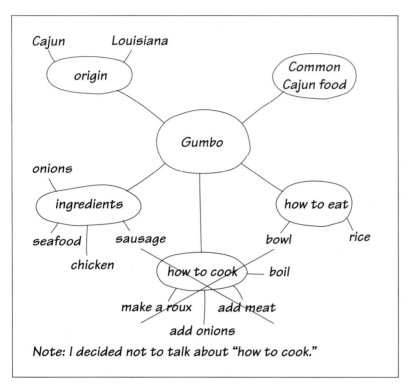

Susan's brainstorming diagram

Step 3: Outline

At this point, some writers want to start writing, but that is not the best plan. After you brainstorm your ideas, the next step is to make an outline. An outline helps you organize how you will present your information. It helps you see which areas of the paragraph are strong and which are weak.

After brainstorming, Susan studied her list of ideas. She then made a simple outline of what her paragraph might look like. Some writers prepare very detailed outlines, but many writers just make a list of the main points and some of the details for each main point.

Read the outline that Susan wrote.

> What is gumbo?
> 1. A simple definition of gumbo.
> 2. A longer definition of gumbo.
> 3. A list of the different ingredients of gumbo.
>   A. seafood or meat
>   B. with vegetables (onions)
>   C. seafood gumbo
> 4. How gumbo is served.

Susan's outline

As you can see, this outline is very basic. There are also some problems. For example, Susan repeats some items in different parts of the outline. In addition, she does not have a concluding sentence. These errors will probably be corrected at the first draft step, the peer editing step, or the final draft step.

Step 4: Write the First Draft

Next, Susan wrote a first draft. In this step, you use the information from your outline and from your brainstorming session to write a first draft. This first draft may contain many errors, such as misspellings, incomplete ideas, and incorrect punctuation. At this point, do not worry about correcting the errors. The main goal is to put your ideas into sentences.

You may feel that you do not know what you think about the topic yet. In this case, it may be difficult for you to write, but it is important to start the process of writing. Sometimes writing helps you think, and as soon as you form a new thought, you can write it down.

Read Susan's first draft, including her notes to herself.

Introduction is weak ??? Use dictionary!

(Rough draft)
Susan Mims

Do you know what gumbo is. It's a seafood soup. However, gumbo is really more than a kind of soup, it's special. ???

Gumbo is one of the most popular of all Cajun dishes.

Combine { It's made with various kinds of seafood or ~~meet~~. meat
This is mixed with vegetables such as onions. + green peppers

Combine { Seafood Gumbo is made with shrimp and crab. ok ???
Also chicken, sausage, and turkey, etc. Regardless of what is in Gumbo, it's usually served in a bowl over the rice.
— Is this correct? Ask teacher!

Susan's first draft

What do you notice about this first draft? Here are a few things that a good writer should pay attention to:

- First of all, remember that this paper is not the final draft. Even native speakers who are good writers usually write more than one draft. You will have a chance to revise the paper and make it better.

- Look at the circles, question marks, and writing in the margin. These are notes that Susan made to herself about what to change, add, or reconsider.

- Remember that the paper will go through the peer-editing process later. Another reader will help you make your meaning clear and will look for errors.

In addition to the language errors that writers often make in the first draft, the handwriting is usually not neat. Sometimes it is so messy that only the writer can read it!

Step 5: Get Feedback from a Peer

Peer editing a draft is a critical step toward the final goal of excellent writing. Sometimes it is difficult for writers to see the weaknesses in their own writing, so receiving advice from another writer can be very helpful.

Ask a colleague, friend, or classmate to read your writing and to offer suggestions about how to improve it. Some people do not like criticism, but constructive criticism is always helpful for writers. Remember that even professional writers have editors, so do not be embarrassed to receive help.

Susan exchanged papers with another student, Jim, in her class. Here is the peer editing sheet that Jim completed about Susan's paragraph. Read the questions and answers.

Peer Editing Sheet

Writer: _Susan_   Date: _2-14_

Peer Editor: _Jim_

1. What is the general topic of the paper? _gumbo_

2. What is the writer's purpose? (in 15 words or less)

   to define gumbo

3. Is the paragraph indented? _yes_

4. How many sentences are there? _6_

5. Is the first word of every sentence capitalized? _yes_
   If you answered *no*, circle the problem(s) on the paper.

6. Does every sentence end with correct punctuation? _no_
   If you answered *no*, circle the problem(s) on the paper.

7. Are there any other capitalization or punctuation errors? _yes_
   If you answered *yes*, circle the problem(s) on the paper.

8. Write the topic sentence here.

   You have two sentences: Do you know what gumbo is. It is a seafood soup.

9. Do you think the topic sentence is good for this paragraph? Comments?

   No, you need one sentence that introduces your topic and purpose better.

10. Does the paragraph talk about just one topic? _yes_

    If you answered *no*, what is the extra topic? _____

    In what sentence is this extra topic introduced? _____

11. Does every sentence have a verb? __no__

If you answered *no*, circle the error(s)on the paper.

12. Write any mistakes that you found. Add appropriate corrections.

Error 1: __it's—don't use contractions in formal writing__

Correction: __it is__

Error 2: __etc.—don't use this__

Correction: __You should list all the kinds.__

Error 3: _____

Correction: _____

13. Did you have any trouble understanding this paragraph? __no__

If you answered *yes*, tell where and/or why.

_____

14. What questions do you have about the content? What other information should be in this paragraph?

__How do you make gumbo? Is it easy to cook? Why do you think people started making gumbo?__

15. What is your opinion of the writing of this paragraph?

__It is good, but the concluding sentence gives new information. It does not conclude! Also, do not repeat the word "gumbo" so much. Do not use "is" so much! Use other verbs.__

16. What is your opinion of the content of this paragraph?

__I like the topic. I think I ate gumbo at a restaurant once.__

Step 6: Revise the First Draft

In this step, you will see how Susan used the suggestions and information to revise her paragraph. This step consists of three parts:

1. React to the comments on the peer editing sheet.
2. Reread the paragraph and make changes.
3. Rewrite the paragraph one more time.

Here is what Susan wrote about the changes she decided to make.

> I read my paragraph again several times. Each time I read it, I found things that I wanted to change in some way. Sometimes I corrected an obvious error. Other times I added words to make my writing clear to the reader. Based on Jim's suggestion, I used "this delicious dish" and other expressions instead of repeating "gumbo" so many times.
>
> I used some of Jim's suggestions, but I did not use all of them. I thought that some of his questions were interesting, but the answers were not really part of the purpose of this paragraph, which was to define gumbo.
>
> I was happy that the peer editor was able to understand all my ideas fully. To me, this means that my writing is good enough.

Susan's notes about changes she decided to make

Step 7: Proofread the Final Draft

Most of the hard work should be over by now. In this step, the writer pretends to be a brand-new reader who has never seen the paper before. The writer reads the paper to see if the sentences and ideas flow smoothly.

Read Susan's final paper again on page 218. Notice any changes in vocabulary, grammar, spelling, or punctuation that she made at this stage.

Of course, the very last step is to turn the paper in to your teacher and hope that you get a good grade!

Editing Your Writing

While you must be comfortable writing quickly, you also need to be comfortable with improving your work. Writing an assignment is never a one-step process. For even the most gifted writers, it is often a multiple-step process. When you were completing your assignments in this book, you probably made some changes to your work to make it better. However, you may not have fixed all of the errors. The paper that you turned in to your teacher is called a **first draft**, which is sometimes referred to as a **rough draft**.

A first draft can almost always be improved. One way to improve your writing is to ask a classmate, friend, or teacher to read it and make suggestions. Your reader may discover that one of your paragraphs is missing a topic sentence, that you have made grammar mistakes, or that your essay needs different vocabulary choices. You may not always like or agree with the comments from a reader, but being open to changes will make you a better writer.

This section will help you become more familiar with how to identify and correct errors in your writing.

Step 1

Below is a student's first draft for a timed writing. The writing prompt for this assignment was "Many schools now offer classes online. Which do you prefer and why?" As you read the first draft, look for areas that need improvement and write your comments. For example, does every sentence have a subject and a verb? Does the writer always use the correct verb tense and punctuation? Does the paragraph have a topic sentence with controlling ideas? Is the vocabulary suitable for the intended audience? What do you think of the content?

The Online Courses

Online courses are very popular at my university. I prefered traditional face-to-face classes. At my university, students have a choice between courses that are taught online in a virtual classroom and the regular kind of classroom. I know that many students prefer online classes, but I cannot adjust to that style of educate. For me, is important to have a professor who explains the material to everyone "live" and then answer any questions that we have. Sometimes students might think they understand the material until the professor questions, and then we realize that we did not understand everything. At that moment, the professor then offers other explanation to help bridge the gap. I do not see this kind of spontaneous learning and teaching can take place online. I have never taken an online course until now. Some of my friends like online courses because they can take the class at his own convenience instead of have to assist class at a set time. However, these supposed conveniences are not outweigh the educational advantages that traditional face-to-face classes offer.

Step 2

Read the teacher comments on the first draft of "The Online Courses." Are these the same things that you noticed?

Your title is OK. Any other ideas?

The Online Courses

Combine first two sentences.

Online courses are very popular at my university. I prefered traditional face-to-face classes.

At my university, students have a choice between courses that are taught online in a virtual

Give more details about CLASSSROOM. Describe it.

classroom and the regular kind of classroom. I know that many students prefer online classes,

WORD FORM   SUBJ?

but I cannot adjust to that style of educate. For me, is important to have a professor who explains

the material to everyone "live" and then answer any questions that we have. Sometimes students

POSES A QUESTION

might think they understand the material until the professor questions, and then we realize that

we did not understand everything. At that moment, the professor then offers other explanation

Which gap???   HOW?

to help bridge the gap. I do not see this kind of spontaneous learning and teaching can take place

Purpose of this sentence? Connected to the topic?

online. I have never taken an online course until now. Some of my friends like online courses

because they can take the class at his own convenience instead of have to assist class at a set

Add more reasons here!

time. ^ However, these supposed conveniences are not outweigh the educational advantages that

traditional face-to-face classes offer.

You have some very good ideas in this paragraph. Your topic sentence and concluding sentence are good. Your title is OK, but can you spice it up? It's rather plain right now. Check to make sure that all of your sentences are relevant. Also, I've circled several grammar errors. You need to change these. I also recommend adding some info in a few places. All in all, it's a good paragraph. I understand why you don't like online courses. The more specific reasons you can provide, the better you can convince your readers.

Step 3

Now read the writer's second draft of the paragraph. How is it the same as the first draft? How is it different? Did the writer fix all the sentence mistakes?

Online Courses

Online courses are very popular at my university, but I prefer traditional face-to-face classes. At my university, students have a choice between courses that are taught online in a virtual classroom and the regular kind of classroom with a room, a professor, and students in chairs. I know that many students prefer online classes, but I cannot adjust to that style of education. For me, it is important to have a professor who explains the material to everyone "live" and then answers any questions that we might have. Sometimes students might think they understand the material until the professor poses a question, and then we realize that we did not understand everything. At that moment, the professor then offers another explanation to help bridge the gap between our knowledge and the truth. I do not see how this kind of spontaneous leaerning and teaching can take place online. Some of my friends like online courses because they can take the class at their own convenience instead of having to attend class at a set time. They also like to save transportation money and time. However, these supposed conveniences do not outweigh the many educational advantages that traditional face-to-face classes offer.

Capitalization Activities
Basic Capitalization Rules

1. Always capitalize the first word of a sentence.

   Today is not Sunday.

   It is not Saturday either.

   Do you know today's date?

2. Always capitalize the word *I* no matter where it is in a sentence.

   John brought the dessert, and **I** brought some drinks.

   I want some tea.

   The winners of the contest were Ned and **I**.

3. Capitalize proper nouns   the names of specific people, places, or things. Capitalize a person's title, including *Mr., Mrs., Ms.,* and *Dr.* Compare these example pairs.

   When our teacher **Mr. Hill** visited his home state of **Arizona**, he took a short trip to see the **Grand Canyon**.

   When our teacher visited his home state, he saw many mountains and canyons.

   The **Statue of Liberty** is located on **Liberty Island** in **New York**.

   There is a famous statue on that island, isn't there?

4. Capitalize names of countries and other geographic areas. Capitalize the names of people from those areas. Capitalize the names of languages.

   People from **Brazil** are called **Brazilians**. They speak **Portuguese**.

   People from **Germany** are called **Germans**. They speak **German**.

5. Capitalize titles of works, such as books, movies, and pieces of art. If you look at the example paragraphs in this book, you will notice that each of them begins with a title. In a title, pay attention to which words begin with a capital letter and which words do not.

Gumbo	*A Lesson in Friendship*	*An Immigrant in the Family*
The King and I	*The Tale of Pinocchio*	*Love at First Sight*

   The rules for capitalizing titles are easy.

   - Always capitalize the first letter of a title.
   - If the title has more than one word, capitalize all the words that have meaning (content words).
   - Do not capitalize small (function) words, such as *a, an, and, the, in, with, on, for, to, above, an,* and *or*.

Capitalization Activities

Activity 1

Circle the words that have capitalization errors. Make the corrections above the errors.

1. the last day to sign up for the trip to são paolo is this Thursday.

2. does jill live in west bay apartments, too?

3. the flight to vancouver left late saturday night and arrived early sunday morning.

4. My sister has two daughters. Their names are rachel and rosalyn.

5. one of the most important sporting events is the world cup.

Activity 2

Complete these statements. Be sure to use correct capitalization.

1. *U.S.A.* stands for the United _____ of _____.

2. The seventh month of the year is _____.

3. _____ is the capital of Brazil.

4. One of the most popular brands of jeans is _____.

5. The first person to walk on the moon was named _____.

6. Parts of Europe were destroyed in _____ (1914–18).

7. My favorite restaurant is _____.

8. Beijing is the largest city in _____.

9. The winter months are _____, _____, and

   _____.

10. The last movie that I saw was _____.

Activity 3

Read the following titles. Rewrite them with correct capitalization.

1. my favorite food _____

2. living in montreal _____

3. the best restaurant in town _____

4. my best friend's new car _____

5. a new trend in hollywood _____

6. why i left my country _____

7. my side of the mountain _____

8. no more room for a friend _____

Activity 4

Read the following paragraph. Circle the capitalization errors and make corrections above the errors.

A visit to Cuba

according to an article in last week's issue of *newsweek*, the prime minister of canada will visit cuba soon in order to establish better economic ties between the two countries. because the united states does not have a history of good relations with cuba, canada's recent decision may result in problems between washington and ottawa. In an interview, the canadian prime minister indicated that his country was ready to reestablish some sort of cooperation with cuba and that canada would do so as quickly as possible. there is no doubt that this new development will be discussed at the opening session of congress next tuesday.

Activity 5

Read the following paragraph. Circle the capitalization errors and make corrections above the errors.

crossing the atlantic from atlanta

it used to be difficult to travel directly from atlanta to europe, but this is certainly not the case nowadays. union airways offers several daily flights to london. jetwings express offers flights every day to frankfurt and twice a week to berlin. other european air carriers that offer direct flights from atlanta to europe are valuair and luxliner. However, the airline with the largest number of direct flights to any european city is not a european airline. smead airlines, which is a new and rising airline in the united states, offers seventeen flights a day to twelve european cities, including paris, london, frankfurt, zurich, rome, and athens.

Activity 6

Read the following paragraph. Circle the capitalization errors and make corrections above the errors.

my beginnings in foreign languages

I have always loved foreign languages. When I was in tenth grade, I took my first foreign language class. It was french I. My teacher was named mrs. montluzin. She was a wonderful teacher who inspired me to develop my interest in foreign languages. Before I finished high school, I took a second year of french and one year of spanish. I wish my high school had offered latin or greek, but the small size of the school body prevented this. Over the years since I graduated from high school, I have lived and worked abroad. I studied arabic when I lived in saudi arabia, japanese in japan, and malay in malaysia. Two years ago, I took a german class in the united states. Because of recent travels to uzbekistan and kyrgyzstan, which are two republics from the former soviet union, I have a strong desire to study russian. I hope that my love of learning foreign languages will continue.

Punctuation Activities
End Punctuation

The three most common punctuation marks found at the end of English sentences are the **period**, the **question mark**, and the **exclamation point**. It is important to know how to use all three of them correctly. Of these three, however, the period is by far the most commonly used punctuation mark.

1. **period (.)** A period is used at the end of a declarative sentence.

   This sentence is a declarative sentence.

   This sentence is not a question.

   All three of these sentences end with a period.

2. **question mark (?)** A question mark is used at the end of a question.

   Is this idea difficult?

   Is it hard to remember the name of this mark?

   How many questions are in this group?

3. **exclamation point (!)** An exclamation point is used at the end of an exclamation. It is less common than the other two marks.

> I cannot believe you think this topic is difficult!
>
> This is the best writing book in the world!
>
> Now I understand all of these examples!

Activity 1
Add the correct end punctuation.

1. Congratulations

2. Do most people think that the governor was unaware of the theft

3. Do not open your test booklet until you are told to do so

4. Will the president attend the meeting

5. Jason put the dishes in the dishwasher and then watched TV

Activity 2
Look at an article in any English newspaper or magazine. Circle every end punctuation mark. Then answer these questions.

1. How many final periods are there? _____ (or _____ %)

2. How many final question marks are there? _____ (or _____ %)

3. How many final exclamation points are there? _____ (or _____ %)

4. What is the total number of sentences? _____

Use this last number to calculate the percentages for each of the categories. Does the period occur most often?

Commas

The comma has several different functions in English. Here are some of the most common ones.

1. A comma separates a list of three or more things. There should be a comma between the items in a list.

> He speaks French and English. (No comma is needed because there are only two items.)
>
> She speaks French, English, and Chinese.

2. A comma separates two sentences when there is a combining word (coordinating conjunction) such as *and, but, or, so, for, nor,* and *yet.* The easy way to remember these conjunctions is *FANBOYS* (*for, and, nor, but, or, yet, so*).

> Six people took the course, but only five of them passed the test.
>
> Sammy bought the cake, and Paul paid for the ice cream.
>
> Students can register for classes in person, or they may submit their applications by mail.

3. A comma is used to separate an introductory word or phrase from the rest of the sentence.

> In conclusion, doctors are advising people to take more vitamins.
>
> First, you will need a pencil.
>
> Because of the heavy rains, many of the roads were flooded.
>
> Finally, add the nuts to the batter.

4. A comma is used to separate an appositive from the rest of the sentence. An appositive is a word or group of words that renames a noun. An appositive provides additional information about the noun.

Washington, the first president of the United States, was a clever military leader.

SUBJECT (NOUN)   APPOSITIVE   VERB

In this sentence, the phrase *the first president of the United States* is an appositive. This phrase renames or explains the noun *Washington*.

5. A comma is sometimes used with adjective clauses. An adjective clause usually begins with a relative pronoun (*who, that, which, whom, whose, whoever,* or *whomever*). We use a comma when the information in the clause is unnecessary or extra. (This is also called a nonrestrictive clause.)

The book <u>that is on the teacher's desk</u> is the main book for this class.

(Here, when you say "the book," the reader does not know which book you are talking about, so the information in the adjective clause is necessary. In this case, do not set off the adjective clause with a comma.)

The History of Korea, <u>which is on the teacher's desk,</u> is the main book for this class.

(The name of the book is given, so the information in the adjective clause is not necessary to help the reader identify the book. In this case, you must use commas to show that the information in the adjective clause is extra, or nonrestrictive.)

Activity 3

Add commas as needed in these sentences. Some sentences may be correct, and others may need more than one comma.

1. For the past fifteen years Mary Parker has been both the director and producer of all the plays at this theater.

2. Despite all the problems we had on our vacation we managed to have a good time.

3. I believe the best countries to visit in Africa are Senegal Tunisia and Ghana.

4. She believes the best countries to visit in Africa are Senegal and Tunisia.

5. The third step in this process is to grate the carrots and the potatoes.

6. Third grate the carrots and the potatoes.

7. Blue green and red are strong colors. For this reason they are not appropriate for a living room wall.

8. Without anyone to teach foreign language classes next year the school will be unable to offer French Spanish or German.

9. The NEQ 7000 the very latest computer from Electron Technologies is not selling very well.

10. Because of injuries neither Carl nor Jamil two of the best players on the football team will be able to play in tomorrow's game.

11. The job interview is for a position at Mills Trust Company which is the largest company in
    this area.

12. The job interview is for a position at a large company that has more than 1,000 employees in
    this area.

13. Kevin's birthday is January 18 which is the same day that Laura and Greg have their
    birthdays.

14. Martina Navratilova whom most tennis fans refer to only as "Martina" dominated women's
    tennis for years.

15. My brother who lives in San Salvador has two children. (I have several brothers.)

16. My brother who lives in San Salvador has two children. (I have only one brother.)

17. This flight is leaving for La Paz which is the first of three stops that the plane will make.

18. No one knows the name of the person who will take over the committee in January so there have been
    many rumors about this.

19. Greenfield Central Bank the most recent bank to open a branch here in our area has tried to establish a
    branch here for years.

20. On the right side of the living room an antique radio sits on top of a glass table that also has
    a flowerpot a photo of a baby and a magazine.

Apostrophes

Apostrophes have two basic uses in English. They indicate either a contraction or possession.

Contractions:	Use an apostrophe in a contraction in place of the letter or letters that have been deleted.
	he's (he is *or* he has), they're (they are), I've (I have), we'd (we would *or* we had)
Possession:	Use an apostrophe to indicate possession. Add an apostrophe and the letter *s* after the word. If a plural word already ends in *s*, then just add an apostrophe.
	Gandhi's role in the history of India yesterday's paper the boy's books (One boy has some books.) the boys' books (Several boys have one or more books.)

Activity 4

Correct the apostrophe errors in these sentences.

1. I am going to Victors birthday party on Saturday.

2. My three cousin's house is right next to Mr. Wilsons house.

3. Hardly anyone remembers Stalins drastic actions in the early part of this century.

4. It goes without saying that wed be better off without so much poverty in this world.

5. The reasons that were given for the childrens' bad behavior were unbelievable.

Quotation Marks

Below are three of the most common uses for quotation marks.

1. To mark the exact words that were spoken by someone:

    The king said, "I refuse to give up my throne." (The period is inside the quotation marks.)*

    "None of the solutions is correct," said the professor. (The comma is inside the quotation marks.)*

    The king said that he refuses to give up his throne. (No quotation marks are needed because the sentence does not include the king's exact words. This style is called indirect speech.)

    * Note that the comma separates the verb that tells the form of communications (*said, announced, wrote*) and the quotation.

2. To mark language that a writer has borrowed from another source:

    The dictionary defines gossip as a "trivial rumor of a personal nature," but I would add that it is usually malicious.

    This research concludes that there was "no real reason to expect this computer software program to produce good results with high school students."

    According to an article in *The San Jose Times*, about half of the money was stolen. (No quotes are necessary here because it is a summary of information rather than exact words from the article.)

    NOTE: See pages 247–248 for more information on citing sources.

3. To indicate when a word or phrase is being used in a special way:

    The king believed himself to be the leader of a democracy, so he allowed the prisoner to choose his method of dying. According to the king, allowing this kind of "democracy" showed that he was indeed a good ruler.

Activity 5

Add quotation marks where necessary. Remember the rules for placing commas, periods, and question marks inside or outside the quotation marks.

1. As I was leaving the room, I heard the teacher say, Be sure to study Chapter 7.

2. It is impossible to say that using dictionaries is useless. However, according to research published in

   the latest issue of the *General Language Journal*, dictionary use is down. I found the article's statement

   that 18.3% of students do not own a dictionary and 37.2% never use their dictionary (p. 75) to be rather

   shocking.

   Source: Wendt, J. (2007). Dictionary use by language students. *General Language Journal*, Volume 3, 72–101.

3. My fiancée says that if I buy her a huge diamond ring, this would be a sign that I love her. I would like to know if there is a less expensive sign that would be a sure sign of my love for her.

4. When my English friend speaks of a heat wave just because the temperature reaches over 80°, I have to laugh because I come from Thailand, where we have sunshine most of the year. The days when we have to dress warmly are certainly few, and some people wear shorts outside almost every month of the year.

5. The directions on the package read, Open carefully. Add contents to one glass of warm water. Drink just before bedtime.

Semicolons

The semicolon is used most often to combine two related sentences. Once you get used to using the semicolon, you will find that it is a very easy and useful punctuation tool to vary your sentences in your writing.

- Use a semicolon when you want to connect two simple sentences.
- The function of a semicolon is similar to that of a period. However, in order to use a semicolon, there must be a relationship between the sentences.

> Joey loves to play tennis. He has been playing since he was ten years old.

> Joey loves to play tennis; he has been playing since he was ten years old.

Both sentence pairs are correct. The main difference is that the semicolon in the second example signals the relationship between the ideas in the two sentences. Notice also that *he* is not capitalized in the second example.

Activity 6

The following sentences use periods for separation. Rewrite the sentences. Replace the periods with semicolons and make any other necessary changes.

1. Gretchen and Bob have been friends since elementary school. They are also next-door neighbors.

_____

2. The test was complicated. No one passed it.

_____

3. Tomatoes are necessary for a garden salad. Peas are not.

_____

4. Mexico lies to the south of the United States. Canada lies to the north.

_____

Activity 7

Look at a copy of an English newspaper or magazine. Circle all the semicolons on a page. The number should be relatively small.

NOTE: If the topic of the article is technical or complex, there is a greater chance of finding semicolons. Semicolons are not usually used in informal or friendly writing. Thus, you might see a semicolon in an article about heart surgery or educational research, but not in an ad for a household product or an e-mail or text message to a friend.

Editing For Errors

Activity 8

Find the 14 punctuation errors in this paragraph and make corrections above the errors.

EXAMPLE PARAGRAPH 83

An Unexpected Storm

Severe weather is a constant possibility all over the globe; but we never really expect our own area to be affected However last night was different At about ten o'clock a tornado hit Lucedale This violent weather destroyed nine homes near the downtown area In addition to these nine houses that were completely destroyed many others in the area had heavy damage Amazingly no one was injured in last nights terrible storm Because of the rapid reaction of state and local weather watchers most of the areas residents saw the warnings that were broadcast on television

Activity 9

Find the 15 punctuation errors in this paragraph and make corrections above the errors.

EXAMPLE PARAGRAPH 84

Deserts

Deserts are some of the most interesting places on earth A desert is not just a dry area it is an area that receives less than ten inches of rainfall a year About one-fifth of the earth is composed of deserts Although many people believe that deserts are nothing but hills of sand this is not true In reality deserts have large rocks mountains canyons and even lakes For instance only about ten percent of the Sahara Desert the largest desert on the earth is sand

Activity 10

Find the 15 punctuation errors in this paragraph and make corrections above the errors.

A Review

I Wish I Could Have Seen His Face Marilyn Kings latest novel is perhaps her greatest triumph In this book King tells the story of the Lamberts a poor family that struggles to survive despite numerous hardships. The Lambert family consists of five strong personalities. Michael Lambert has trouble keeping a job and Naomi earns very little as a maid at a hotel The three children range in age from nine to sixteen. Dan Melinda and Zeke are still in school This well-written novel allows us to step into the conflict that each of the children has to deal with. Only a writer as talented as King could develop five independent characters in such an outstanding manner The plot has many unexpected turns and the outcome of this story will not disappoint readers While King has written several novels that won international praise *I Wish I Could Have Seen His Face* is in many ways better than any of her previous works.

Additional Grammar Activities
Verb Tense

Activity 1

Fill in the blanks with the verb that best completes the sentence. Be sure to use the correct form of the verb. Use the following verbs: like, cut, break, stir, *and* spread.

A Simple Sandwich

Making a tuna salad sandwich is not difficult. Put two cans of flaked tuna in a medium-sized bowl. With a fork, _____ the fish apart. _____ up a large white onion or two small yellow onions. _____ in one-third cup of mayonnaise. Then add salt and pepper to taste. Some people _____ to mix pieces of boiled eggs into their salad. Once you finish making the salad, _____ it between two slices of bread. Now you are ready to eat your easy-to-make treat.

Activity 2

Fill in the blanks with the correct form of any appropriate verb.

Who Killed Kennedy?

One of the most infamous moments in U.S. history _____ in 1963.

In that year, President John F. Kennedy _____ assassinated in Dallas,

Texas. Since this event, there _____ many theories about what

_____ on that fateful day. According to the official U.S. government report,

only one man _____ the bullets that _____ President

Kennedy. However, even today many people _____ that there

_____ several assassins.

Activity 3

Fill in the blanks with the correct form of any appropriate verb.

A Routine Routine

I have one of the most boring daily routines of anyone I _____. Every

morning, I _____ at 7:15. I _____ a shower and

_____ dressed. After that, I _____ breakfast and

_____ to the office. I _____ from 8:30 to 4:30. Then

I _____ home. This _____ five days a week without fail.

Just for once, I wish something different would happen!

Activity 4

Fill in the blanks with the correct form of the verbs in parentheses.

The Shortest Term in the White House

William Henry Harrison (be) _____ the ninth president of the United States. His presidency was extremely brief. In fact, Harrison (be) _____ president for only one month. He (take) _____ office on March 4, 1841. Unfortunately, he (catch) _____ a cold that (become) _____ pneumonia. On April 4, Harrison (die) _____. He (become) _____ the first American president to die while in office. Before becoming president, Harrison (study) _____ to become a doctor and later (serve) _____ in the army.

Activity 5

Fill in the blanks with the correct form of the verbs in parentheses.

The History of Brownsville

Brownsville, Texas, is a city with an interesting history. Brownsville (be) _____ originally a fort during the Mexican-American War. During that war, American and Mexican soldiers (fight) _____ several battles in the area around the city. As a matter of fact, the city (get) _____ its name from Major Jacob Brown, an American soldier who was killed in a battle near the old fort. However, Brownsville's history (be) _____ not only connected to war. After the war, the city was best known for farming. The area's rich soil (help) _____ it become a thriving agriculture center. Over time, the agricultural industry (grow) _____, and today Brownsville farmers (be) _____ well-known for growing cotton and citrus. In sum, both the Mexican-American War and farming have played important historical roles in making Brownsville such an interesting city.

Articles

Activity 6
Fill in the blanks with the correct article. If no article is required, write an X in the blank.

_____ Simple Math Problem

There is _____ interesting mathematics brainteaser that always amazes _____ people when they first hear it. First, pick _____ number from _____ 1 to _____ 9. Subtract _____ 5. (You may have a negative number.) Multiply this answer by _____ 3. Now square _____ number. Then add _____ digits of _____ number. For _____ example, if your number is 81, add 8 and 1 to get an answer of _____ 9. If _____ number is less than _____ 5, add _____ 5. If _____ number is not less than _____ 5, subtract _____ 4. Now multiply this number by _____ 2. Finally, subtract _____ 6. If you have followed _____ steps correctly, _____ your answer is _____ 4.

Activity 7
Fill in the blanks with the correct article. If no article is required, write an X in the blank.

_____ Geography Problems among _____ American Students

Are _____ American high school students _____ less educated in _____ geography than high school students in _____ other countries? According to _____ recent survey of _____ high school students all over _____ globe, _____ U.S. students do not know very much about _____ geography. For _____ example, _____ surprisingly large number did not know _____ capital of _____ state in which they live. Many could not find _____ Mexico on a map even though Mexico is one of _____ two countries that share _____ border with _____ United States. Some _____ educators blame this lack of _____ geography knowledge on the move away from memorization of material that has taken _____ place in _____ recent years in American schools. Regardless of _____ cause, however, the unfortunate fact appears to be that American _____ high school students are not learning _____ enough about this subject area.

Activity 8

Fill in the blanks with the correct article. If no article is required, write an X in the blank.

_____ Homeowners Saving _____ Money with a New Free Service

People who are concerned that their monthly electricity bill is too high can now take _____ advantage of _____ special free service offered by the local electricity company. _____ company will do _____ home energy audit on any house to find out if _____ house is wasting _____ valuable energy. Homeowners can call _____ power company to schedule _____ convenient time for _____ energy analyst to visit their home. The audit takes only about _____ hour. _____ analyst will inspect _____ home and identify potential energy-saving _____ improvements. For _____ example, he or she will check _____ thermostat, the air-conditioning, and _____ seals around doors and windows. The major energy-use _____ problems will be identified, and _____ analyst will recommend _____ ways to use _____ energy more efficiently.

Activity 9

Fill in the blanks with the correct article. If no article is required, write an X in the blank.

_____ Great Teacher

To this day, I am completely convinced that _____ main reason that I did so well in my French class in _____ high school was the incredible teacher that I had, _____ Mrs. Montluzin. I had not studied _____ foreign language before I started _____ Mrs. Montluzin's French class. _____ idea of being able to communicate in a foreign language, especially _____ French, intrigued me, but _____ idea also scared me.

_____ French seemed so difficult at first. We had so much _____ vocabulary to memorize, and we had to do _____ exercises to improve our grammar. While it is true that there was _____ great deal of work to do, _____ Mrs. Montluzin always tried her best to make French class very interesting. She also gave us _____ suggestions for learning _____ French, and these helped me a lot. Since this French class, I have studied a few other languages, and my interest in _____ foreign languages today is due to _____ success I had in French class with _____ Mrs. Montluzin.

Activity 10

Fill in the blanks with the correct article. If no article is required, write an X in the blank.

_____ Surprising Statistics on _____ Higher Education
in _____ United States

Although _____ United States is a leader in many areas, it is surprising that _____ number of Americans with _____ college degree is not as high as it is in some _____ other countries. Only about 22 percent of _____ Americans have attended college for four or more years. To _____ most people, this rather low ratio of one in five is shocking. Slightly more than _____ 60 percent of _____ Americans between _____ ages of 25 and 40 have taken some _____ college classes. Though

these numbers are far from what _____ many people would expect in _____

United States, these statistics are _____ huge improvement over figures at _____

turn of _____ last century. In _____ 1900, only about _____ 8 percent of

all Americans even entered _____ college. At _____ present time, there are about

16 million students attending _____ college.

Editing for Errors

Activity 11

This paragraph contains 8 errors. They are in word choice (1), article (1), modal* (1), verb tense (1), subject-verb agreement (3), and word order (1). Mark these errors and write the corrections above the errors.

A Dangerous Driving Problem

Imagine that you are driving your car home from mall or the library. You come to a bend in the road. You decide that you need to slow down a little, so you tap the brake pedal. Much to your surprise, the car does not begin to slow down. You push the brake pedal all the way down to the floor, but still anything happens. There are a few things you can do when your brakes does not work. One was to pump the brakes. If also this fails, you should to try the emergency brake. If this also fail, you should try to shift the car into a lower gear and rub the tires against the curb until the car come to a stop.

*Modals are *can, should, will, must, may,* and *might.* Modals appear before verbs. We do not use *to* between modals and verbs. (*Incorrect:* I should to go with him. *Correct:* I should go with him.) Modals do not have forms that take *-s, -ing,* or *-ed.*

Activity 12

This paragraph contains 10 errors. They are in prepositions (3), word order (1), articles (2), and verb tense (4). Mark these errors and write the corrections above the errors.

The Start of My Love of Aquariums

My love of aquariums began a long time ago. Although I got my first fish when I am just seven years old, I can still remember the store, the fish, and salesclerk who waited on me that day. Because I made good grades on my report card, my uncle has rewarded me with a dollar. A few days later, I was finally able to go to the local dime store for spend my money. It was 1965, and dollar could buy a lot. I looked a lot of different things, but I finally chose to buy a fish. We had an old fishbowl at home, so it seems logical with me to get a fish. I must have spent 15 minutes pacing back and forth in front of all the aquariums before I finally choose my fish. It was a green swordtail, or rather, she was a green swordtail. A few weeks later, she gave birth to 20 or 30 baby swordtails. Years later, I can still remember the fish beautiful that got me so interested in aquariums.

Activity 13

This paragraph contains 8 errors. They are in prepositions (1), articles (3), word forms (2), verb tense (1), and subject-verb agreement (1). Mark these errors and write the corrections above the errors.

An Effect of Modern Technology on Drivers

One of the recent developments in the modern technology, cellular phones, can be threat to safety. A recent study for Donald Redelmeier and Robert Tibshirani of the University of Toronto showed that cellular phones pose a risk to drivers. In fact, people who talk on the phone while driving are four time more likely to have an automobile accident than those who do not use the phone while drive. The Toronto researchers studied 699 drivers who had been in an automobile accident while they were using their cellular phones. The researchers concluded that the main reason for the accidents is not that people used one hand for the telephone and only one for driving. Rather, cause of the accidents was usually that the drivers became distracted, angry, or upset by the phone call. The drivers then lost concentration and was more prone to a car accident.

Activity 14

This paragraph contains 7 errors. They are in verb tense (1), articles (2), word forms (3), and subject-verb agreement (1). Mark these errors and write the corrections.

Problems with American Coins

Many foreigners who come to the United States have very hard time getting used to America coins. The denominations of the coins are 1, 5, 10, 25, and 50 cents, and 1 dollar. However, people used only the first four regularly. The smallest coin in value is the penny, but it is not the smallest coin in size. The quarter is one-fourth the value of a dollar, but it is not one-fourth as big as a dollar. There is a dollar coin, but no one ever use it. In fact, perhaps the only place to find one is at a bank. All of the coins are silver-colored except for one, the penny. Finally, because value of each coin is not clearly written on the coin as it is in many country, foreigners often experience problems with monetarily transactions.

Activity 15

This paragraph contains 7 errors. They are in word order (1), articles (2), preposition (1), subject-verb agreement (1), and verb tense (2). Mark these errors and write the corrections.

An Oasis of Silence

Life on this campus can be extremely hectic, so when I want the solitude, I go usually to the fourth floor of the library. The fourth floor has nothing but shelves and shelves of rare books and obscure periodicals. Because there are only a few small tables with some rather uncomfortable wooden chairs and no copy machines in this floor, few people are staying here very long. Students search for a book or periodical, found it, and then take it to a more sociable floor to photocopy the pages or simply browse through the articles. One of my best friends have told me that he does not like this floor that is so special to me. For him, it is a lonely place. For me, however, it is oasis of silence in a land of turmoil, a place where I can read, think, and write in peace.

Citations and Plagiarism

Imagine this: You have invited some friends over for dinner. Because you did not have time to make a dessert, you stop at a local bakery and pick up a cake. After dinner, your friends compliment you on the delicious cake you made. How do you respond? Most people would give credit to the person who made the cake: "I'm glad you liked it, but I didn't make it. I bought it at Sunshine Bakery." By clarifying that the cake was not yours, you are rightfully giving the credit to Sunshine Bakery. The same concept holds true in writing.

When you write a paragraph or an essay, you should use your own words for the most part. Sometimes, however, writers want to use ideas that they have read in another piece of writing. For example, a writer may want to use a quotation from a famous politician if he or she is writing a paragraph about a recent election. In this case, the writer must indicate that the words are not his or her own, but that they came from someone else, and give credit to that writer. The action of indicating that a writer's words are not original but rather they are from another source is called **citing**. In academic writing, it is *imperative* for a writer to cite all sources of information that is not original.

If writers do not give credit for borrowed ideas or borrowed words, they make a serious error. In fact, it is academic theft, and such stealing of ideas or words is not tolerated at all. It is not acceptable to use even a few words from another source without citing the source—the amount of information that you borrow is irrelevant. Stealing is stealing. If you steal one sentence or even one phrase from another source, it is still considered stealing. Stealing someone else's ideas or words and using them in a piece of writing as if they were your original ideas is called **plagiarism**. In an academic setting, plagiarism is considered a very serious offense. In most schools, there are serious academic consequences for plagiarizing any work. For example, some schools require the paper to receive a score of 0 (zero). Other schools will expel the student permanently. In some instances, schools will take both of the above steps.

Does this mean then that writers cannot use other people's words or ideas? No, not at all. In fact, a writer's key points can be strengthened by using facts from outside sources or quotes from experts. Consequently, writers are encouraged to borrow appropriate information. The key to avoiding plagiarism is to cite the source of the information.

Many students have a difficult time knowing when to use a citation, especially if they believe the information is general knowledge. For example, Hessa, a student from the United Arab Emirates (UAE), is writing an essay about her country. She knows that the UAE is made up of seven emirates. Does she need to cite this information? If Hessa is writing this essay in an English-speaking country where people may not know that there are seven emirates, she needs to cite the information. If, however, the information is common knowledge in Hessa's academic community, she would not have to cite the information. In the end, it is better to cite the information than to risk being accused of plagiarism. Before turning in any piece of writing, it is helpful to mark any information that is not your original writing. For any information that you mark, you need to give credit to the person, organization, or Web site that originally wrote it by citing those sources.

Citing: Using a Direct Quotation or Paraphrasing

When you use material from another source, you have two choices: using a **direct quotation** or **paraphrasing**. If a writer uses the exact words (a direct quotation) from a source, the borrowed words must be placed in quotation marks. If a writer borrows an idea from a source but uses his or her original words to express this idea, the writer has used a method called paraphrasing. Paraphrasing does not require quotation marks because the writer is not using the exact words from the original source. However, whether a writer is using an exact quotation or a paraphrased version, the information is not original and must be cited.

Example of a Direct Quotation

Notice that this paragraph from *Vocabulary Myths* (Folse, 2004) contains a direct quotation. When you use a direct quotation, you must state the name of the author, the date of the publication, and the page number of the direct quotation.

> One of the first observations that second language learners make in their new language is that they need vocabulary knowledge to function well in that language. How frustrating it is when you want to say something and are stymied because you do not know the word for a simple noun even! In spite of the obvious importance of vocabulary, most courses and curricula tend to be based on grammar or a combination of grammar and communication strategies rather than vocabulary. As a result, even after taking many courses, learners still lack sufficient vocabulary knowledge. Vocabulary knowledge is critical to any communication. Wilkins (1972) summarizes the situation best with "While without grammar very little can be conveyed, without vocabulary *nothing* can be conveyed" (p. 111).

Example of a Paraphrase

Notice that this paragraph from *Vocabulary Myths* (Folse, 2004) contains a paraphrase, or summary, of a concept from a work written by Eskey in 1988. Instead of using any phrases or sentences from Eskey's work, Folse uses a sentence in the paragraph that summarizes Eskey's work and connects that idea to the current paragraph and audience. When you paraphrase material, you must state the name of the author and the date of the publication.

> While lack of vocabulary knowledge is a problem across all skill areas, it is especially apparent in ESL reading. Eskey (1988) found that not being able to recognize the meaning of English words automatically causes students who are good readers in their native language to do excessive guesswork in the second language and that this guessing slows down the process of reading.

Bibliography

In addition to providing information on sources in places where they are used within your writing, you should also list all the works, or sources, of the words and ideas you used in the final **bibliography**, or **list of works cited**, at the end of your paper.

Citation methods vary according to academic professions and fields, so you should ask your instructor about the citation system that is required in your coursework.

Study the following example of a bibliography that lists the four works used in the preceding examples. The first, third, and fourth entries are books. The second entry is a chapter in an edited volume.

Bibliography

Carter, R., and M. McCarthy. 1988. *Vocabulary and language teaching*. New York: Longman.

Eskey, D. 1988. Holding in the bottom: An interactive approach to the language problems of second language readers. In *Interactive approaches to second language reading*, edited by P. Carrell, J. Deveine, and D. Eskey. Cambridge: Cambridge University Press.

Folse, K. 2004. *Vocabulary myths: Applying second language research to classroom teaching*. Ann Arbor: University of Michigan Press.

Wilkins, D. 1972. *Linguistics in language teaching*. London: Edward Arnold.

Appendices

Appendix 1   **Building Better Sentences**   250

Practice 1	Unit 1	251
Practice 2	Unit 1	252
Practice 3	Unit 2	253
Practice 4	Unit 3	253
Practice 5	Unit 3	254
Practice 6	Unit 3	255
Practice 7	Unit 4	255
Practice 8	Unit 4	256
Practice 9	Unit 5	257
Practice 10	Unit 5	257
Practice 11	Unit 6	258
Practice 12	Unit 6	258
Practice 13	Unit 7	259
Practice 14	Unit 7	260
Practice 15	Unit 8	260
Practice 16	Unit 8	261
Practice 17	Unit 9	262
Practice 18	Unit 9	262
Practice 19	Unit 10	263
Practice 20	Unit 10	264

Appendix 2   **Peer Editing Sheets**   265

Peer Editing Sheet 1	Unit 1, Activity 17	267
Peer Editing Sheet 2	Unit 2, Activity 8	269
Peer Editing Sheet 3	Unit 3, Activity 14	271
Peer Editing Sheet 4	Unit 4, Activity 13	273
Peer Editing Sheet 5	Unit 5, Activity 16	275
Peer Editing Sheet 6	Unit 6, Activity 12	277
Peer Editing Sheet 7	Unit 7, Activity 10	279
Peer Editing Sheet 8	Unit 8, Activity 16	281
Peer Editing Sheet 9	Unit 9, Activity 12	283
Peer Editing Sheet 10	Unit 10, Activity 11	285
Peer Editing Sheet 11	Unit 11, Activity 9	287

Appendix 1

 Building Better Sentences

Being a good writer involves many skills, such as being able to write with correct grammar, use variety in vocabulary selection, and state ideas concisely. Some student writers like to keep their sentences simple because they feel that if they create longer and more complicated sentences, they are more likely to make mistakes. However, writing short, choppy sentences one after the other is not considered appropriate in academic writing. Study the examples below.

The time was yesterday.

It was afternoon.

There was a storm.

The storm was strong.

The movement of the storm was quick.

The storm moved towards the coast.

The coast was in North Carolina.

Notice that every sentence has an important piece of information. A good writer would not write all these sentences separately. Instead, the most important information from each sentence can be used to create ONE longer, coherent sentence.

Read the sentences again; this time, the important information has been circled.

The time was (yesterday.)

It was (afternoon.)

There was a (storm.)

The storm was (strong.)

The (movement) of the storm was (quick.)

The storm moved towards the (coast.)

The coast was in (North Carolina.)

Here are some strategies for taking the circled information and creating a new sentence.

1. Create time phrases to introduce or end a sentence: *yesterday + afternoon*

2. Find the key noun: *storm*

3. Find key adjectives: *strong*

4. Create noun phrases: *a strong + storm*

5. Change word forms: *movement = move; quick = quickly*

   moved + quickly

6. Create prepositional phrases: *towards the coast*

   towards the coast (of North Carolina)

   or

   towards the North Carolina coast

Now read this improved, longer sentence:

Yesterday afternoon, a strong storm moved quickly towards the North Carolina coast.

Here are some additional strategies for building better sentences:

7. Use coordinating conjunctions (*and, but, or, nor, yet, for, so*) to connect two sets of ideas.

8. Use subordinating conjunctions, such as *after, while, since,* and *because,* to connect related ideas.

9. Use clauses with relative pronouns, such as *who, which, that,* and *whose,* to describe or define a noun or noun phrase.

10. Use pronouns to refer to previously mentioned information.

11. Use possessive adjectives and pronouns, such as *my, her, his, ours,* and *theirs.* These words can make your writing flow more smoothly.

Study the following example.

(Susan) (went) somewhere. That place was (the mall.) Susan wanted to (buy new shoes.) The shoes were for (Susan's mother.)

Now read the improved, longer sentence:

Susan went to the mall because she wanted to buy new shoes for her mother.

Practices

This section contains practices for the example paragraphs in Units 1–10. Follow these steps for each practice:

1. Read the sentences. Circle the most important information in each sentence.

2. Write an original sentence from the information you circled. Use the strategies listed above.

3. Go back to the page in the unit to check your sentence. Find the sentence on that page. Compare your sentence with the original sentence. Remember that there is more than one way to combine sentences.

Note that the first exercise in Practice 1 has been done for you.

Practice 1 Unit 1, page 9

A. page 2

1. Braille is a (system.)

2. The system is (special.)

3. It is a system of (writing.)

4. It is a system of (reading.)

5. It is a system for (people.)

6. The people are (blind.)

   Braille is a special system of writing and reading for blind people.

B. page 2

1. Braille uses a code.
2. The code is special.
3. It is a code of characters.
4. There are sixty-three of them.

_____

_____

C. page 4

1. First, boil eggs.
2. There are two eggs.
3. Do this for five minutes.

_____

_____

Practice 2 Unit 1, page 21

A. page 13

1. Computers are machines.
2. The machines are excellent.
3. These machines can help students.

_____

_____

B. page 15

1. Many battles occurred in South Carolina.
2. These battles were important.
3. These were the battles of the Revolution.
4. The Revolution was American.

_____

_____

C. page 16

1. Jim Thorpe won medals.
2. The medals were Olympic medals.
3. They were gold medals.
4. He won them in 1912.
5. He was not allowed to keep the medals.

_____

_____

Practice 3 Unit 2, page 39

A. page 39

    1. Mimi is a teacher.

    2. She teaches kindergarten.

    3. She is a teacher at a school.

    4. The school is King Elementary School.

_____

_____

B. page 39

    1. She teaches children.

    2. The children are very young.

    3. There are twenty-two children.

_____

_____

C. page 39

    1. Mimi must attend meetings.

    2. Mimi must create lessons.

    3. The lessons are new.

    4. Mimi must do this after school.

_____

_____

Practice 4 Unit 3, page 49

A. page 46

    1. The season is winter.

    2. This season is the best.

    3. This season is for kids.

_____

_____

B. page 47

    1. This dictionary contains words.

    2. The dictionary is monolingual.

    3. There are more than 42,000 words.

_____

_____

C. page 48

1. The crash of a jet baffled investigators.

2. The crash was shocking.

3. The jet was a 747 jumbo jet.

4. The crash was off the coast of New York.

_____

_____

Practice 5 Unit 3, page 55

A. page 48

1. Research has confirmed that eating vegetables, such as broccoli, may reduce the risk of some types of cancer.

2. The research is recent.

3. The vegetables are dark green ones.

4. The vegetables are leafy vegetables.

5. Another example of this is cabbage.

_____

_____

B. page 50

1. Flowers grow during the summer.

2. There are only four kinds of flowers.

3. The summers are short.

4. The summers are in Alaska.

_____

_____

C. page 53

1. A heart is necessary for life.

2. The heart is good.

3. The heart is strong.

4. The life is long.

5. The life is healthy.

_____

_____

Practice 6 Unit 3, page 59

A. page 55

1. Malaysia is a country.

2. Thailand is a country.

3. These two countries are in Asia.

4. They are in Southeast Asia.

_____

_____

B. page 55

1. Malaysia has beaches.

2. There are miles of beaches.

3. The beaches are beautiful.

4. These beaches attract tourists.

5. This is true about Thailand, too.

_____

_____

C. page 57

1. Students can choose to major in art.

2. They are at a university.

3. Only a small number choose to major in this subject.

4. This number is low for a reason.

5. The reason is that they are concerned about job possibilities.

6. The job possibilities are in the future.

_____

_____

Practice 7 Unit 4, page 68

A. page 65

1. One of the cities to visit is Washington, D.C.

2. It is one of the best cities.

3. It is on a coast of the United States.

4. The coast is in the east.

_____

_____

B. page 66

    1. Flight attendants receive training.

    2. It is a large amount of training.

    3. The training is for their job.

_____

_____

C. page 68

    1. Texas is home to snakes.

    2. There are several kinds of snakes.

    3. These snakes are poisonous.

_____

_____

Practice 8 Unit 4, page 80

A. page 73

    1. Music is popular.

    2. The music is Baroque.

    3. It is popular because it helps students.

    4. It helps students study better.

_____

_____

B. page 74

    1. Giraffes have eyelashes to protect their eyes.

    2. The eyelashes are thick.

    3. They protect their eyes from dust.

    4. The dust is in their habitat.

    5. Their habitat is dry.

_____

_____

C. page 77

    1. I was in high school.

    2. I hardly ever studied.

    3. My grades were fairly good.

_____

_____

Practice 9 Unit 5, page 88

A. page 84

1. Only tourists attempt to cross the bridge.

2. The tourists are adventure-seeking.

3. The bridge is narrow and swinging.

4. This happens today.

_____

_____

B. page 86

1. Hockey is a sport.

2. It is a popular sport.

3. It is popular in Canada.

4. It is popular in the United States.

_____

_____

C. page 87

1. Sweet tea is a drink that is popular.

2. The drink is very easy to make.

3. It is popular in the southern United States.

_____

_____

Practice 10 Unit 5, page 94

A. page 88

1. Coins were left under the mast.

2. The mast was part of the ship.

3. There were a small number of coins.

4. This happened when a new ship was built.

_____

_____

B. page 88

1. Scientists find evidence of this tradition.

2. The evidence is in a variety of locations.

3. The tradition is long-standing.

4. This happens today.

_____

_____

C. page 93

1. Floods provided the marsh with water to support its plants and animals.

2. These floods always did this.

3. The water was new.

4. The marsh had a wide variety of plants and animals.

_____

_____

Practice 11 Unit 6, page 105

A. page 104

1. The pretzel became popular.

2. This event happened rapidly.

3. This event happened throughout Europe.

_____

_____

B. page 104

1. Pretzels were made in a monastery.

2. They were the first pretzels made.

3. It was an Italian monastery.

4. This happened in A.D. 610.

_____

_____

C. page 104

1. The pretzel is a snack.

2. It is especially popular.

3. This is true in Germany.

4. This is true in Austria.

5. This is true in the United States.

6. It is true today.

_____

_____

Practice 12 Unit 6, page 118

A. page 112

1. A hurricane is a storm.

2. The storm is dangerous.

3. The storm features winds and rain.

4. The winds are high.

5. The rains are heavy.

_____

_____

B. page 112

1. A hurricane resulted in thousands of deaths.

2. The hurricane surprised the residents of Galveston, Texas.

3. This happened in 1900.

_____

_____

C. page 116

1. A folly is an action.

2. This action is costly.

3. The action has a result.

4. The result is bad or absurd.

_____

_____

Practice 13 Unit 7, page 126

A. page 124

1. The step is to choose several schools.

2. This is the first step.

3. These are schools that you are interested in attending.

_____

_____

B. page 124

1. One piece of advice is to start early.

2. This is the last piece of advice.

3. You should do this because students are all applying.

4. The students are in high school.

5. There are thousands of them.

6. They are all doing this at the same time.

_____

_____

C. page 125

    1. Give everyone a glass to drink with the coffee.

    2. The glass is small.

    3. The glass has water.

    4. The water is cold.

    5. The coffee is hot and thick.

    6. Do this before you serve the coffee.

Practice 14 Unit 7, page 132

A. page 128

    1. Hit the ball into the box.

    2. The box is small.

    3. It is on the opposite side of the net.

B. page 128

    1. The racket should be near your knee.

    2. The racket is yours.

    3. It is the knee on the left.

    4. Do this after you have completed your serve.

C. page 130

    1. You will need a quart jar.

    2. The jar must be clean.

    3. The jar must have a tight lid.

    4. You will need some tape.

    5. You will need a goldfish.

    6. You will need some water.

    7. You will need a few plants.

    8. The plants need to be green.

    9. You need all this for the experiment.

Practice 15 Unit 8, page 146

A. page 138

    1. A mother is standing.

    2. She is to your left.

3. Her child is standing.

4. The child is crying.

_____

_____

B. page 140

1. The tornado used its power to uproot trees.

2. The tornado used its power to toss cars around.

3. The trees were huge.

4. The cars were tossed around as if they were toys.

_____

_____

C. page 142

1. Mother also trimmed the flowers.

2. She did this to make room for their replacements.

3. The flowers were old.

4. Their replacements were bright.

_____

_____

Practice 16 Unit 8, page 158

A. page 148

1. The trees are gray.

2. The trees are brittle.

3. The trees are old.

4. The trees are near the river.

_____

_____

B. page 154

1. A cat is curled up in a ball.

2. The cat is fat.

3. The cat is striped.

4. The cat has whiskers.

5. The whiskers are long.

6. The cat is on the right side of the sofa.

_____

_____

C. page 156

   1. The Statue of Liberty has a crown on her head.

   2. The crown has seven spikes.

   3. These spikes symbolize the oceans and the continents.

   4. There are seven oceans.

   5. There are seven continents.

Practice 17 Unit 9, page 169

A. page 163

   1. I am in favor of a ban.

   2. The ban is on cell phone use.

   3. This use is by drivers.

   4. I am in favor of a ban because cell phones and driving are a deadly mix.

B. page 164

   1. Texting is certainly very common.

   2. This fact is true now.

   3. This is because texting is convenient.

   4. This is because texting is fast.

C. page 166

   1. School uniforms should be mandatory.

   2. This should be for all students.

   3. This is for a number of reasons.

Practice 18 Unit 9, page 173

A. page 170

   1. Too much time can cause damage.

   2. The time is in the sun.

   3. The damage is to the skin.

   4. The damage is severe.

   5. This occurs especially in young children.

B. page 172

1. She parked a car.

2. It was her car.

3. She parked illegally.

4. She got a ticket.

5. The ticket was for $30.

C. page 173

1. One source is the newspaper.

2. The source is good.

3. It is for topics.

4. The topics are for paragraphs.

5. The paragraphs are opinion paragraphs.

Practice 19 Unit 10, page 188

A. page 178

1. I practiced my speech.

2. I did this with my notes.

3. I did this in front of a mirror.

4. I did this in front of my cat.

5. I did this in front of my husband.

B. page 183

1. Everything changed.

2. This happened when I was sixteen years old.

3. This happened because my parents decided to move.

4. The move was to Florida.

C. page 186

1. I was in a building.

2. I was on the third floor.

3. It was a six-story building.

4. I thought the building was going to collapse.

_____

_____

Practice 20 Unit 10, page 194

A. page 188

1. The man waited until a guard gave him a number.

2. He did this patiently.

3. The number was to enter the building.

4. The building was warm.

_____

_____

B. page 191

1. It looked like a net.

2. The net was for fishing.

3. The net was old.

_____

_____

C. page 193

1. My best friend was sitting on a train.

2. I was sitting on a train.

3. The train was in Frankfurt.

4. The train was bound for Paris.

5. This is when the nightmare began.

_____

_____

Appendix 2
Peer Editing Sheets

Writer: _____ Date: _____

Peer Editor: _____

1. What is the general topic of the paragraph? Does the title relate to this general topic? _____

   _____

2. What is the more specific topic? _____

   _____

3. If you can find the topic sentence, write it here. _____

   _____

4. How many sentences does the paragraph have? _____ Do all the sentences relate

   to the same topic? _____ If any sentence is not about the topic, write it here.

   _____

   _____

5. Can you understand the meaning of every sentence? _____

6. If you answered *no* in Item 5, write the unclear sentence(s) here.

   _____

   _____

7. Does every sentence have a verb? _____ If any sentence

   does not have a verb, write that sentence here and add a verb.

   _____

   _____

   _____

8. Is the paragraph indented? _____ If it is not, circle the area where it should be indented.

9. Are any key nouns repeated? If so, give an example.

_____

_____

10. If you have ideas or suggestions for making the paragraph better, write them here.

_____

_____

_____

Peer Editing Sheet 2 Unit 2, Activity 8, page 42

Writer: _____ Date: _____

Peer Editor: _____

1. What is the general topic of the paragraph? _____

_____

2. What is the specific topic? _____

_____

3. Write the topic sentence here. _____

_____

4. Is there any sentence that is not related to the topic? If so, write it here. _____

_____

5. Does every sentence have a verb? _____ If any sentence does not have a verb, write it here and

add a verb. _____

_____

_____

6. Did you notice an error in subject-verb agreement? _____ If so, write the sentence with the

error here and make the correction. _____

_____

7. Is there any sentence that is unclear to you? If so, write it here. _____

_____

8. Is the paragraph indented? _____ If it is not, circle the area where it should be indented.

9. Do you have any suggestions for improving this paragraph? If so, write them here.

_____

_____

_____

Peer Editing Sheet 3 Unit 3, Activity 14, page 62

Writer: _____ Date: _____

Peer Editor: _____

1. What is the general topic of the paragraph? (Circle one.)

    food   conservation   jobs   computers

2. What is the specific topic? _____

    _____

3. Write the topic sentence here. _____

    _____

4. Do all the sentences relate to one topic? _____ If not, which sentence has extra material?

    _____

5. Is the paragraph indented? _____ If it is not, circle the area where it should be indented.

6. Does every sentence end with correct punctuation? _____

7. Is the first word of every sentence capitalized? _____

8. Are there any other capitalization errors? _____ If yes, circle them on your classmate's paper.

9. If you answer *yes* to any of the following questions, circle the error on your classmate's paper.

    a. Is any sentence missing a verb? _____

    b. Is there any problem with subject-verb agreement? _____

    c. Did you notice any comma splices? _____

    d. Are there any sentence fragments? _____

10. If you had trouble understanding any part of this paragraph, write the unclear part here.

_____

_____

_____

11. If you have any suggestions for improving this paragraph, write your comments here.

_____

_____

_____

Writer: _____ Date: _____

Peer Editor: _____

1. What is the topic of the paragraph? _____

2. Write the topic sentence here. _____

   _____

3. Circle the controlling ideas in the topic sentence.

4. Do all the sentences in the paragraph add information about the controlling ideas? _____

   If you answered *no*, describe any problems here. _____

   _____

   _____

5. Look at the pronouns. Do they each refer correctly to a noun? List any problems here.

   _____

   _____

6. Do all the sentences begin with a capital letter? _____ If you answered *no*, write the

   errors here. _____

   _____

7. Check for comma splices. If you find any errors, write them here.

   _____

   _____

8. If you found any sentence-fragment errors, list them here.

   _____

   _____

9. Write the concluding sentence of the paragraph here.

_____

_____

10. Compare the topic sentence and the concluding sentence. Are they similar? If so, how?

_____

_____

11. Is the paragraph missing any important information? If so, write any questions that you think should be answered in this paragraph.

_____

_____

_____

12. Do you have any other suggestions for improving this paragraph? Write them here.

_____

_____

_____

Writer: _____ Date: _____

Peer Editor: _____

1. Check for these features:

   a. Does the paragraph have a topic sentence? _____

   b. Do all the sentences in the paragraph relate to one topic? _____

   c. Is the first line of the paragraph indented? _____

2. If you answered *no* to the first two questions above, write comments here.

   Topic sentence: _____

   _____

   One topic: _____

   _____

3. What is the general topic of the paragraph? _____

4. Check for these errors. Circle them on your classmate's paper. Write the letters in parentheses above the circled word(s).

   sentence fragment (SF)   subject-verb agreement (S-V)

   comma splice (CS)   possessive pronoun reference (PR)

   capitalization (C)

5. Underline all the articles in the paragraph. Make sure each one is correct. Explain any corrections that

   are needed. _____

   _____

6. What is your overall impression of the paragraph?

_____

_____

7. Do you have any ideas or suggestions for improving the paragraph?

_____

_____

_____

Peer Editing Sheet 6 Unit 6, Activity 12, page 120

Writer: _____ Date: _____

Peer Editor: _____

1. What is the general topic of the paragraph? _____

2. Write the topic sentence here. _____

   _____

3. Is the topic sentence a definition? _____

   Can you suggest any improvements for the topic sentence?

   _____

   _____

4. Is the paragraph indented? _____ If it is not, circle the area where it should be indented.

5. Does the writer use quotation marks? If so, are they used correctly?

6. Check for these errors. Circle any you find on your classmate's paper. Write the letters in parentheses above the circled word(s).

   sentence fragment (SF)   subject-verb agreement (S-V)

   comma splice (CS)   possessive pronoun reference (PR)

   capitalization (C)   end punctuation (EP)

   articles (A)

7. Write one sentence from the paragraph that has an adjective clause. Is the clause correct?

   _____

   _____

8. Do you see any short, choppy sentences that could be combined for sentence variety? If so, write them and a suggested combination here. _____

_____

_____

9. Did you have any trouble understanding this paragraph? _____ If yes, tell where and why.

_____

_____

10. What questions do you have about the content? What other information should be in this paragraph?

_____

_____

_____

Writer: _____ Date: _____

Peer Editor: _____

1. What process does this paragraph describe? _____

2. Write the topic sentence here. _____

   _____

3. How many steps does this process have? _____

4. Do you believe that the steps are in the correct order? _____

   If you answered *no*, what can the writer do to put the steps in the correct order?

   _____

   _____

5. What time or transition words or phrases does the writer use? Are they used correctly? (Review page 127 if you need help with these words.) _____

   _____

6. Is there a comma after all the introductory time words or phrases? _____

   If not, mark the errors on your classmate's paper.

7. Does the writer include any technical terms? Do you understand what they mean, or do they need more explanation? _____

   _____

8. Check for these errors. Circle any you find on your classmate's paper. Write the letters in parentheses above the circled word(s).

sentence fragment (SF)	subject-verb agreement (S-V)
comma splice (CS)	possessive pronoun reference (PR)
capitalization (C)	end punctuation (EP)
articles (A)	adjective clauses (AC)

9. What suggestions do you have for improving this paragraph?

_____

_____

_____

_____

Writer: _____ Date: _____

Peer Editor: _____

1. What does this paragraph describe? _____

2. Write the topic sentence here. _____

   _____

   _____

3. Underline all the descriptive adjectives. How many are there? _____

4. Is every adjective placed in the correct position? If not, make corrections on your classmate's paper.

5. Read the adjectives again. Do you understand the connotation for each one? If you have questions about the precise meaning of any adjective, write your question here.

   _____

   _____

   _____

6. Check for these errors. Circle them on your classmate's paper. Write the letters in parentheses above the circled word(s).

sentence fragment (SF)	subject-verb agreement (S-V)
comma splice (CS)	possessive pronoun reference (PR)
capitalization (C)	end punctuation (EP)
articles (A)	adjective clauses (AC)

7. Is the paragraph indented? _____ If it is not, circle the area where it should be indented.

8. Do you have a positive or a negative impression of the topic? What word(s) gave you this impression?

Positive: _____

Negative: _____

9. Write any suggestions you have for improving the paragraph.

_____

_____

_____

Writer: _____ Date: _____

Peer Editor: _____

1. What is the general topic of this paragraph? _____

2. What is the writer's opinion about this topic? _____

   _____

3. Write the topic sentence here. _____

   _____

4. Check for correct word forms. Write any problems here. _____

   _____

   _____

5. Does the writer include an opposing opinion, or counterargument? If so, is this opinion refuted? Make notes about this on your classmate's paper.

6. Check for these errors. Circle any you find on your classmate's paper. Write the letters in parentheses above the circled word(s).

   sentence fragment (SF)   subject-verb agreement (S-V)

   comma splice (CS)   possessive pronoun reference (PR)

   capitalization (C)   end punctuation (EP)

   articles (A)   adjective clauses (AC)

   adjective placement (AP)

7. Do the supporting sentences give enough facts to support the writer's opinion? _____

   Are there any supporting sentences that do not fit? _____ Write any comments you have

   about the writer's supporting facts.

   _____

8. Read the concluding sentence. Does it restate the topic sentence or make a prediction? If not, make a revision suggestion for the writer.

9. What other suggestions do you have for improving the paragraph?

Writer: _____ Date: _____

Peer Editor: _____

1. Write the topic sentence of the paragraph here. _____

   _____

2. Is this a narrative paragraph? _____

3. Look for the beginning, middle, and end of the story. Summarize these parts here.

   Beginning: _____

   _____

   Middle: _____

   _____

   End: _____

   _____

4. Is there any part of the paragraph that is unclear to you? If so, write it here. What do you think the

   problem is? _____

   _____

   _____

5. Are the verb tenses consistent? If not, write any problems here. _____

   _____

   _____

6. Check for these errors. Circle any you find on your classmate's paper. Write the letters in parentheses above the circled word(s).

sentence fragment (SF)   subject-verb agreement (S-V)

comma splice (CS)   possessive pronoun reference (PR)

capitalization (C)   end punctuation (EP)

articles (A)   adjective clauses (AC)

adjective placement (AP)   word forms (WF)

7. Sometimes a narrative needs more information to sound complete or clear. Does this story need any more information? If so, what?

_____

_____

8. Write any other suggestions or comments you have about the paragraph.

_____

_____

_____

Writer: _____ Date: _____

Peer Editor: _____

1. How many paragraphs are in the essay? _____ What is the topic of the essay?

   _____

2. Is there a thesis statement? _____ If yes, write it here. _____

   _____

   _____

3. Read the second paragraph. Does every supporting sentence connect to the first sentence of the

   paragraph (the topic sentence)? _____ If not, circle any sentence that is not related to the topic

   sentence.

4. Read the third paragraph. Write all the adjectives you find in the paragraph. _____

   _____

   _____

5. Find a sentence that contains a comma. Write the sentence here. _____

   _____

   _____

   In your opinion, is the comma used correctly? If not, correct the error on your classmate's paper.

6. Find the transition words in the essay and write them here. _____

   _____

   _____

   In your opinion, are all the transition words used correctly? _____

   If not, suggest corrections on your classmate's paper.

Index

a/an, 94
adjective
  definition of, 143
  in descriptive paragraphs, 136-141, 145-147
  position of, 144
  possessive, 131
  predicate, 144
adjective clauses, 111, 114
adverb, 115, 171-172
adverb clauses, 114
an/a, 94
appositives
  and use of commas, 233
apostrophes, 234
articles, 94-95, 241-243

bibliography, 248
bilingual dictionaries, 146
brainstorming, 29, 31-32, 173, 210-211, 220
  cluster, 32-33
  negative-positive, 173
Building Better Sentences, 9, 21, 39, 49, 55, 59, 68, 80, 88, 94, 105, 118, 126, 132, 146, 158, 169, 173, 188, 194, *See also* Appendix 1, 250-264
Building Better Vocabulary, 26, 40, 60, 80, 96, 118, 132, 159, 174, 195, 213

capitalization, 228-230
chronological (time) order, 127
citing works, 247-248
clauses
  simple adjective, 111
cohesion
  by repetition of nouns, 3, 74
  by use of pronouns, 74
comma splice, 56-57
commas, 232-233
common mistakes
  comma splice, 56-57
  sentence fragments, 56-57
  subject-verb agreement, 37-38
concluding sentences, 10, 75

and main idea, 76
  and opinion, 76
  and prediction, 76
  and suggestion, 76
connotation and denotation, 147-150
contractions
  and use of apostrophe, 234
contrasting (opposing) opinions, 167, 173
controlling ideas
  in topic sentences, 47-48
count nouns
  and articles, 94-95

definition paragraphs, 99
denotation and connotation, 147-150
descriptive paragraphs, 135
dictionaries
  bilingual, 146
direct quotation, 247-248
draft
  final, proofing, 224
  first, 221
    and peer editing, 28, 221
    revising, 224

end punctuation (exclamation point, period, question mark), 231-232
essay
  definition of, 199
  example of, 202-203
  outline of, 204
  reasons for writing, 199
  versus paragraph, 200
examples
  inclusion of, in paragraphs, 110
exclamation point, 232

final draft, proofing, 224
fragment, 23, 56-57
first draft, 221

and peer editing, 28, 221
revising, 224

ideas
   brainstorming, 31-32
   controlling, 47
   for opinion paragraphs, 173
   using a journal for, 54
   supporting, 205
imperative sentence, 6
indentation
   of first line of paragraph, 10

key nouns
   repetition of, 3
   replacing with pronouns, 74

last sentence (*see* concluding sentences)

main idea
   restated in concluding sentence, 75

narrative paragraphs, 177-178
noun
   and articles, 94-95
   definition of, 171
   in prepositional phrases, 37
   replacing with pronoun, 74

opinion paragraphs, 162
   sources for topics, 173
opinions, opposing (contrasting), 167, 173
opposing (contrasting) opinions, 167, 173
outline of essay, 220

paragraphs
   definition, 99
   description of, 1
   descriptive, 122
   features of, 1, 9-10, 83
   including examples in, 110
   narrative, 177-178
   opinion, 162
   process analysis, 121
   steps in writing, 219
   versus essays, 200
paraphrasing, 247-248

parts of speech (word forms), 171
peer editing, 28, 221
periods, 231
plagiarism, 107, 110, 247
possession
   and use of apostrophe, 234
possessive adjective, 131
predicate adjective, 144
predictions in concluding sentences,
   10, 76
process analysis paragraphs, 121
   organization of, 127
pronoun
   consistent use of, 74
   relative, in adjective clause, 111
   replacing key noun, 74
proofing final paper, 224
proofreading, 85
punctuation, 231-235
   apostrophes, 234
   commas, 232
   exclamation points, 232
   periods, 231
   question marks, 231
   quotation marks, 105, 235
   semicolons, 236

question marks, 231
quotation marks, 105, 235

relative pronoun
   in adjective clause, 111
repetition
   of key nouns, 3, 74
revising the first draft, 224

semicolons, 236
senses, five
   in descriptive paragraphs, 136
sentence fragment, 23, 56-57
sentences
   combining, 114-115
   concluding, 10, 75-77
   imperative, 6
   supporting, 63, 82
      kinds of, 67
   topic, 9, 47-51
   variety of, 114-115
steps in the writing process, 219
steps in writing a paragraph, 219-224

subject-verb agreement, 37-38
supporting ideas in essays, 205
supporting sentences, 63-66
  kinds of, 67

technical terms, 129
that versus *which* versus *who*
  in simple adjective clauses, 111
the, 94
thesis statement, 204
time (chronological) order, 127
time/transition words, 127
Timed Writing, 29, 42, 62, 82, 98, 120, 134,
  161, 176, 197, 215
titles
  capitalization of, 21, 228

topic sentence, 9, 47-51, 179
transition/time words, 127

verb
  check for, 23
  consistency in tense of, 188
  definition of, 171
  tense, 188, 238-240
vocabulary, 204

which versus *that* versus *who* in simple
  adjective clauses, 111
who versus *that* versus *which* in simple
  adjective clauses, 111
word forms (parts of speech), 171-172

Photo Credits

Unit 1
Page 10: © Michael Newman/
   PhotoEdit Inc.
Page 13: © David Deas/Getty Images
Page 14: © AKG-Images/The Image
   Works
Page 16: © 2006 Mark Rucker/
   Transcendental Graphics/Getty
   Images
Page 20: © Jeremy Frechette/Getty
   Images
Page 23: © Udoudo/Dreamstime.com

Unit 2
Page 33: Left: © Guy Cali/
   Photolibrary; Left center:
   © Tracy Whiteside/Shutterstock;
   Right center: © Patrick Breig/
   iStockPhoto; Right:
   © Photos.com/RF
Page 34: Top left: © Barbara
   Boensch/Photolibrary; Top Right:
   © Greg Pease Photography/Getty
   Images; Bottom left: © Vicenzo
   Lombardo/Getty Images;
   Bottom center: © A. Ramey/
   PhotoEdit Inc.; Bottom right:
   © Cloki/iStockPhoto
Page 35: Top left: © Photos.com/
   RF; Top right: © Wilson Valentin/
   iStockPhoto; Bottom left: © Photos.
   com/RF; Bottom center: © Kenneth
   C. Zirkel/iStockPhoto; Bottom
   right: © John Verner/iStockPhoto
Page 38: © Masterfile

Unit 3
Page 44: © Pascual Ferrandis/
   Photolibrary
Page 47: © Skjold Photographs/
   PhotoEdit Inc.

Page 48: Left: © Dan Brandenburg/
   iStockPhoto; Right:
   © Photos.com/RF
Page 50: © Moustyk/Dreamstime.com
Page 53: © Tony Latham
   Photography Ltd./Getty Images
Page 54: © Rocter/iStockPhoto
Page 58: © David Deas/Getty Images

Unit 4
Page 65: Top left: © Steve Maehl/
   iStockPhoto; Bottom left: © Dennis
   O'Clair/Getty Images; Right:
   © Russell McBridge/iStockPhoto
Page 74: © Theo Allofs/Getty Images
Page 76: © Michael Newman/
   PhotoEdit Inc.
Page 79: © Dan Brandenburg/
   iStockPhoto

Unit 5
Page 86: © Vospalej/Dreamstime.com
Page 91: © Steven Kazlowski/Getty
   Images
Page 92: © Michael Burke/
   Photolibrary

Unit 6
Page 100: © Michael Burke/
   Photolibrary
Page 101: Left: © Kilkk/Dreamstime
   .com; Center: © Tdoes1/
   Dreamstime.com;
   Right: © Photos.com/RF
Page 104: © Dreambigphotos/
   Dreamstime.com
Page 111: © James Camp/
   iStockPhoto
Page 112: © Anne Griffiths Belt/
   Getty Images

Page 113: © Daniel J. Cox/Getty
   Images

Unit 7
Page 122: © Douglas Johns/Getty
   Images
Page 125: © Igor Smichkov/
   iStockPhoto

Unit 8
Page 136: © Steve Gorton/Getty
   Images
Page 138: © Chris Stowers/Getty
   Images
Page 140: © Alan R. Moller/Getty
   Images
Page 156: © Samecia24/Dreamstime
   .com

Unit 9
Page 163: © A.B./Getty Images
Page 166: © Per-Anders Pettersson/
   Getty Images
Page 170: © Don Bayley/iStockPhoto

Unit 10
Page 180: © Alex Segre/Alamy
Page 181: © Peter Galbraith/
   iStockPhoto
Page 183: © Dave Nagel/Getty
   Images
Page 186: © Time & Life Pictures/
   Getty Images
Page 188: © Photos.com/RF
Page 190: © Steven Hoeck/Getty
   Images
Page 192: © Chris Rogers/
   iStockPhoto

Unit 11
Page 202: © Richard Price/Getty Images